THE LIFE *of*

JOHN A. RAWLINS

Lawyer, Assistant Adjutant-General, Chief of Staff, Major General of
Volunteers, and Secretary of War

BY

JAMES HARRISON WILSON

1916

Contents

PREFACE

THE purpose of this narrative is fully set forth in the following pages, the preparation of which was begun, at his request, shortly after the death of General Rawlins, and has been continued at various intervals of a busy life up to the present time. I have explored every possible source of information which promised to throw any light whatever on the services and relations of General Rawlins with General Grant. I have consulted the Official Records, the *Memoirs* of General Grant, General Sherman, and General Sheridan; the "Personal History" of General Grant by Badeau, as well as those by Coffee, Richardson, Deming, Dana and Wilson; the "Recollections of Charles A. Dana"; the newspapers and magazines of the period, and especially the correspondence of General Rawlins.

I am particularly indebted to S. Cadwallader, Esquire, of California, formerly war correspondent of the New York Herald, for access to his valuable work in manuscript, entitled *Four Years with Grant*; to Hempstead Washburne, Esq., of Chicago, for copies of his father's correspondence with Rawlins, and to David Sheean, Esq., of Galena, Illinois, for collecting the letters of Rawlins to the various members of his family, for furnishing me with the family records, and for giving me his assistance with the manuscript and proofs at every stage of their preparation.

I am also greatly indebted to the late J. Russell Jones, of Chicago, and to the late Major General John E. Smith and the late Doctor E. D. Kittoe, of Galena, who were all lifelong friends of Rawlins and Grant and familiar with the history of their relations in both military and civil life.

I am under special obligation to Major General Grenville M. Dodge, who from the rich stores of his memory and his records has helped me with valuable facts and references, covering many incidents in Rawlins's career from the time he entered the army till his death as Secretary of War to each of these gentlemen I extend my grateful thanks, with the statement that I have used the matter furnished me according to my own judgment, and that I am solely

1

responsible for the statements and opinions contained in this book, as well as for the time of its publication.

Finally, having served with Rawlins on the staff of General Grant from the beginning of the operations against Vicksburg until the close of the Chattanooga and Knoxville campaigns and having maintained the closest intimacy with him to the end of his career, I had ample opportunity to become acquainted with his services and to form a correct estimate of his extraordinary character. As will be more fully explained in its proper place, Rawlins asked me shortly before his death to become his literary executor and to see that justice should be done to his memory when he was gone. This touching and solemn request is my special warrant for becoming his biographer.

JAMES HARRISON WILSON.

Wilmington, Delaware, January, 1916.

INTRODUCTORY

JOHN A. RAWLINS, all things considered, was the most remarkable man I met during the Civil War, and although he came from the plain people and always held a subordinate position in the army, it was his good fortune to exert a tremendous influence not only upon persons of high rank but upon events of transcendent importance. He never commanded troops in the field nor became charged with the supreme control of great movements. Whatever he did was upon and through others, as aid, counsellor, and Adjutant General to General Grant, as Chief of Staff of the Army, and as Secretary of War. It is certain that in all these positions he exerted a very great influence upon men and events. This was especially the case during the war for the reestablishment of the Union.

While Rawlins was a man of extraordinary qualities and character, it cannot be claimed that he was to General Grant what Berthier was to Napoleon, or even what Gneisenau and Muffling were to Blücher. It will be remembered that Berthier was a professional soldier of great experience in both America and Europe, and that Gneisenau and Muffling were highly-educated Prussian regulars who were expected to guide and direct their sturdy but thick-headed chief. According to the history of the times, they conceived the plans and worked out the details which he executed. He was from first to last merely a typical dragoon of the old school, always ready to march and fight even when beaten, as well as after he had become worn down with years. It is said that he scarcely knew either how to use a map or write an order, but had the good sense to submit himself to the guidance of those officers of his staff who were able to make plans and frame the instructions for carrying them into effect. Rawlins was but a country lawyer who had had no military training whatever when he entered the volunteer army, and never, even to his dying day, made the slightest pretensions to technical education in the profession of arms. His was a special and peculiar field, which will be defined with the progress of this narrative. It is believed that it was in many respects unlike that of any other man recorded in history.

Grant was a soldier of another sort. It will be recalled that he was a graduate of West Point and had served inconspicuously but with credit in the regular army during the Mexican War, after which he had the usual tour of duty in the Indian Country, and then had left the service under a cloud. It is a part of the history of the times that he had fallen for a season into the evil ways of military men serving on the remote frontier and that his return to civil life was commonly believed to have been a choice between resignation and a court-martial. Rejoining his family in Missouri, Grant settled on a farm, which after a series of minor business disappointments he gave up in order to accept the position of clerk at six hundred dollars per year in the leather and harness store of his kinsmen at Galena, Illinois. After the outbreak of the war between the States, his public services became too important and too well known to require recital here, but I shall show in the course of this narrative that in some respects his character had not been fully understood and that in certain particulars it was happily supplemented by that of his friend and adjutant, John A. Rawlins.

Grant was of course proficient in the military profession as taught at West Point. While his services with the troops had made him familiar with the use of maps and plans, as well as with the details of army administration, it has never been claimed that he was learned in military history or in the higher branches of tactics, logistics, and strategy as set forth in the military textbooks. Indeed, it is improbable that he had ever, during his active service, read any military treatise more complex than the drill book or the army regulations. That he had not done so was doubtless due to the fact that the higher branches of the art of war were not taught at the Military Academy in his day, and it had not become the fashion for infantry officers to read such authors at any time up to the outbreak of the War between the States. After that it was impossible for him to give attention to the theoretical study of his profession. He was, from the first day of his participation in the war, occupied with the routine work of administration and of active campaigning, in which he got no help except from his own experience, or from current observation, or from others who had read and studied more than had he himself.

4

But it was not in respect to technical or strictly professional matters that Rawlins or any other officer contributed materially to Grant's success, and indeed it was not in respect to these that he required assistance, or that his character was supplemented by others. He had as much of the education supposed to be essential to the exercise of high command as had most of his contemporaries; yet this is paying him no great compliment, for it cannot be claimed that either our government or our generals habitually conducted war either economically or in accordance with the practice and precept of the great masters of the art. It is well known that our military policy and volunteer system, largely inherited from the mother country, were crude and costly in the highest degree, that our administration was capricious and extravagant, and that our plans of campaign and their execution were frequently unscientific to an extent rarely exceeded in modern warfare. Finally, the tactics of our battles were as a general rule of the simplest and most primitive description. But, notwithstanding all this, we were victorious over the public enemy, whose inexperience was as great as our own, and came out of the four years' struggle with both success and honor. We owed our triumph primarily, however, to our superiority in numbers and resources, and secondarily to the exalted spirit of patriotism and love for the Union which inspired our people and impelled our army to renewed exertions after repeated failure and defeat.

It was in respect to the qualities that constitute character in the individual, as well as in the nation at large, that Rawlins as their exponent became a potent factor in the struggle, and supplemented and sustained the general to whom his services were given and with whom his fortunes were allied from the first to the final hour of the conflict. The relations which existed between him and his Chief were unusually close and intimate. They were due to his fidelity, his intense earnestness, his severe morals, his aggressive temper, his unselfish devotion to the duties of his position, his clear perception of what ought to be done from time to time, his sound and unfailing judgment, his quick and unerring grasp of the needs of the army, his keen insight into character, his fearless contempt for vice and vicious men, his love of justice and fair dealing, his prodigious energy, his resolute will and his unfaltering self-denial and

5

patriotism, and especially his natural capacity for war. In these high qualities he had few equals and no superiors. In all the great emergencies they conspired to make his influence irresistible.

It cannot be maintained that Rawlins was, or ever became, a tactician, for he not only never set a squadron in the field but never read a book on either grand tactics or strategy. He was not learned in military administration nor military organization, and he knew absolutely nothing of the duties of either the staff or of the line when he entered the army. He was merely a plain citizen of average education and a lawyer by profession, all of whose thoughts, aspirations, and pursuits were those of peace up to the outbreak of the war between the States. He was not even in sympathy with the party whose candidate had been elected to the Presidency, and yet it may be doubted if it was the lot of any man who did not actually reach the command of an army, or become a member of the Cabinet, to render the country greater or more valuable services than did Rawlins in the four years' war for the Union.

Holding always the position of a confidential staff-officer, it was Rawlins's pleasure as well as his duty, so far as possible, not only to efface himself but to merge his individuality in that of his Chief. The Official Records contain but few reports over his own name. It is true that that name appears frequently on the returns to the War Department and on the records of the armies with which he served, but in nearly every case as the Adjutant or the Chief of Staff of General Grant. For this reason the events of his life and the influence exerted by him must be gathered mostly from family records, private correspondence, and the recollections of his comrades and personal friends.

It is not to be thought that an officer of Rawlins's impatient and aggressive temper should have entirely escaped the enmity of smaller souls, for such is not the case. There were those who were doubtful of his great qualities, and did what they could to minimize his influence and to belittle his services.

It is perhaps natural that the superficial observer of later times should fail to recognize his remarkable personality or to give him his true place in the career of the great general for whom he did so much. It is the duty of the staff officer to efface himself, and this duty Rawlins performed without stint or hesitation. But it is equally the duty of those who are familiar with the truth to make it known when there is no longer a just excuse for concealing it.

It is my purpose, therefore, so far as the materials within reach will permit, to set the life and services of this good citizen and fearless officer before his countrymen in their true light; and I do this all the more confidently because I knew him intimately, was daily associated with him during three of the greatest campaigns of the war, and held the most friendly relations with him to the end. He was indeed a man without guile, whose only aim was to serve his country faithfully and leave an honored name behind him. While he was fortunate in his friendships and opportunities, his fight for life against an insidious disease clouded his closing years with pain and apprehension. I record it with sorrow, mingled with satisfaction, that when the end was near at hand and he was prone on the bed of sickness, from which he never arose, he sent for me, a thousand miles away, and with a pitiful appeal, which I shall never forget, requested me—and I promised without hesitation or reserve—to become his literary executor and to see justice done to his memory when he was gone.

EARLY LIFE

JOHN AARON RAWLINS was the second child in a family of eight brothers and one sister. He was born at East Galena, Jo Daviess County, Illinois, on February 13, 1831, and was of Scotch-Irish extraction. His father, James D. Rawlins, the son of a Virginian, was born in Clark County, Kentucky, February 28, 1801, and removed when eighteen years of age to Howard County, Missouri, where on October 5, 1828, he married Lovisa Collier. She was the daughter of a Revolutionary soldier of Irish descent, and was born in Lincoln County, Kentucky, May 2, 1803.

Shortly after marriage the young couple removed from Missouri to the lead-mine district of Illinois, then the center of frontier enterprise and activity. The tide of immigration was then flowing strongly into that region, dotting it with villages and towns and filling it with the homes of agricultural people. The Mississippi was the ample highway by which it was reached. Railroads had not yet penetrated the wilderness, but the spirit which opened the lead mines was astir throughout the country. It received a further impulse in 1849 from the discovery of gold in California, and among the first to make the overland trip was James D. Rawlins, who for three years led an adventurous but unsuccessful life as a gold seeker. During his absence the care of the farm and family fell almost entirely upon the shoulders of the wife and her son John. The struggle for existence was sharp and discouraging. Poverty and hardship were the lot which confronted this typical family, and the only consolation was that they were no worse off than their neighbors. The means of communication with the older States were the steamboat and the canvas-covered wagon; the implements of industry were the plow, the axe, and the spinning wheel; the food of the people was mostly Indian corn and bacon, while their clothes were of homespun cloth. The church and schoolhouse were costly luxuries that came later and were but poorly patronized. A large family, early taught to labor in field and forest, was the poor man's greatest wealth.

It was into this active, earnest, intense, and robust life that John A. Rawlins was born, and it was this life, in its varying stages of evolution, that surrounded him until the outbreak of the Civil War. His parents first settled at Ottawa, in the town of East Galena, and afterwards removed to a farm in what is at present the town of Guilford, where they resided the rest of their lives. James D. Rawlins took part with his neighbors in transporting supplies to the troops engaged in the Black Hawk War, and after it was ended returned to the laborious and uneventful life of a farmer and charcoal burner. As can well be understood, the family never acquired wealth nor high social position, but remained as they began, plain, hardy and industrious people of but little means and of limited education.

The father was a man of determined will, but of unsettled purpose and roving disposition, which received but little if any benefit from his life in California. It is said that it was the knowledge of this that early caused his son John to adopt and live up to the rule of total abstinence, except when his doctor ordered otherwise. Be this as it may, it is certain that from his earliest manhood John A. Rawlins exhibited an earnest and uncompromising hatred for strong drink, and during his military life waged constant warfare against its use in the army. His dislike of it amounted to a deep and abiding abhorrence, and while he was in no sense a pharisee, he was often heard to declare that he would rather see a friend of his take a glass of poison than a glass of whiskey.

His mother, who survived him, from all accounts was a woman of strong and exemplary character. She is described as having had excellent judgment, an even temper, and a most kindly and benevolent heart. It is also said that she impressed herself deeply on the character of her children and that her son John was especially indebted to her for his moral training and ambition, while he owed his steady courage and determination to the virile qualities of his father.

An anecdote, which has been preserved by one who knew the family well, presents in a favorable light not only the piety of the mother but the intelligence of the child. A Sunday-school teacher, who had come from a distance to instruct the children, promised a book as a prize to such as would commit the Ten Commandments to memory within a fortnight. When the appointed time came around, little John, the smallest of the lot,—so small indeed that he had neither learned to read nor to talk plainly,—declared that he could say them, and this he did, to the delight of his teacher and with no fault but one of pronunciation. Eager to get the promised prize, he had beset his mother to read the Commandments to him, and after this had been done, at most but three times, he had them by heart and repeated them triumphantly.

The Rawlins family, sometime prior to the year 1838, located a homestead on government land, in the town of Guilford. This farm consists of about two hundred acres of timber and grass-land and at the government land sales in April, 1847, bought in by John, who early became the mainstay of the family. They were not over-thrifty, and their principal income was from the sale of wood and charcoal produced on their forest land. The cultivated portion was small, and the food produced was barely enough for the family's use.

As has already been indicated, young Rawlins early began to show the characteristics of the sturdy and aggressive race, the Scotch-Irish, from which he was descended, and which has given so many distinguished names to English and American history. His family on both sides, as far back as it can be traced, were pioneers and farmers in the settlement of Virginia and the Western States, and while they, like their neighbors, were lacking in the refinement and education which pertain to older communities, it is apparent that they have been in some degree compensated for it by the possession of the hardier and more robust characteristics which encouraged them to fell the forest and subdue the soil of the frontier world, at a time when their race and perhaps their very kindred were conquering the people and regenerating the civilization of India and the Far East.

Bosworth Smith, in the "Life of Lord Lawrence," the great Indian administrator during and after the Sepoy rebellion, says, with an insight which our American experience shows to be true:

. . . The people who have sprung from that sturdy mixture of Scotch and Irish blood are not without their conspicuous faults. No race which is at once so vigorous and so mixed is ever free from them. A suspiciousness and caution which often verges on selfishness, an ambition which is as quiet as it is intense, a slow and unlovable calculation of consequences, these are some of the drawbacks which those who know and love them best are willing to admit. On the other hand, there have been formed amongst them men who under the most widely different circumstances in Great Britain itself, in that Greater Britain which lies across the Atlantic, and amongst our widely scattered dependencies, last not least, in that greatest dependency of all, our Indian Empire, have rendered the noblest service to the state as intrepid soldiers, as vigorous administrators, as wise and far-seeing statesmen.

Among the Scotch-Irish there have been found men who have combined in their own persons much of the rich humor and the strong affections, the vivacity and the versatility, the genius and generosity of the typical Irishman, with the patience and the prudence, the devotion and the self-reliance, the stern morality and the simple faith of the typical Scotchman. In some families one of these national types seems to predominate throughout, almost to the exclusion of the other. In others the members differ much among themselves, one conforming mainly to the Scotch, another to the Irish type of character, although each man manages to retain something which is distinctive of the other.

As this story develops, it will be seen that Rawlins was a striking embodiment of these characteristics. From the time he was big enough to work at all he passed his life on the family farm, performing the various tasks suited to his age and strength. Living within reach of the lead mines, where concentrated fuel was in constant demand, the principal occupation of father and sons was cutting wood, burning it into charcoal and hauling it to the furnaces and smelting works. John did his full share of this uninviting work, and from his own account took special interest in tending the pits during the night watches. The life was rough, yet not without beneficent influences in the shaping of his character. It seems to have made a deep and lasting impression upon him. But the hardship and exposure, the rough habits and language of his companions and the meagre profits of the business gave him a distaste for it and early set him to thinking of how he should get out of it into something better. In the silent hours of the night he pondered long and deeply upon life and its problems.

Looking about him, John soon saw, as does every American boy, that his own condition was but the circumstance of a day, and that he might fairly hope by industry and study, education and character, not only to escape from it but to rise to the highest place in the land. Lifted by this hope and by the numerous examples of success, under even more discouraging conditions, which abound in American history, which he read with avidity, he resolved that nothing should keep him in ignorance or bind him to the lot of hardship and toil wherein his awakening ambition found him.

John's parents were too poor to send him to the neighboring school continuously even in childhood. He began his first term in the winter of 1838, when only seven years old, and from that time to the winter of 1849-50 he attended eight terms of three months each, or two years in all. From the day he learned to read he became a lover of poetry, biography and history. Whenever he could find time, or get books, he devoured and absorbed them so that when he reached the age of twenty he had gathered an unusual but heterogeneous store of general information, and was much better prepared for the struggle of life than many young men who had enjoyed superior opportunities. He did his best at the neighborhood school and got out of it all its range of instruction, with his irregular attendance, would permit. As has been seen from the incident of the Ten Commandments, from childhood he had a tenacious memory, and fortunately it remained with him throughout life, holding firmly whatever engaged its attention. It was accurate in little things as well as in great, and aided by industry, concentration and acute powers of observation, it was always easy for him to acquire knowledge and retain it. His tendency and preference seem to have been for history, rhetoric, logic and language, rather than for mathematics and science; but there is no doubt that his mind was capable of mastering all branches of learning, which, with proper opportunity and means, he would have explored to their utmost limits.

But the country schools of those days dealt merely with the rudiments of education. Spelling, reading, writing, arithmetic, and grammar were as much as the average teacher was expected to know. Few boys counted upon passing beyond them, but young Rawlins could not be confined to such narrow limits, and so, at the beginning of the winter of 1850-51, he went to Galena, and was received into the house of Mr. Hallett, where he became the schoolmate and friend of his son Moses, late the distinguished Judge of the United States Court for the District of Colorado.

John attended the high school for only one term, but the change had stimulated the country boy's ambition. During the remainder of the year, he again assisted on the farm and at the charcoal pits, saving his earnings for the purpose of paying his sister's expenses at the Galena Academy and his own at the Rock River Seminary, an institution of local reputation, situated at Mount Morris, in Ogle County, Illinois. He entered this Seminary in January, 1852, and remained there until the following April, when he was compelled by the exhaustion of his slender purse to return home to work on the farm and at charcoal burning. This lasted till September of the same year, when he reentered the Seminary at Mount Morris and resumed his studies with renewed ardor and determination, continuing them till the end of the academic year in June, 1853. He occupied a room at Mount Morris with his friend, Moses Hallett, and amongst their fellow students were Shelby M. Cullom, late the venerable senior Senator from Illinois; G. C. Barnes, late Circuit Judge at Lacon, Illinois; Greenbury L. Fort, late member of Congress from Wisconsin; R. R. Hitt, long a congressman from Illinois; Smith D. Atkins, Colonel of the Ninety-second Illinois Infantry, and a number of other youths who subsequently distinguished themselves in the army or in civil life.

During his stay at the Seminary, Rawlins studied Geometry, Moral Science, and Political Economy, and read part of both Caesar and Virgil. Politics and debating, however, occupied a great part of his time, as they did that of his associates. His room was the scene of many hot controversies, and, having a strong voice, he never failed to make himself heard above the din, no matter how loud it became.

He was an earnest and vehement debater, with cordial and open manners, which emphasized the strength of his convictions without producing the slightest impression of dogmatism. His sole desire seemed to be that others should accept the truth as fully as he believed it. His friend, Hallett, aptly said many years afterwards: "His flashing black eyes were more eloquent than his tongue. In private life he was a most engaging person, strong for every good work and beloved by all who knew him."

At that time political discussion turned mostly upon slavery in the territories, and Rawlins, who was an ardent Democrat and a great admirer of Senator Douglas, took an active part in all the academic controversies. At the close of the year he delivered an original oration in which patriotism was his theme. His manner upon that occasion is described as impassioned and eloquent and as showing powers which, if cultivated, could not fail to bring him distinction as an orator. While attending the Mount Morris Seminary he was a member of the "Amphictyonic" Society and seldom failed to speak at its weekly meetings. He was also a leading member of a private club known as the "Hekadelphoi." These circumstances serve to show that, notwithstanding his disadvantages, he not only made noticeable progress in his academic work but impressed himself upon his associates as a youth of unusual ability and promise.

When he left the Seminary in June, 1853, it was his intention to return and graduate, but, like many another poor young man, he could not get the necessary money for his expenses. His family could not furnish it, and he was too proud to ask a loan of it from his friends. Without hesitation or delay he therefore returned to burning charcoal, cutting his own wood, preparing his own pits, and finally, in the absence of other help, hauling his own coal to market. Starting with his last load on a hot September day, although he had two yoke of oxen, the heavy load and the hot weather proved too much for them. To go on was impossible, and there was nothing left for him but to lie by for the night. Starting again in the cool of the next morning, he went on till he reached the Galena branch of the Illinois Central Railroad, which was then under construction. There his team again gave out, but receiving an offer from the contractors for his oxen and wagon, he accepted it on the condition that the charcoal should also be included in the sale at its market value. With the proceeds, amounting to something like two hundred and fifty dollars, he pushed on to town and on the way made up his mind to give up charcoal burning forever.

He was then in his twenty-third year, and casting about for a new occupation more congenial to his taste and aspirations, he concluded to study law as the profession of his life. He had gained confidence in himself by associating with his fellow-students at the Seminary, and although painfully conscious of the insufficiency of his education, he saw no help for it but to devote himself to his law books all the more closely, and by industry and application to gather professional knowledge as he gathered experience, and so he left the farm forever and definitely located at Galena. After some discouragements from well-meaning friends, he began studying law under the instruction of Isaac P. Stevens, Esquire, then a practicing attorney of excellent character and standing at the bar of Jo Daviess County.

Rawlins was at that time blessed with a strong, robust body, a vigorous constitution, and a mind which, although but partly developed, was self-reliant and confident. He had already made many friends and attracted the attention of the leading men, and this, together with the hopefulness of youth, encouraged him to apply himself to his studies with such assiduity that by October, 1854, or at the end of a single year, he was not only admitted to the bar but was taken into partnership by his preceptor, with whom he continued till August, 1855, when the latter retired, leaving his entire business to his young partner. From that time Rawlins had a remunerative practice, and a rising reputation, which spread farther and farther as his abilities expanded and his acquaintance increased. He soon became known throughout the county as an excellent lawyer and a rising man.

In March, 1857, he was elected City Attorney, in which capacity he served for one year, with credit to himself and benefit to the city. In February, 1858, he formed a partnership with David Sheean, who had been reading law with him since July, 1856, and had just been admitted to the bar. This partnership continued with mutual satisfaction till January, 1862, Mr. Sheean conducting the business of the firm alone from August, 1861, at which time Rawlins was preparing to enter the army.

Rawlins had developed rapidly as a general practitioner, but his special distinction was in jury trials. In one of his earliest cases he acted as assistant to John M. Douglas, later president of the Illinois Central Railroad, a lawyer of high character and standing, and after the witnesses had been examined, Mr. Douglas, feeling especially pleased with the skill displayed by his young assistant in bringing out the points of the case, said:

"Now, John, I want you to talk to the jury; to sum up the proofs and apply the law to this case."

Rawlins replied with trepidation:

"But I can't make such a speech as this case requires, Mr. Douglas."

"Oh, yes, you can, John," said the old counsellor; "but I did not ask you to make a speech, I merely asked you to 'talk to the jury.' I want you to tell them quietly all the facts, just as you would tell your mother, and then, after citing the law, we shall get a decision in our favor."

And John, catching the lesson promptly, did as he was told, with such clearness and cogency as to secure a judgment for his client.

But it would be wrong to suppose that Rawlins's style was uniformly colloquial and quiet, for such was far from the fact. He could assume a quiet manner whenever necessary, but he was naturally passionate, vehement, and emphatic; and yet, his words were generally well chosen and deliberately uttered. While they sometimes poured forth like a torrent, each was in its proper place to convey the idea he had in mind. They did not become confused and tumble over one another in the fervid rush of passion or indignation, as is too frequently the case with impetuous young lawyers, but even in the midst of the hottest debate each was so

16

clearly and distinctly enunciated as to carry his hearers forcibly along with him.

Notwithstanding the fact that most of his life had been passed in farming, wood-chopping, and charcoal-burning, he rapidly acquired unusual prominence as a clear-headed and successful lawyer. He became known in due time as a formidable and earnest advocate and a close, logical reasoner. Like many another great lawyer of the state, he was more or less ignorant of the technicalities and refinements of the profession at first and therefore minimized their importance or swept them contemptuously aside when they were in his way. A close observer of human nature, and a careful and indefatigable student of his cases, he made it a rule to master every detail, not only of his own side but also of his opponent's. But as he was always terribly in earnest, like all such men, he occasionally emphasized the merits of his cause by appealing to common sense and the eternal principles of justice. While he had the faculty of marshalling the main points at issue, he permitted no detail, however insignificant, to drop from its proper place, nor to fail of its due effect upon the cause he was arguing. His popularity was enhanced from the first by the sturdiness with which he stood up for the rights of his clients, however humble they might be. He was, according to his partner, most persistent in demanding every courtesy and consideration for them, and would permit neither Judge nor opposing counsel to minimize their just deserts. The very thought of injustice or of wrongdoing filled him with anger, while at the slightest show of rights denied to him or to his client he poured forth a vehement and impassioned flood of protest, which rarely ever failed to secure what he was contending for.

And yet in the preparation and management of his cases he exhibited the greatest tact and good judgment. He never annoyed witnesses nor fatigued the court by piling proof upon proof. His rule was to bring in sufficient evidence for his purpose and then to allow his witnesses to be discharged. The weak points on his own side he guarded and concealed with consummate skill, while he exposed those of his adversary with unusual quickness and attacked them with tremendous vigor. His patience was unwearying and his

17

application and industry quite beyond the common. He was preeminently a man of vigilance and clear perceptions, who readily understood the character of men and divined their motives and purposes with intuitive but unerring certainty. Honorable and chivalric by nature, free from envy and malice, and scorning all selfish and immoral purposes, he was unrelenting in exposing the want of those virtues in others, and was rarely ever mistaken when he uttered a sentence of condemnation.

According to all accounts, he was eminently successful not only in getting but in winning cases; and yet he was always financially poor. Generous and free with money, he seemed to care but little for collecting it, and still less for saving it. His controlling sentiment was ambition, but ambition always subordinate to patriotism and to the aspirations of an honest and generous heart. He desired fame and dreamed of it and worked for it, and it is altogether to his credit that he bent all his energies to its achievement even to the total disregard of his financial interests. To prepare and try his case well, to make a good argument, and to succeed in the trial were more important to him than the money he was to get for his services. The consciousness of duty well performed and the credit of having won his client's commendation were far more gratifying to him than any fee, however great, or however freely bestowed.

Struggling upwards constantly, and yet conducting himself everywhere with becoming modesty, he gained the good will of all with whom he came in contact, so that within half a decade no man in the community enjoyed its confidence and respect more fully than did Lawyer Rawlins. He was popular with old and young, for although a man of decided views, and always ready upon proper occasions to state and enforce them, he never failed to pay due deference and becoming respect to the character and opinions of his elders.

One of his earliest and best friends, whom he met first at Galena in 1853 while he was still a student, says:

His personal appearance was even then such as to arrest attention. I passed him on the sidewalk. A strong, sturdy looking young fellow, swarthy in complexion, with hair and eyes black as night, which

18

when they looked at you looked through you. But in those youthful days they had in them a merry and kindly twinkle which at once impressed you with the notion that they were the windows of a large and generous soul. After he had passed I turned and looked at him and my mental comment was: "There goes a fellow worth knowing." It was not long until I did know him and from that time until he went to the war, which was at least a year before I went, our acquaintance and association were intimate. It is needless to say that my first guess about him was right.

After these young men became acquainted they formed an association with two others, Sheean and McQuillan, and Captain (afterwards Judge) John M. Shaw of Minneapolis were accustomed to meet of evenings in Rawlins's office, where they read the standard books, criticised the leading men, and discussed the great questions of the day. Rawlins, with a fine and sonorous voice, read poetry with much feeling and effect. He was specially fond of Burns, and his thrilling rendition of "A Man's a Man for a' That" stirred the souls and lingered long in the memory of his companions. Three of the party were Democrats, while only one was an out-and-out abolitionist. Their discussions were an epitome of what was taking place during that decade everywhere throughout the United States, and not only gave them a clearer view of the great principles involved, the great interests at stake, and of the great men upon the stage, but heightened their skill in debate, and stimulated both their patriotism and their ambition.

POLITICAL CONNECTIONS

IT may be doubted if there is any occupation which more quickly develops character than that of a lawyer in a growing Western town such as Galena was in the decade of 1850 and 1860. It was the seat of an active commerce not only with the lead mines and surrounding country, but also with the towns and cities on both the Mississippi and Ohio rivers, with which it was connected by steamboat lines owned and controlled mostly by its own citizens. The population contained an unusual number of men of prominence and ability. Both Elihu B. Washburne, who so long represented the Galena district in Congress and afterwards held with high honor the position of Minister Plenipotentiary at Paris, and J. Russell Jones, Lincoln's United States Marshal for the Northern District of Illinois and Grant's United States Minister at Brussels for seven years, resided there. The latter was the wise and sagacious friend of both Lincoln and Grant, and was noted throughout the region for his ability and success as a business man. John M. Douglas, for many years a distinguished lawyer, and president of the Illinois Central Railroad, John E. Smith, a successful business man and afterwards a Colonel, Brigadier General and Major General of Volunteers, and finally Colonel and Brevet Major General in the Regular Army, and Dr. Edward D. Kittoe, an Englishman belonging to a historical family, a learned and successful practitioner of surgery and medicine, born and educated abroad, but a thorough American both by adoption and conviction, were also at that time citizens of that thrifty town. Along with Maltby, [Augustus] Chetlain, and Rowley, all of whom entered the Volunteers, they early became the staunch friends of Rawlins. They gave character and direction to the social as well as the professional and business life of the place and surrounding country. While they differed in politics from one another, and most of them differed widely from Rawlins, the white heat of the great war soon burnt down all party lines, leaving nothing but Union men and patriots in all that region.

It should be remembered that Rawlins was by birth, association, and conviction a Democrat and that in the exciting political canvass which resulted in the election of Lincoln to the Presidency, he gave

20

his support to the principles of the Democratic party as set forth by Senator Douglas, the author of the Kansas-Nebraska Bill, but the vigilant opponent of the Lecompton Constitution in the United States Senate.

By 1860 Rawlins, the charcoal burner, had become so prominent a lawyer and public speaker that he was almost unanimously nominated for the office of presidential elector on the Douglas ticket for the first Congressional district of Illinois, and with characteristic fearlessness he challenged the Republican candidate, Allen C. Fuller, one of the most eloquent speakers in the State, to a series of joint discussions. The challenge was accepted, and the opponents met in every county of the district. Party feeling ran high; the people were thoroughly aroused, and while it is fair to admit that a large majority of both parties was entirely loyal and patriotic, it is equally certain that even the wisest men were far from agreed as to just what was best to be done to ensure public tranquillity, and to preserve the national Union. Slavery as an institution was abhorrent to the feelings of many Democrats as well as to most Republicans, and to no one more so than to Rawlins; but he, like many other worthy and patriotic citizens, considered it as having been established in the earlier days of the country, under the sanction of custom and law older than the Constitution itself, and that it was not only tolerated but protected in terms by that great instrument of government.

No party at that time, except the abolitionists, thought of disturbing slavery in the States where it existed. Both Lincoln and Douglas were willing to give it every legal and constitutional protection so long as it should be confined to the old slave States. The great object and aim of the Republican party was to prevent its further spread and to preserve the Union of the States at all hazards. They were unwilling that any new States should be admitted into the Union with slavery as one of its institutions, no matter whether it was situated north or south of the Missouri Compromise line. They claimed that in the interest of justice and humanity Congress, which under the Constitution has absolute power and control over the territories, should by law prohibit the introduction of slavery into any of them and by that means restrict its extension.

The Southern, or pro-slavery, Democrats claimed the absolute right for citizens of the slave States to remove to any new territory with their slaves and to keep them there indefinitely under the protection of the laws. They also claimed that all States which should be thereafter organized south of the old line of the Missouri Compromise, should be slave States absolutely, and that all others should be free to adopt slavery if they chose. Douglas and his followers held a middle position, and contended for the so-called doctrine of "Popular Sovereignty"; the substance of which was that the settlers and inhabitants of the new territories should have the right to decide for themselves whether or not they would have slavery amongst them, and that this right should inhere without reference to the territory's immediate or ultimate admission into the Union of States. The idea was both ingenious and popular. Besides, it was not inconsistent with what had been the policy and practice of the people in earlier days; but, like all half or intermediate measures in times of great excitement, it was favored by neither of the extremes. It did not satisfy such of the Northern people as believed with Garrison and Phillips that slavery was "the sum of all villainies," and that no new community of Americans, whether from the South or North, should have the right to adopt it under any form of sovereignty. It was equally unsatisfactory to a large majority of the Southern Democrats; for it conceded the right of settlers, or "squatters" as they were derisively called, to exclude slaves from any territory of which the majority of the population might happen to be composed of people from the North.

In the joint debate which took place between Rawlins and Fuller, the whole ground of the controversy was fought over before the electors. The political history of the country from the days of the Revolution down to the time of the discussion was laid before the people and the two candidates, with great fervor, urged them, each according to his ideas of propriety and duty, to gravely consider and wisely decide what should be done in the crisis then upon them. Every town in the district was visited, and each candidate in turn, under the rules adopted, strove to his utmost to enlighten his hearers and confute the arguments of his opponent. From the published accounts of the debates it is evident that Rawlins threw his whole soul into them, relying altogether upon the Constitution of the United States, the laws enacted by Congress thereunder, the decisions of the Supreme Court, and the speeches and writings of Jefferson, Madison, Clay, Webster, Cass, and Douglas to support him in his contentions.

In the discussion at Freeport on September 29, 1860, Rawlins displayed powers of reasoning and a ready familiarity with the facts and arguments pertaining to the slavery question which surprised not only his supporters but his opponents. He began with the earliest records, and showed that Congress had not legislated against slavery in the territories previous to the passage of what was known as the Missouri Compromise Bill, and that many of the wisest statesmen of that day, amongst them both Jefferson and Madison, had deprecated that measure as unwise and dangerous to the peace and unity of the country. He then discussed the Wilmot Proviso and the Compromise Measures of 1850, following the line of argument and supporting the positions taken by Douglas in that memorable controversy. He justified the Compromise of 1850, brought forward by Henry Clay and carried through by the aid of Daniel Webster; defended the Kansas-Nebraska Bill, which repeated the Missouri Compromise of 1820, and supported the doctrine of Popular Sovereignty, under which new states were to decide whether they would have slavery or not. It was during the discussion of 1850 that Seward in the United States Senate first proclaimed a "Higher Law" than the Constitution of the United States; and while this doctrine was a favorite one with the abolitionists, Rawlins condemned it as both dangerous and unsound. He contended with force and ingenuity that it was better for the cause of freedom itself, as well as more in consonance with precedent, that the people of the territories should exclude or adopt slavery in each case than that Congress should arbitrarily dispose of it in either way.

Now that Slavery has been abolished by the conflict of arms and at the cost of so much blood and treasure, it is difficult for the people of this day to perceive how there could have been such wide differences of opinion about it between the North and the South; but it was a question of profound and growing interest to all parts of the

Great Republic. When it is recalled that, although it might be "the sum of all villainies" and opposed to the spirit of the Golden Rule, it was distinctly recognized by the Constitution as existing in the original States and as entitled to the protection of the laws passed by Congress for the arrest and return of fugitive slaves to- their masters, and finally that those laws had been pronounced by the Supreme Court to be in accordance with the Constitution, it is easy to understand how Rawlins, himself a lawyer, as well as hundreds of thousands of good citizens who abhorred slavery, could advocate the doctrine that it should not be interfered with directly or indirectly by the Congress or by the people themselves in the older States, and that the people of the inchoate States claiming admission into the Union should be left free to adopt or reject it as a majority of them, ascertained in the usual way, should decide. It is a fact creditable to human nature, however, that the majority of the people of the free States were firmly opposed to the spread of slavery, no matter under what pretext or color of law that end might be sought. They felt that if the Constitution as it stood favored the extension of slavery, it should be so amended as to forever prohibit its extension, while the more uncompromising abolitionists, who were fortunately never very numerous, openly claimed that the Constitution was "a covenant with death and an agreement with hell" and should therefore be destroyed along with the Union itself if no other way could be found to rid the country of that hated institution.

From 1850 to 1860 this all-absorbing question monopolized the attention of the pulpit and the press, as well as of Congress and the State Legislatures, to the exclusion of almost every other topic, and Rawlins but followed the example of his elders in familiarizing himself with every phase of the discussion, so that when he was called upon to take part in it, he was familiar with every view that had been taken of slavery, as well as with every argument that could be made for or against it. His speeches, which were closely reasoned and impressively delivered, won a great local reputation for him as a public speaker. They included all that could be said in favor of the middle ground occupied by Douglas; and while these arguments failed to carry the people of his district with him, they were not without great effect upon them as well as upon Rawlins himself.

They showed both the futility of trying to settle a question affecting the very foundations of human society by the quiet methods of the Constitution, and made clear the course they should pursue in case the arbitrament of arms, the last argument of people as well as of kings, should be forced upon them by their brethren of the Southern States.

No precept or statement, no appeal to the Constitution, no authority of scripture or law, no example of custom or history, however antiquated or sacred, could convince Rawlins or the people that slavery itself, mild and mitigated as it might be, was essentially right, or could ever be regarded as beneficial to either slave or master. His very soul revolted against the idea of property in human beings. His whole life so far was at war with a condition of society in which such an idea could prevail; and yet it does not appear that he denounced it in its moral aspects in any public speech. But, on the other hand, I have failed to find a single word ever uttered by him in its favor. He evidently saw none of the advantages claimed for slavery by its advocates, and recognized none of its so-called blessings. Indeed, so far as can be discovered, he never felt called upon to consider or discuss it as an abstract question of morals, or even of economics, much less to uphold it as an ideal condition of society. It was a concrete fact, for which neither he nor any living citizen of the Republic could be held primarily responsible. He therefore considered it merely as an established institution, which it was his duty as a citizen to assist in protecting by such means and in such way as would not interfere with vested and established rights, but which should best promote the peace and prosperity of the whole country as well as of the people more immediately concerned.

Rawlins came out of the joint discussion with increased strength and confidence in himself. He had met an able and experienced debater, before large and deeply interested gatherings of intelligent citizens; he had acquitted himself as a logician and orator to the satisfaction of his own party, and had gained the respect of his opponents as an honest, fearless, and able advocate of the cause which he had espoused. But he also came out of the discussion with grave apprehensions as to the future. Like Douglas, his great leader, he feared that the day for argument had gone by and that the hot heads of the South and the extremists of the North would speedily bring on a conflict in which all minor questions would be lost sight of, and the very existence of the Union itself would be imperiled.

BEGINNING OF THE WAR

AFTER the canvass was over and the election of Lincoln to the Presidency had become known, Rawlins returned to the practice of his profession, feeling that he had done his whole duty to his fellow-citizens. He had striven with all his abilities to guide them aright through the political crisis which was upon them. He was inspired throughout by love for the Union and respect for the wisdom and patriotism of the Fathers who had established it. He was entirely free from sectionalism or bigoted partisanship. He loved his whole country, and knew "no North, no South, no East, no West." He revered the Constitution as the greatest charter of Government ever framed by human wisdom. His sole desire was to preserve it unchanged and hand it down to posterity unviolated, and in full force and effect throughout the land. He had done his very best, according to his light, to cultivate a feeling of moderation and compromise and to avert the war which now seemed about to burst forth. Reflecting on all this, without reference to party allegiance or to the course of others, he saw plainly what his duty as a citizen might require, and when the dread hour came his course lay clear before him.

On April 12, 1861, the Secessionists of South Carolina fired on Fort Sumter in Charleston Harbor. The whole country was aroused as if by the shock of an earthquake. There was no longer any doubt or hesitation in the minds of loyal men. All knew that war was at hand, and that the forts must be repossessed and the rebellion put down, no matter at what cost in blood and treasure. Some few hesitated till they could learn what course their favorite leaders would adopt. Douglas, although friendly with the President and opposed to disunion, had not publicly declared for coercion, but Rawlins was one of those who did not wait. He was aroused, indignant, and outspoken in denunciation of the lawless and sacrilegious act of the "fire-eaters" and Secessionists. On the 15th the news, which had been flashed over the country by telegraph, reached Galena that Sumter had fallen. On the 16th the stores were closed, business was suspended, and the country people from far and near hurried into town. The greatest excitement prevailed, bands paraded the streets playing the national airs, and the stars and stripes were unfurled amid the cheers of the aroused and patriotic multitude. In the evening the citizens, without regard to past party differences, assembled in mass convention. The Mayor undertook to explain the objects of the meeting. His remarks were desultory, uncertain, and disappointing. He was followed by E. B. Washburne, the Republican member of Congress, whose commanding figure and resounding voice proclaimed that the hands of the legally elected President must be upheld at every cost; that the day of compromise had passed, and that "the wicked and unjustifiable war" which had been begun by the South Carolinians must be fought through to the bitter end, till the rebellious States had been coerced back into the Union, and the authority of the Constitution and the laws should be admitted to be paramount throughout the land. Amid loud cheering the sturdy Washburne took his seat, and then a cry arose from all sides for "Rawlins—Rawlins!" And it may not be doubted that many who joined in the meeting hoped that he would take the "Democratic view" of the crisis and show that there was no legal or constitutional power in the National Government "to coerce a sovereign State," that "war could not reestablish the Union," and that it was better if no compromise should be found, that the discontented sister States should be permitted to "depart in peace" rather than that war should be made upon them.

On the day of the meeting a doubting Democratic friend said to Rawlins, in words which had already become familiar: "It is an abolition meeting. Do not mix up in it, for if you do, it will injure both you and your party." Another advised him to abstain from speaking, because the time had not yet come for war measures; still another claimed that the General Government had no authority "to coerce a state"; but Rawlins was deaf to all such appeals. With flashing eye and clenched fist he declared:

"I shall go to the meeting, and if called upon, I shall speak. I know no party now; I only know that traitors have fired upon our country's flag."

And so, when he heard the call of his fellow-citizens, from his modest place at the rear, he elbowed his way through the dense and excited throng to the little open space on the platform and took his stand before them, quivering in every muscle with excitement and patriotic fervor.

Rawlins was at that time barely thirty years of age, his form was spare but muscular and erect, his face pale but swarthy, his hair black and brushed back from a high and ample forehead, his eyes dark as night and flashing with anger at the cowardly advice of his political friends. Looking the audience squarely in the face, he began his address with deliberation. Silence fell at once upon the meeting, for the orator was a favorite of both parties in the community. Speaking with a deep, rich, and penetrating voice, every word he uttered reached its mark, and had the audience been ten times as large, every man of it would have heard all he had to say. For three-quarters of an hour, amidst the profoundest silence, he described the history and provisions of the Constitution, the nature and growth of political parties, and the transcendent advantages of the Union. He reviewed the past, from the foundation of the Government, repeated the real and the fancied wrongs of the slave holders, dwelt upon the good faith with which the Northern Democrats had fought their battles under the Constitution, and commended the cheerfulness with which the minorities, hitherto out-voted, had submitted to the will of the majority, as in the case of the Missouri Compromise, the Mexican War, and the Kansas-Nebraska Bill. He showed his fellow-citizens that the American way was to submit to the will of the majority and to trust the future, the good sense, the justice and sober second thought of the people, in every emergency. He then pointed out the wickedness of the overt act which had been committed against the sovereignty of the National Government, and declared that it was the work of "fire-eaters" and "hot heads," entirely without legal right or justification. Finally, in the full glow of patriotic fervor, his voice ringing out like a trumpet through the open space into the narrow streets beyond, he rose to his splendid climax in words that should never be forgotten:

... I have been a Democrat all my life; but this is no longer a question of politics. It is simply Union or disunion, country or no country. I have favored every honorable compromise, but the day for compromise is past. Only one course is left for us. We will stand by the flag of our country and appeal to the God of Battles! . . .

The effect was electric and instantaneous. The audience, springing to its feet, gave cheer after cheer for the Union and for its defence and maintenance at whatever cost. No opposing voice was heard; party lines were forgotten in the wild tumult of applause, and Major [Robert] Anderson, the gallant defender of Fort Sumter, became at that moment the hero alike of both Democrats and Republicans. The white heat of patriotic eloquence had for the time fused all opinions into an united, unquestioning love of the Union, which would brook no rebellious resistance to its Constitution or its laws. The speech was a genuine surprise to the Republicans. They knew that Rawlins was earnest and able, but they were not prepared for such a flood of cogent argument or its thrilling climax. As for the Democrats, they were simply amazed and overwhelmed. They had come to the meeting in hesitation and doubt, but they left it to doubt no longer.

Among the citizens present was Captain U. S. Grant, late of the regular army and a graduate of West Point. He was then a clerk in his brother's leather store, but neither a politician nor a partisan, though he had always called himself a Democrat, and had cast his only vote for President, four years before, for James Buchanan. How he felt when he went to that meeting is not recorded; whether he was for Douglas or for Breckenridge in the late election is also unknown. He was at that time nearly forty years of age, a modest, quiet citizen who had lived at Galena less than the requisite time to acquire the right to vote. He had but few acquaintances in the community and fewer intimate friends. Lawyer Rawlins was attorney for the leather store, and had met Captain Grant both socially and on business, but as yet there had been no intimacy between them. Rawlins was favorably known to nearly every man and woman of the district. He had lived and grown up among them, and had by his own energy and industry made himself a conspicuous figure; so that at this time it is but the simple truth to say that he was a much more considerable man in the public estimation at Galena than was Captain Grant. So much is certain, for General Grant told me, when the speech was still fresh in his memory, that he had listened to it with rapt attention, that it had stirred his patriotism and rekindled his military ardor. But this is not all. It appears to have removed all doubt from his mind, if any existed, as to the course he should pursue, and it is a notable fact that from that day forward he supported the doctrines of coercion which Rawlins had so eloquently proclaimed.

We are told by Richardson,* who was Grant's first authorized biographer and whose work was corrected by Rawlins, that on his way home from the first Galena mass meeting, Grant said to his brother Orville that he thought he ought to reenter the army.

*Albert Richardson was a respected correspondent for the New York Tribune. He was captured during an attempt to run the batteries at Vicksburg and spent time in Confederate prisons. He'd also been a spy for the Union. See his The Secret Service, the Field, the Dungeon, and the Escape.—Ed. 2015

The next day a company of volunteers was enrolled, and the former captain of the regular army, being the only man in town who even knew the manual of arms or had had any military experience whatever, was asked to drill it. Four days later he was on his way with this company to Springfield, where through the recommendation of Russell Jones and other home friends, he was temporarily employed by Governor Yates as a clerk in the Adjutant General's office. He appears to have been the only person within reach who knew how to make out a requisition for arms or other supplies in proper form, or to what bureau of the War Department it should be sent, and hence his assistance at that particular juncture was invaluable.

It is also worthy of note that about this time Grant addressed an official letter to the Adjutant General at Washington, telling him who he was and offering his services again to the country, but, curiously enough, he never received the courtesy of a reply. Shortly after reaching Springfield family business took him to Covington, Kentucky, where his father resided, and while there he called twice on Major- General McClellan, just appointed to command the Ohio militia, with headquarters at Cincinnati. The ex-captain of infantry entertained the hope that a casual acquaintance with that distinguished officer during the Mexican War would secure for himself an offer of employment, but in this he was also disappointed. He then returned to Springfield, where Governor Yates gave him further employment in connection with the organization, equipment and supply of the volunteers, then being enrolled under President Lincoln's first call. While he was there teaching others, from his abundant experience, how to get clothing, arms, and military munitions, and instructing the green and untrained officers how to organize and drill their newly enrolled companies and regiments, the Battle of Bull Run was fought, the country was plunged into still greater excitement, and more troops were called for by the President. In a short time the modest ex-captain, by his industry and knowledge of military details, had gained the confidence of the Governor, who at the suggestion of others, but with some hesitation, gave him the appointment of Colonel to the Twenty-first Regiment of Illinois Infantry Volunteers on June 21, 1861, in place of Colonel Goode, a volunteer of the Mexican War and a participant in Lopez's filibustering expedition to Cuba, who, in accordance with the custom of the day, had been elected first by the men to that important office. As a measure of instruction and discipline, and for lack of rail transportation, the new Colonel, when the proper time came, asked permission to march his regiment from its camp near Springfield, across country to the town of Mexico in northeastern Missouri, and obtained authority to do so, as the best means of getting it under discipline and giving it practical military instruction.

Meanwhile Rawlins had been invited by his friends, John E. Smith and James A. Maltby, to help them raise an independent cavalry regiment, with the understanding that he was to have the rank of major, but owing probably to the indifference of General Scott to that arm of service this fell through, whereupon he helped them with the Forty-fifth Illinois Infantry, known later as "The Lead Mine Regiment," and it is certain that his name had quite as much influence as that of either of his seniors in attracting the best class of men to the organization, which afterwards gained much distinction in the Army of the Tennessee.

In the midst of the excitement of recruiting, Rawlins was called to Goshen, New York, to attend the bedside of his dying wife, who had long been ill of consumption. She was the daughter of Hiram Smith of that place, and had returned to her father's house in the hope that a change of climate and scenery would have a beneficial effect, but in this she and her husband were doomed to grievous disappointment.

In those exciting days, events occurred rapidly. The Government was organizing armies and arranging in earnest for suppressing the outbreak against the Union. [John C.] Fremont, as a popular hero, had been assigned to the command at St. Louis, and had general charge of all military operations in the region south and west of that place. New generals were required, and Congressmen of influence were called upon to make nominations. Mr. Washburne of the Galena district, who was always active and vigilant in looking out for the public interests, gave prompt consideration to the qualifications and claims of his own constituents and the necessity for military training and experience. Amongst others he bethought him of Captain Grant, even before the latter had received his commission of colonel. West Point men of experience were but few, and specially in demand. At Washburne's request the other members of the Illinois delegation joined in recommending this modest and comparatively obscure man to the favorable consideration of the President. In a few weeks, and apparently without reference to the fact that the Governor had already given him a colonel's commission, the President appointed him a brigadier general of volunteers to date from May 17, 1861, or but one month back of his colonel's commission. On account, however, of the precedence which this State Commission gave him over other colonels with commissions of later date, serving in the same field, Grant found himself commanding a brigade of volunteers in the Department of Missouri. He had evidently not forgotten his neighbor's patriotic war speech at Galena a few months before, and although the latter had at that time never seen a company of uniformed soldiers and was absolutely without technical military knowledge, Grant hastened, on the same day, to send Rawlins a formal letter offering him the position of aid-de-camp, and asking him to get a lieutenant's commission in the

33

Galena regiment then about ready for the field, and to report to him for duty at his earliest convenience. As this was probably the very first letter Grant wrote giving a position on his staff to anyone, it seems to show that he had even at that early day become a good judge of men, and makes it certain, at all events, that Rawlins had by one means or another already made a profound impression upon the future army commander.

To this letter Rawlins replied only five days later as follows:

Galena, August 12, 1861.

BRIGADIER GENERAL U. S. GRANT,

Saint Louis, Missouri.

DEAR SIR:

Your letter bearing date St. Louis, Missouri, August 7th, A. D. 1861, tendering me the position of aid-de-camp on your staff is before me. It is a compliment unexpected; but fully appreciating your kindness and friendship for me, and believing from your long experience in and knowledge of the military service, and its duties, you would not have offered me the position were you not satisfied it is one I could fill, gladly and with pleasure I accept it and whatever the duties and responsibilities devolved upon me by virtue of the same, I will with the help of God discharge them to the best of my ability.

Wishing you success in the cause of Constitutional freedom for which you are fighting, I remain,

Yours obediently,

JOHN A. RAWLINS.

But before he could complete his arrangements to take the field it became necessary for Rawlins to rejoin his wife at Goshen, where she died, August 30, leaving one son and two daughters, the eldest only five years of age.

Meanwhile Grant's appointment to the actual rank of Brigadier General of Volunteers reached him, and this entitled him under the law to an Adjutant, Quartermaster, and Commissary, all with the rank of Captain of United States Volunteers, besides two aids-de-camp to be selected from his actual command. True to the prepossessions already noted, the new general now made haste to offer the first of those offices to Rawlins, and this gave him in due time the first and most important position on Grant's staff. This, it should be noted, he retained with the increasing rank which came to him in due course, as his chief was promoted from grade to grade, and from command to command. To the infinite credit of both, there was never any suggestion of change, and the close relations which grew up between them from the start remained unbroken to the end. The correspondence relating to the position of Adjutant General has not been found, though its character can well be inferred from that already given in reference to the appointment of aid-de-camp. Rawlins frequently mentioned it with satisfaction in his conversations with me while we were intimately associated— as will be more fully referred to hereafter—on the same staff during the Vicksburg Campaign.

But all doubt, if any exists, as to Grant's feelings towards Rawlins as well as towards Congressman Washburne, their common friend, is fully removed by a letter from Grant to Washburne now in possession of the Library of Congress. It runs as follows:

Cairo, Illinois,

September 3, 1861.

HON. E. B. WASHBURNE,

Galena, Illinois.

DEAR SIR:

Your very kind letter was duly received . . . and would have been answered at once but for the remark that you were about to start for New York City and would not receive it for some days. I should be most pleased to have you pay me the visit here, or wherever else I may be, that you spoke of paying me there.

In regard to the appointment of Mr. Rawlins I never had an idea of withdrawing it so long as he felt disposed to accept, no matter how long his absence. Mr. Rawlins was the first one I decided upon for a place with me, and I very much regret that family affliction has kept him away so long. The post would have been a good school of instruction for him in his new duties; the future bids fair to try the backbone of our volunteers. I have been kept actively moving from one command to another, more so, perhaps, than any other officer. So long as I am of service to the cause of our country, I do not object however.

General Fremont has seen fit to entrust me with an important command here, embracing all the troops in southeast Missouri, and at this place. ... A little difficulty of an unpleasant nature has occurred between General Prentiss and myself relative to rank, he refusing to obey my orders, but it is to be hoped that he will see his error and not sacrifice the interest of the cause to his ambition to be Senior Brigadier General of Illinois, as he contends he is.

In conclusion, Mr. Washburne, allow me to thank you for the part you have taken in giving me my present position. I think I see your hand in it, and admit that I had no personal claims for your kind office in the matter. I can assure you, however, my whole heart is in the cause which we are fighting for, and I pledge myself that if equal to the task before me, you shall never have cause to regret the part you have taken.

Yours very truly,

U. S. GRANT,

Brig. Gen. Vols.

It is probable that Rawlins's letter of appointment came to Galena and was remailed to him at Goshen. His acceptance was doubtless written at the same place, about the first of September, for it is known that as soon as he could arrange for the care of his young children he started for Cairo, and was there on September 14. Thenceforth he was the constant companion of his chief and always on duty, except for two months, between August and October, 1864. During this period he was absent on sick leave under medical treatment for what he and the staff surgeon persistently believed to be merely a severe bronchial affection contracted in service, but which finally developed into pulmonary tuberculosis and proved fatal four years after the war. But even during this absence, his faithful friend and assistant, Lieutenant Colonel Theodore S.

Bowers, of Mt. Carmel, Illinois, kept him constantly informed of what was going on at headquarters, with the understanding that in case of any movement of the Army or any emergency in its affairs, or in those of General Grant, he would return at once to his post.

FIRST MILITARY SERVICES

As heretofore stated, Rawlins at the time of his entry into the Army knew absolutely nothing of military affairs, and indeed it was impossible that it should have been otherwise. His life had been passed far from military scenes, or the thought of military employment. He had never even seen a company of regular infantry, a battery of artillery or a squadron of cavalry. He knew nothing whatever of tactics, organization, or military administration, and never even thought of the functions of the staff and staff corps, or of the relations and uses of the various arms of service to one another. It would seem almost incredible that a civilian of such limitations should have been assigned at such a time to the most important duties, after those of the commanding general, connected with the troops in that military district; and yet the sequel will show that General Grant had made no mistake in his choice. The young lawyer, while lacking the very rudiments which he would find necessary for the correct performance of his daily duty, had every natural qualification for his place. His study and practice of law, especially of the Constitution, had taught him the relations between the civil and the military powers of the State, as well as the rights and duties of the several States and of their citizens towards one another and towards the general Government. Besides, he was thoroughly in earnest, and had the sagacity to see that he must first learn what his position required of him before he could be expected to fill it worthily. Like all volunteers, he was at the outbreak of the war perhaps unduly impressed by the superior knowledge of the regular officers, but as there were only a small number of them then or afterwards in General Grant's Western command, he lost no time in regretting his own ignorance, but forthwith began to learn from his chief and the army regulations what was expected of him, and how to make himself useful.

Fortunately Grant's military education and his services in the regular army in actual warfare had made him thoroughly familiar with military life and with the duties of both the staff and the line, while his even temper and clear head especially qualified him to act as an instructor not only to his own staff but to the troops under his command. From the date of his own arrival at Cairo, September 2, 1861, he had been compelled to perform the duties of adjutant general, quartermaster, commissary, ordnance officer, and drill master. He had worked almost alone from morning till midnight for two weeks, and was nearly worn out when his uninstructed but willing adjutant general reported for duty. New regiments were arriving daily and required to be encamped, fed, brigaded, and prepared for active service, and Rawlins found himself at once in a military school of the most practical character. Precept and instruction went hand in hand with the necessity for daily action. Of course, the adjutant general was compelled to give his first attention to the duties of his own department, which comprehended the returns, reports, correspondence and orders of the command, but at the same time he took a deep interest in everything else going on about him and soon became in fact as well as in theory the main dependence of his Chief. He made it his practice to see that everyone else performed the service assigned him. He was from the first active, inquisitive, vigilant, and terribly in earnest. Consequently he soon came to be looked upon by subordinate commanders, with whom he was naturally sympathetic, as scarcely less important than Grant himself.

Having been deeply engaged in public life during the excitement immediately preceding the outbreak of the war, he knew many of the leading men who were now coming forward as field officers and generals, especially those from Illinois, as well as from the neighboring region of Wisconsin and Iowa. Through them, aided by an exceedingly frank and sociable disposition, he made new acquaintances readily, and in this way, as well as through the daily routine of business, he soon came to know every important and influential officer in the command. With an unusually keen insight into the character and motives of men, he rarely made a mistake in his estimates of their moral and intellectual worth, or of their military capabilities. While he was rigid and austere in his own principles and practices, he was liberal and sensible with reference to the conduct of others. What he looked for and insisted upon having was prompt and unquestioning obedience to orders and a trustworthy sobriety of behavior at all times on the part of both officers and men. On the other hand, he was far from being a martinet, and never forgot that the army was chiefly composed of citizens who were called forth in a great emergency to perform the duty of soldiers, and of whom the rigid and machinelike discipline of regulars could neither be expected nor exacted. In this he and his Chief were in hearty accord, but it is well known that Rawlins was far the more exacting of the two.

Grant has been credited in the popular mind with having shown particularly good judgment in the selection of his subordinates and in surrounding himself with a specially able staff, and while it is true that he finally became fairly successful in both respects, his success was doubtless due as much to the selection of Rawlins in the first place, and to the influence which that officer exerted ever afterwards, as to any extraordinary perspicacity or discrimination on his own part.

Rawlins always took a most earnest and active interest in seeing that none but worthy men should have command, and that his Chief should not be long imposed upon by such officers as were weak, corrupt, or inefficient.

This was especially true in regard to the staff and the clerical force at headquarters. In the first days of Grant's arrival at Cairo, he was too busy, and perhaps too poorly acquainted with the personnel of his command, to choose his assistants and aids-de-camp from the volunteers with proper discrimination. Those were taken who were nearest at hand, and perhaps some put themselves forward by solicitation or through the influence of their friends, for the purpose of finding easy and conspicuous places. At all events it is certain that with the exception of Rawlins, at first, and of Colonel Webster, an ex-regular, and Captain Rowley, of Galena, a little later, Grant's first staff was but poorly constituted and contained several officers who were not only ignorant but unworthy of respect and confidence. Rawlins was not long in picking them out, though it took him more than a year, with all the help he could get, to overcome the General's partiality for some and to get rid of others. During their connection with the staff several gave much trouble and were the source of constant anxiety. They were roystering, good-hearted, good-natured, hard-drinking fellows, with none of the accomplishments and few of the personal qualities of good soldiers, and did not hesitate, when opportunity offered, to put temptation in the way of those they thought would meet it halfway. Grant himself was preoccupied with his own responsibilities, or had a sympathetic side for them when off duty. Or perhaps, like most men, he was more or less subject to flattery and to the kind attentions such "jolly dogs" knew how to bestow acceptably upon those with whom they desired to curry favor. But Rawlins was too serious, too stern and unrelenting, to countenance or encourage them. He had no patience with them, but from the start kept close watch upon them, and as they became more and more indiscreet or reckless, and he better and better informed as to their real qualities, he induced the general to send them away one after the other, till all the objectionable ones were gone.

It was in this, as well as in other respects, that he was always the complement and counterpart of his taciturn but kind-hearted Chief, and was enabled to render him most invaluable services throughout the war. He appeared to know instinctively a worthless or vicious man, and to abhor his example and influence. But his highest function was in protecting Grant from himself as well as from others, in stimulating his sense of duty and ambition, and in giving direction and purpose to his military training and aptitudes. It was Rawlins, more than any other man, who aroused Grant's sensibilities and gave his actions that prompt, aggressive, and unrelenting character which so distinguished them. In fact, it has been frequently and truthfully said that the two together constituted a military character of great simplicity, force, and singleness of purpose, which has passed into history under the name of Grant. This character, while achieving extraordinary results, was not without fault, nor did it get through to the end without serious mistakes and checks. Its plans, as might have been expected, were in some degree rude and unscientific, while its practical operations were occasionally marred by faults both of logistics and tactics. It was, in fact, far from possessing all the attributes of the ideal captain, but, without reference to the part contributed by either or by the attendant circumstances, it may be truthfully said that it was patient, even-tempered, prompt, courageous, and altogether patriotic. What is still more noteworthy is the fact that for four years of active and costly campaigning it escaped any great disaster, and was uniformly successful.

When it is considered that the result was the same whether Grant was confronted by Pillow or Polk, as at Belmont; by Floyd, or Buckner, as at Donelson; by Albert Sidney Johnston or Beauregard, as at Shiloh; by Joseph E. Johnston or Pemberton, as in the Vicksburg Campaign; by Bragg or Longstreet, as at Missionary Ridge, or by the hitherto invincible Lee, as in the wonderful series of operations from the Rapidan to Appomattox Court House, it must be admitted that he was favored by something more than mere luck or fortune or even a preponderance of resources which gave him one of the most remarkable series of victories recorded in history. No suggestion nor criticism can explain away this extraordinary result. It cannot be contended that Rawlins was greater or wiser than Grant, in any respect, nor can it be properly claimed that he made the plans or "supplied Grant with brains," as some have declared, but it seems to be certain that Rawlins, an untrained man of the plain people, was different from Grant, and furnished him with qualities and characteristics which Grant did not possess at all, or which he possessed in a limited degree, and without which, either from Rawlins or from some other source in whom he had confidence, it would have been impossible for him to succeed as he did.

In military matters perhaps more than in any others, no one man can devise all the plans, make all the dispositions, think out all the movements or play all the parts. Official cooperation, loyal help and personal support are necessary, not only in the daily administration of an army but throughout every campaign and in every battle, and it is the province of organization and of discipline not only to draw these from the army but to make them effective wherever found. And yet, all combined may fail to command success for a general, no matter how great his army nor how well it is supplied, unless he is, himself, guided by a high moral purpose, quick and just perceptions, alert intelligence, and an active, ready, fearless, and aggressive temper. It is but just to add that in respect to all the necessary qualities of leadership, except only such as were based upon military experience and technical knowledge, Rawlins, by common consent, was regarded by those who knew him as easily the peer of any man in the army. It is but natural that the high qualities conceded to him, aided by his intimate personal and official relations with his Chief, should have furnished him with abundant opportunity to render such support and assistance as the varying circumstances which surrounded them seemed to call for from time to time. During the progress of this narrative it will appear that those moral perceptions and aggressive qualities, which are so greatly the characteristics of the successful general, were possessed to a marked degree by Rawlins, and that he contributed them ungrudgingly to the support of his Chief and to the advancement of the cause for which they were fighting.

EVENTS IN KENTUCKY, 1861

PADUCAH and Smithland, situated within a few miles of each other on the lower Ohio River in Western Kentucky, were occupied by Grant, September 6, 1861, and the Battle of Belmont, a few miles below the confluence of the Ohio and the Mississippi, was fought two months later, November 7. The first of these movements resulted in breaking the neutrality which Kentucky was at that time striving to maintain. Rawlins saw through the shallow pretense upon which this policy was based and often declared afterward that, considering "conditional neutrality as absolute hostility to the Government," he had from the first urged Grant to disregard it entirely, if it should at any time or in any manner interfere with the operations of his command. This radical advice was acted upon with boldness and promptitude and the consequences were both startling and far reaching.

The Secessionists under General Leonidas Polk at that time occupied Columbus, a strongly fortified position some twenty miles below Cairo, on the east bank of the Mississippi, as the left flank of their defensive line, of which Fort Henry on the Tennessee and Fort Donelson on the Cumberland, near the Kentucky and Tennessee State line, were the left center; Bowling Green, Kentucky, on the Louisville and Nashville Railroad, the right center, somewhat thrown forward, and Cumberland Gap, near the eastern corner of Kentucky and Tennessee, the extreme right. The seizure of Paducah, at the mouth of the Tennessee, and of Smithland, at the mouth of the Cumberland, was a direct menace to both the extreme left and left-center of their line, and was followed by great commotion among the Confederate leaders.

Fremont, who was relieved by Halleck on November 2 from the command of the Union forces in Missouri and Southern Illinois, had been engaged in conducting certain desultory operations in Southeastern Missouri against the Confederate General Thompson. Grant was cooperating from Bird's Point and Cape Girardeau, but fearing that Polk would send a force from Belmont, opposite Columbus, to cut off the Union columns, he resolved to make a preliminary dash at Belmont, and did so with about thirty-five hundred men, whom he commanded in person. This was Grant's first actual battle with the Confederates, and was entirely successful in its main object. He captured the hostile camps, but the Confederate commander promptly reinforced the outlying detachment at Belmont, which was easy to do, as it lay within the range of his heavy guns on the other side of the Mississippi, at Columbus, and in turn forced Grant and his audacious followers to cut their way back to their transports. This was the first fighting that Rawlins ever took part in or saw, and in addition to giving him and his Chief confidence in their men and in each other, it was important in turning the enemy's attention to the exposed situation of the garrison at Columbus, and in exerting considerable influence upon its ultimate withdrawal to Island Number Ten.

Writing to his mother from Cairo on November 15, Rawlins described his feelings and the action as follows:

> I have been in one battle, heard the whistling of bullets and the whizzing of cannon balls, and I tell you I thought no more of the first than of the last; still I never thought of running. Any man with half a soul must be somewhat brave on the battle field. Your mind is filled more with a desire of winning victory than of personal safety, and this is felt more strongly when the chances appear against you. Success is the paramount feeling. I was in the midst of danger and within the reach of the rebel fire more than once during the day. I was by the side of General Grant when his horse was shot under him. Just the moment before he was trying to urge his horse up to the ranks of our men, and his horse not being very bridle-wise, refused to go ahead, and my horse being one that will go any place, I rode ahead, the General following. Just then I turned to look towards him, when the General said his horse was shot so severely that it was necessary to leave him on the field.

> Our troops fought well and bravely. We had three thousand men all told, the effective and well men of five regiments, commanded by Colonels Buford, Logan, Fouke, Dougherty and Lauman, the three first under General McClernand, the other two under Colonel Dougherty, while all were under the command of General Grant. All of the above mentioned officers, except Colonel Lauman, whose politics I do not know, are Democrats. I mention this to show that Democrats will fight

(I mean Union Democrats) for the country, Washington and the stars and stripes. Our loss was, killed 85, wounded 218. This is official.

The enemy had the effective men of eleven regiments, consisting of Tennessee, Arkansas and Louisiana troops, the flower of Southern chivalry, according to their own figures, and lost in killed and wounded 543, not including the loss of one regiment not yet ascertained.

We met and defeated them on their own ground, took possession of and burnt all their tents and camp equipage, captured six pieces of artillery and brought away two with us, all under the guns of the strongest fortified position on the Mississippi River. Upon our return to the boats from which we had debarked, they rallied their scattered forces and with fresh troops from Columbus, undertook to cut off our retreat, when another battle ensued, in which we a second time defeated them and continued our march uninterrupted to our transports. Just as we were all aboard, they having in the meantime crossed over more troops from Columbus, arrived on the shore and commenced firing at our boats wounding two men on board the steamer *Memphis*. The gun-boats then poured into their ranks several broadsides of canister and grape shot doing great execution.

Belmont is entirely abandoned by the enemy and thus the Southeastern portion of Missouri is without a rebel army.

I am glad old Guilford is for the Union. I am as you are a Democrat, but I am also for the Union of the States and the triumph of my country in arms against whomsoever may oppose us.

This letter is important not only because it is the first one of the kind written by Rawlins, but because it shows also that he as well as Grant, with both officers and men, behaved with spirit and courage in their first battle for the Union.

Followed, as the affair was, by the occupation of Paducah by a force sufficiently large to overrun the neighboring country, it produced an effect on the extreme left of the enemy's defensive line similar to that produced by Thomas's brilliant victory over Crittenden and Zollicoffer at Mill Springs, on the right center. It was in addition good practice for the troops, and aroused in them a healthy show of enthusiasm. It secured for Rawlins his first mention in the Official Reports, taught him, as well as his General, the advantage of taking the initiative, and made him always afterwards the earnest advocate of striking the first blow.

But while the occupation of Paducah and Smithland and the Battle of Belmont brought Grant's name prominently before the country as an aggressive and enterprising general, they stimulated envy and malice at once to spread rumors prejudicial to his sobriety and trustworthiness. The army contractors, who had undertaken to furnish supplies to his troops, were prompt to resent his efforts to make them deliver supplies of full weight and proper quality. They complained to the reporters, and the reporters gave the story to the newspapers. The facts connected with Grant's retirement from the regular army were noised about at that early day, and, in one way or another, prejudicial rumors based thereon were set afloat and soon reached Washburne at his seat in Congress. As he was both an ardent patriot and a man of austere and correct habits himself, who felt more or less responsible for the good character of Grant and the other officers who owed their appointment to his recommendation, naturally enough he made haste to write to Rawlins for the real facts of the case. The latter replied fully and in detail, without delay:

Headquarters, District of Cairo,

December 30, 1861.

DEAR WASHBURNE:

Yours of the 21st is at hand. I was no less astounded at the contents of your note than you must have been at the information reported to you.

I thank you for the confidence manifested by you in the frank manner of your inquiry. I feel that you of all other men had the right, as you would feel it your duty, to investigate the charge. I know how much you have done for General Grant and how jealous you are of his good name, and assure you it is appreciated not only by General Grant but by all his friends.

I will answer your inquiry fully and frankly, but first I would say unequivocally and emphatically that the statement that General Grant is drinking very hard is utterly untrue and could have originated only in malice.

47

When I came to Cairo, General Grant was as he is today, a strictly total abstinence man, and I have been informed by those who knew him well, that such has been his habit for the last five or six years.

A few days after I came here a gentleman made him a present of a box of champagne. On one or two occasions he drank a glass of this with his friends, but on neither occasion did he drink enough to in any manner affect him. About this time General Grant was somewhat dyspeptic and his physician advised him to drink two glasses of ale or beer a day. He followed this prescription for about one or two weeks (never exceeding the two glasses per day) and then being satisfied it did him no good, he resumed his total abstinence habits, until some three or four weeks after the Battle of Belmont, while he was rooming at the St. Charles Hotel, Colonel Taylor of Chicago, Mr. Dubois, Auditor of State, and other friends, were visiting Cairo, and he was induced out of compliment to them to drink with them on several occasions but in no instance did he drink enough to manifest it to anyone who did not see him drink. About this time Mr. Osborne, President of the Illinois Central Railroad Company, our mutual friend J. M. Douglas, and several of their friends made a visit to Cairo, and gave a dinner (or lunch) on the cars, to which the General and I were invited with others; champagne was part of the fare. Sitting near the General I noticed that he did not drink more than half a glass. The fact of his drinking at all was remarked simply because of his usual total abstinence.

But no man can say that at any time since I have been with him has he drunk liquor enough to in the slightest unfit him for business, or make it manifest in his words or actions. At the time I have referred to, continuing probably a week or ten days, he may have taken an occasional drink with those gentlemen and others visiting Cairo at that time, but never in a single instance to excess, and at the end of that period he voluntarily stated he should not during the continuance of the war again taste liquor of any kind, and for the past three or four weeks, though to my knowledge frequently importuned on visits of friends, he has not tasted any kind of liquor. Ever since I have been with General Grant he has sent his reports in his own handwriting to Saint Louis, daily when there was matter to report, and never less than three times a week, and during the period above referred to he did not at all relax this habit.

If there is any man in the service who has discharged his duties faithfully and fearlessly, who has ever been at his post and guarded the interest confided to him with the utmost vigilance, General Grant has done it. Not only his reports, but all his orders of an important character are written by himself, and I venture here the statement there is not an officer in the Army who discharges the duties of his command so nearly without the intervention of aides, or assistants, as does General Grant.

Some ten or twelve days ago an article was published in the *Chicago Tribune,* charging frauds on the Quartermaster's Department here, in the purchase of lumber at Chicago. General Grant immediately sent Captain W. S. Hillyer, a member of his staff, to Chicago, with instructions to thoroughly investigate and report the facts. That report and a large mass of testimony substantiating the charge had been forwarded to St. Louis when orders came from Washington to investigate the charge. The investigation had already been made. Thus time and again has he been able to send back the same answer when orders were received from St. Louis in reference to the affairs of this District.

I am satisfied from the confidence and consideration you have manifested in me that my statement is sufficient for you, but should the subject be mooted by other parties, you can refer them to Colonel J. D. Webster, of the 1st Illinois Artillery, General Grant's Chief of Staff, who is well known in Chicago as a man of unquestionable habits. He has been counsellor of the General through this campaign, was with him at and all through the Battle of Belmont, has seen him daily and has had every opportunity to know his habits. I would further refer them to General Van Renssalaer, who was specially sent to inspect the troops and investigate the condition of the District by Major General McClellan, and Generals Sturgis and Sweeny, who were sent here by Major General Halleck for the same purpose. These gentlemen after a full and thorough investigation returned to St. Louis some two weeks ago. I know not what report they made; but this I do know, that a few days after their return an order arrived from St. Louis creating the District of Cairo, a District including Southeast Missouri, Southern Illinois, and all of Kentucky west of the Cumberland, a District nearly twice as large as General Grant's former command. I would refer them to Flag Officer A. H. Foote of the U. S. Mississippi Naval Fleet, a man whose actions and judgments are regulated by the strictest New England standard, a strict and faithful member of the Congregational Church who for months has had personal as well as official intercourse with the General.

If you could look into General Grant's countenance at this moment you would want no other assurance of his sobriety. He is in perfect health, and his eye and intellect are as clear and active as can be.

That General Grant has enemies no one could doubt, who knows how much effort he has made to guard against and ferret out frauds in his district, but I do not believe there is a single colonel or brigadier general in his command who does not desire his promotion, or at least to see him the commanding general of a large division of the army, in its advance down the Mississippi when that movement is made.

Some weeks ago one of those irresponsible rumors was set afloat, that General Grant was to be removed from the command of the District, and there was a universal protest expressed against it by both officers and men.

I have one thing more to say, and I have done, this already long letter.

None can feel a greater interest in General Grant than I do; I regard his interest as my interest, all that concerns his reputation concerns me; I love him as a father; I respect him because I have studied him well, and the more I know him the more I respect and love him.

Knowing the truth I am willing to trust my hopes of the future upon his bravery and temperate habits. Have no fears; General Grant by bad habits or conduct will never disgrace himself or you, whom he knows and feels to be his best and warmest friend (whose unexpected kindness toward him he will never forget and hopes some time to be able to repay). But I say to you frankly, and I pledge you my word for it, that should General Grant at any time become an intemperate man or an habitual drunkard, I will notify you immediately, will ask to be removed from duty on his staff (kind as he has been to me), or resign my commission. For while there are times when I would gladly throw the mantle of charity over the faults of friends, at this time and from a man in his position I would rather tear the mantle off and expose the deformity.

Having made a full statement of all the facts within my knowledge, and being in a position to know them all and I trust done justice to the character of him whom you and I are equally interested in, I remain, your friend,

JOHN A. RAWLINS.

This letter speaks for itself and gives the best account extant of Grant's habits as they existed at that time. It needs no comment.

The Battle of Belmont seems to have called attention to the necessity for reinforcements, and these in turn brought Rawlins increased work in helping to organize and instruct them as they came pouring in from the Northwestern States. They were, of course, formed into regiments before leaving home; but many of them were unarmed when they arrived, and all were not only ignorant of their military duties, but poorly equipped and supplied for active field service. They were necessarily assigned to brigades as soon as they arrived, placed in camp, and put at once under such instruction as circumstances permitted. Meanwhile the older troops, under C. F. Smith and McClernand, were used in making reconnaissance and demonstrations against the enemy's position in Western Kentucky.

On February 6, 1862, Fort Henry was taken by a combined naval and land attack, and ten days thereafter Fort Donelson, with its garrison of over 15,000 men for duty, were captured by the forces under General Grant. During these operations Colonel Webster continued to act as chief of staff while Rawlins's duties as assistant adjutant general were confined to issuing orders, sending out instructions and making returns. These orders announced the staff, the creation of brigades and divisions, and the assignment of regiments thereto, but the greater number of them were dictated verbally by General Grant from his own personal experience, and related to the discipline of the troops in camp and on the march, prohibiting them from leaving camp or going outside of the line of sentinels except upon duty, forbidding them to straggle, maraud, or fire away ammunition upon any pretext except in battle; prescribed advanced guards of cavalry and rear guards of infantry; directed that roll calls should be held on the march at least twice a day, and that every man should be accounted for on the daily returns. They also provided that loyal refugees coming into the Union lines at Cape Girardeau, Paducah, Smithland, and Cave-in-Rock should be gathered together and be furnished with food and quarters by contributions to be levied upon and collected from their disloyal neighbors. In addition to all this, details of engineers, pilots, and gunners were made from the soldiers who had enlisted from the river towns, to provide crews for the improvised gunboats and rams, which were now coming from the boat-yards ready for offensive and defensive operations.

After the capture of Fort Henry and pending the capture of Fort Donelson many new regiments were rushed forward to reinforce those in the field. They had also to be assigned to brigades and divisions, and furnished with orders and instructions. On February 9 an order was issued requiring officers to remain with their commands and forbidding them and their men alike from going aboard the transports except upon duty.

On February 17 Grant's command was designated as the District of West Tennessee, and orders were issued congratulating the army upon its great victory, prohibiting officers and men from appropriating captured property, or from going into the town of Dover, and distributing to the various divisions the guard duty and other work to be performed by them. On the 21st the force had swollen to such great numbers as to require a larger organization, and accordingly four divisions were announced, together with a partial redistribution of regiments. On the next day Colonel Mortimer D. Leggett, a learned and discreet lawyer of Ohio, was detailed as Provost Marshal General, and notice was given that no courts would be allowed to sit under State authority and that order would be maintained throughout the District of West Tennessee by martial law. In all doubtful cases Colonel Leggett was required to consult with General [Stephen] Hurlbut, a distinguished lawyer from Northern Illinois, whose decision should be final. On the 26th an order was issued referring to frequent applications on the part of citizens for permission to enter the Union camps for the purpose of seeking for fugitive slaves, and all officers were forbidden to grant permits of that kind.

Such slaves as were within the lines at the time of the capture of Fort Donelson, and such as have been used by the enemy in building the fortifications, or in any way hostile to the Government, will not be released nor permitted to return to their masters, but will be employed in the Quartermaster's Department for the benefit of the Government.

This is noticeable as the first order issued in the West forbidding the return of fugitive slaves to the service of their former masters, and providing for their employment in the Union army.

Owing to the hurry and confusion of the campaign, and the suspension or interruption of mail and telegraphic communications with Halleck's headquarters at St. Louis, and also to the failure of colonels not yet assigned to brigades to make prompt report of their junction with the army, and proper returns of the number of men in their regiments, Grant failed to keep Halleck as fully informed as to the strength of his command and the details of his organization and operations as was desired, and was not only severely censured therefor, but virtually suspended from active command. In spite of all these orders, he was blamed also for reported lawlessness and irregular conduct on the part of the troops, for absence from his command without the authority or knowledge of General Halleck, and finally, on March 4, 1862, Halleck, from St. Louis, telegraphed McClellan, at Washington:

> A rumor has just reached me that since the taking of Fort Donelson, General Grant has resumed his former bad habits. If so, it will account for his neglect of my often repeated orders. I do not deem it advisable to arrest him at present, but have placed General [C. F.] Smith in command of the expedition up the Tennessee. I think Smith will restore order and discipline.

The substance of the foregoing message was evidently communicated to the President, for on March 10 the Adjutant General of the Army telegraphed to Halleck as follows:

> It has been reported that soon after the Battle of Fort Donelson Brigadier General Grant left his command without leave. By direction of the President, the Secretary of War desires you to ascertain and report whether General Grant left his command at any time without proper authority, and if so for how long; whether he has made to you proper reports and returns of his force; whether he has committed any acts which were unauthorized, or not in accordance with military subordination or propriety, and if so, what.

To this minatory message Halleck on March 15, replied:

In accordance with your instructions of the 10th instant, I report that General Grant and several officers of high rank in his command immediately after the Battle of Fort Donelson, went to Nashville without my authority or knowledge. I am satisfied, however, from investigation that General Grant did this from good intentions and from a desire to subserve the public interests. Not being advised of General Buell's movements and learning that General Buell had ordered Smith's division of his (Grant's) command to Nashville, he deemed it his duty to go there in person. During the absence of General Grant and a part of his general officers, numerous irregularities are said to have occurred at Fort Donelson. These were in violation of the orders issued by General Grant before his departure, and probably under the circumstances were unavoidable.

General Grant has made the proper explanation and has been ordered to resume his command in the field. As he acted from praiseworthy although mistaken zeal for the public service in going to Nashville and leaving his command, I respectfully recommend that no further notice be taken of it. There never has been any want of military subordination on the part of General Grant, and his failure to make returns of his forces has been explained as resulting from the failure of colonels of regiments to report to him on their arrival, and partly from an interruption of telegraphic communication. All these irregularities have now been remedied.

The Official Records published by the War Department do not show any explanations or reports from Grant to Halleck between March 4 and 15, nor any of an earlier date, touching the rumor mentioned in Halleck's despatch of the 4th to McClellan and it will be observed that Halleck's telegram of the 15th to Thomas, the Adjutant General, is entirely silent in regard thereto, and that while it exonerates Grant from blame for leaving his command without authority, and declares that "there had never been any lack of military subordination on the part of Grant," it ignores the alleged "acts not in accordance with military propriety," and makes no explanation whatever touching the rumor or the underlying facts.

It is to be observed that while Halleck and Grant were never intimate, it is not impossible—indeed, it is altogether likely—that such a purely personal matter as Grant's habits in the field would have been discussed, if at all, in an unofficial way through the medium of private correspondence, and it has been suggested that such a correspondence took place, but there is no trace of it in the published records. Indeed, the latter contain nothing touching this delicate subject except the three telegrams already quoted. As far as now known, Grant's spirited assertion that he had gone to Nashville solely in the public interest and had not started on the trip till he had reported through the proper channels that such was his intention, supported and emphasized as it was by an indignant and manly request to be relieved from further duty under Halleck, was the only "proper explanation" ever offered by him. It was an all-sufficient reason why he should be restored to the command of which he had been so unjustly deprived.

It will be observed that this statement is not inconsistent with the telegraphic correspondence between Halleck, McClellan, and the Adjutant General at Washington. There is not the slightest doubt that a great wrong had been done to Grant, by relieving him, on an unsupported rumor of this character, from active command in the full tide of a successful campaign, and ordering him to remain at Fort Henry while a large portion of his army was sent forward into the enemy's country under his subordinate, C. F. Smith. Nothing less than the confirmation of the rumor could have justified such treatment, and Rawlins always declared that this rumor was entirely without foundation.

Grant's own account of this important episode is given in a letter to his wife as follows:

> . . . All the slander you have seen against me originated away from where I was. The only foundation was the fact that I was ordered to remain at Fort Henry and send the expedition up the Tennessee River under command of Major General C. F. Smith. This was ordered because General Halleck received no report from me for nearly two weeks after the fall of Fort Donelson. The same occurred to me. I received nothing from him, and the consequence was I apparently totally disregarded his orders. The fact was he was ordering me every day to report the condition of my command and I was not receiving the orders, but knowing my duties, was reporting daily, and when anything occurred to make it necessary, two or three times a day.

When I was ordered to remain behind it was the cause of much astonishment among the troops of my command and also a disappointment. When I was again ordered to join them they showed I believe heartfelt joy.

The precise date or author of this "slander" cannot now be discovered, but that it had been set afloat can hardly be considered as strange. That a rumor prejudicial to Grant's character was on its way and doing its baneful work was fully known to the leading officers in that district, and especially to Rawlins, as early as December 30. This is shown by his letter of that date to Washburne.

This rumor and those which followed had an important influence upon Grant's career not only then but for many months thereafter, and necessarily resulted in establishing still closer and more intimate relations between him and Rawlins. There could be no concealment as to the rumor, or the slander, or as to the real facts between the commanding general and

It has been suggested by General [Grenville] M. Dodge that much of the correspondence between Grant and Halleck pertaining to the Donelson campaign went to the end of the telegraph line where the operator was a rebel, who deserted, taking with him all the despatches in his possession. This may account for the fact that there are so few despatches found in the "Official Records" for this period his confidential friend and staff officer. Whether the rumor was true or false, is not now the question, but it had certainly reached Halleck, who made haste to repeat it to the General-in-Chief at Washington. Without reference to its date, its origin, or its truthfulness, there seems to be no doubt that disappointed contractors, reporters, camp followers, and even rival generals, concurred in giving it currency. Unfortunately it came to be widely believed, and this belief, more than anything else, caused Grant, in spite of his great victories, to be looked upon with suspicion and disfavor in both public and private life. Nor is there any doubt that the rumor, however started, was primarily the cause of the distrust which was shown by both McClellan and the Secretary of War, as well as by Halleck, throughout the Shiloh, Corinth, Tallahatchie, and Vicksburg campaigns, until the fall of Vicksburg at length relieved the public mind of all anxiety on that account and brought the President, with characteristic humor, to declare to a delegation of worthy citizens who came to counsel with and advise him about the matter:

"I can't say whether Grant is a drinking man or not, but if he is, I should like to know where he buys his liquor as I wish to present each one of my army commanders with a barrel of the same brand."

In justice to Grant, it should be here clearly stated that Rawlins continued to declare, as in the Washburne letter, that the damaging rumor had been put into circulation by Grant's enemies and rivals for the purpose of injuring him with the Washington authorities. Be this as it may, it was the foundation for a widespread apprehension that if not true, it might become true at any time, and this was doubtless the source of constant anxiety not only to Rawlins but to many other friends of Grant. It therefore became the duty of Rawlins, as staff officer and friend, to be ever watchful and vigilant; and it is a fact worthy of all praise that he performed that duty till the end of the war with such fidelity and courage as to effectually protect the interests of his Chief, and at the same time to shield the national cause from all injury which might be brought upon it by Grant's habits or by exaggerated reports as to their actual character and importance. No student of history can read the journals and correspondence of that period without perceiving that rumors were a significant factor, affecting not only Grant's reputation but his relations with those in authority over him, as well as with the great events then taking place. In view of the fact that such was certainly the case and that both Rawlins and Grant are long since dead, it would be an inexcusable omission for the biographer of either of those important characters to ignore or minimize its importance.

Unfortunately I shall have occasion to advert to this subject again before concluding this narrative, but for the present, whether its actual importance was great or small, it may be truthfully declared that, so far as known, it never injuriously influenced Grant's action or his plans in regard to either a campaign or a battle. It has never been charged that it at any time induced him to march or fight when he ought not to have done so, nor to refrain from marching or fighting when circumstances were favorable to this course. Moreover, it is confidently claimed that it never caused Grant to blunder or to seriously neglect a duty, nor to perform one in a manner different from that which would have been adopted had he been the most abstemious of men. On the other hand, it is not to be denied that it materially increased the influence and responsibility of Rawlins at headquarters, or that it led to a sort of moral supervision over Grant and his surroundings which, however, unusual or inconvenient, although self-imposed by Rawlins, was of the greatest advantage both to Grant and to the country. This fact, which was no less creditable to the Chief than to the subordinate, was generally known to the leading officers of the army at the time, and did much to secure not only their support and respect for Rawlins but their loyal cooperation in all measures of discipline as well as in all of the great movements which were conducted by Grant.

During the Donelson campaign, in addition to acting as adjutant general of the forces and, upon important occasions, as senior aid-de-camp, Rawlins also performed the delicate and important duties of censor over the telegraphic press despatches. Smarting under the injury inflicted upon him by rumors which he believed to be malicious, Grant specially directed that no reports reflecting upon C. F. Smith should be permitted to go over the telegraph lines. That distinguished veteran was a Regular of great experience and the highest quality, but "rumor" also reported him as having been drunk during the campaign, and Grant did not hesitate to resort to the most arbitrary measures to prevent the spread of such reports. He declared that any criticism of Smith was "sure to be a lie." He bitterly denounced all who took part in setting such rumors afloat, and especially the contractors, whom he had thwarted at Cairo, and who had early begun to cry out against the "red tape" and the "bad habits" of the Regular officers. He went so far in his efforts to reach and punish that class of offenders, who were also the chief scandalmongers, as to seriously recommend in his correspondence with Halleck the enactment of a law which would permit the impressment of "all fraudulent contractors into the ranks, or, still better, into the gunboat service where they could have no chance of deserting."

The Donelson campaign, with its strange experiences, gave Rawlins a clear insight into the difficulties and dangers of military life. It taught him the necessity of full and accurate knowledge on his part and of a complete record in his office not only of what went on throughout the command but of what took place in and about headquarters. If he had not already learned from regulations and books, or from the commanding general, that the adjutant should have charge and supervision of every order and communication from headquarters, whether with the troops, the surrounding country, the Department or Division headquarters, or with the Government at Washington, his experience during this period of rumor and detraction would have taught him the absolute necessity for such an exercise of authority and responsibility. He was an apt pupil, and although he found himself in a strange environment, amidst unexpected scenes and complications, he grasped the elements of the problem with which he had to deal and at once became an acknowledged factor of great power and influence in the daily administration of the army, as well as in the personal and official fortunes of its Chief.

Notwithstanding the capture of Fort Henry and the extraordinary victory at Fort Donelson, the period which followed was one of great discouragement to Grant. The distribution of military authority at that time was peculiar. Halleck had general control over Missouri, Southern Illinois, West Tennessee, and West Kentucky; Buell had similar control over the rest of Kentucky, while Grant himself, who had been in command of a district including Southeastern Missouri, Southern Illinois, and Southwestern Kentucky, and had by a bold and masterly stroke broken the enemy's main defensive line in its most important strategic section, was now assigned to the command of the new District of West Tennessee; but the limits of these widely distributed commands were necessarily vague and ill-defined, while the relations between the commanders were, if possible, still more uncertain. It should not be forgotten that Grant was under the direct orders of Halleck, whose headquarters were at St. Louis, and made his reports and returns to that officer, while both Halleck and Buell reported to and received their general instructions from McClellan, who was then General-in-Chief at Washington. At the same time it should be remembered that all territorial commanders for certain administrative purposes, also had direct communication with the War Department through the adjutant general of the army. And what is still more curious, it now appears from the published records that McClernand, who had been an important Democratic politician and member of Congress from Illinois, and a fellow townsman of Lincoln, but was now one of Grant's subordinates, from the beginning had important if not frequent correspondence with both McClellan and the President.

The situation was at best a complicated one, and as a consequence, neither the military administration nor the practical operations of the armies in the field were conducted upon any well-matured system or plan. They lacked unity as well as force, and much valuable time was lost, after the capture of Fort Donelson, in desultory suggestions and movements or in waiting for formal orders. The difficulties so far as Grant was concerned, were still further exaggerated by the petulant complaints and exactions of Halleck, by his manifest lack of confidence in his lieutenant and finally by the fact that the army itself had become penetrated by a feeling of distrust towards a commander of whom it had heard the "rumor" alluded to in Halleck's despatch to McClellan. This army was made up of the most intelligent men from all parts of the Northwestern States, who had by their home correspondence doubtless given these rumors wide and authoritative circulation. The result was that they were just as effective in shaking the confidence of the country in Grant as if they had been true. New troops were coming forward almost daily; the war correspondent was on the alert, and both troops and correspondent gave immediate currency to every rumor that was started. A state of anxiety and distrust prevailed in the minds of both officers and men, which did much to arouse apprehension at home. The history of what actually took place during the next two months was difficult enough to follow in detail till the Records were published in full, but when all the orders issued, and countermanded, by Halleck from his headquarters at St. Louis, two or three hundred miles away, are considered, it will be seen that an almost hopeless state of confusion existed in his mind as well as in that of the country at large.

On March 5, 1862, Grant's headquarters were removed from Fort Donelson to Fort Henry, and C. F. Smith, in pursuance of Halleck's instructions, was ordered to take command of the expedition which Grant, by virtue of his seniority, had naturally expected to conduct in the direction of Eastport on the Tennessee River. This expedition was at first ordered to destroy the railroad bridge over Bear Creek near that town, and then to break up the railroad connections and crossings at Corinth, Jackson, and Humboldt, in the order named. Shortly after starting, Smith fell sick, and was badly injured by a fall, whereupon Grant, who had at last been credited with making "satisfactory explanations," was, as before stated, permitted to resume command. Absurd as it may appear, the orders then at hand required him on the completion of the designated work, to withdraw his force, "return to Danville and move on Paris." These places it will be observed had never been occupied by any part of his command, but lay in Buell's command, several hundred miles to the northeast in the heart of Kentucky. On the very next day, Halleck sent orders that "there should be no delay in destroying the bridge at Corinth or Bear Creek," and that if successful the expedition would not return to Danville, "but encamp at Savannah unless threatened by superior numbers."

Shortly afterwards Buell's army in Kentucky, whose front had been freed from the presence of the enemy by Grant's victory at Donelson, was put in motion and without serious opposition, found itself soon in Nashville, where Grant in the rightful exercise of his discretion as the commander of a cooperating army, met Buell for a conference, the final result of which was that the latter was wisely instructed by McClellan to march across the country in the direction of Savannah on the Tennessee for the purpose of forming a junction with Grant and thus concentrating an overwhelming force against the enemy.

Thus certainty began to take the place of uncertainty, order the place of disorder; and thus both Grant and his adjutant general saw the plans of operation in that region assuming definite shape, while the administration of the force in the field under their direction was rapidly becoming systematic and effective. They were again in command of a moving and confident army which was daily growing in strength, but they were beset by gathering dangers of another sort of which they were more or less unconscious but which imperiled their future, taught them at the same time lessons of self-reliance and wisdom and gave them that practical experience in military operations without which they could not hope to gain complete or permanent success.

SHILOH

THE battle of Pittsburgh Landing or of Shiloh Meeting House took place on Sunday, April 6, 1862. It was brought on by the Confederate forces, about 40,000 strong, advancing from Corinth, the railroad center against which two Federal armies had been directed, but which neither had reached as yet.

Buell had marched slowly from Nashville, but was within a few miles on the opposite side of the Tennessee. Grant had notified him, on his approach, that there was no special reason for hurrying, but feeling somewhat uneasy about the real plans of the enemy, he took the precaution of sending a note to Sherman at the front, by McPherson asking for a report of the condition of things and whether it was safe for him to remain at Savannah for a conference with Buell. Sherman replied with the information that the enemy had appeared in his front with cavalry, infantry and artillery "six miles out," but he did not "apprehend anything like an attack on our position." Relying fully on Sherman's judgment, Grant wrote Halleck the same evening that he had "scarcely the faintest idea of a general attack," but would be "prepared should such a thing take place." But the fact is that the enemy had been three days floundering through the mud from Corinth, less than twenty miles away, and was by Saturday night within two miles of the Union lines, where no preparations whatever had been made to resist him or even to make him disclose his purposes. The Union troops were encamped without special reference to a defensive battle and in total disregard of the necessity for mutual support and defense. No entrenchments or earthworks of any kind had been constructed, and neither the pickets nor the grand guards were sufficiently far out or sufficiently in touch with each other to give adequate warning or to make adequate resistance to the enemy's advance.

The enemy moved to the attack on Sunday morning as soon as it was light enough to see, and although he did not find many of the Union soldiers in their beds, nor fall upon them before they could form their lines, as has frequently been stated, it was in a military sense a complete surprise. The truth of this statement is established beyond controversy by the simple fact that nearly every general's

63

and field officer's official report admits or declares in terms that the organization to which it refers was surprised by the enemy's attack in force. It is but fair to observe, however, that both Grant and Sherman persisted in denying to the day of their death in face of overwhelming evidence, that such was the case.

As has been shown, Grant himself was not on the field when the battle began, but received his first knowledge of it at Savannah, some seven or eight miles further down the river, from the booming of distant artillery. Knowing too well the significance of that sound, he sent word at once to Buell to hasten his advance, and went forward by boat to Pittsburgh Landing, stopping on the way at Crumps' Landing, between four and five miles from the scene of battle, and there gave Lew Wallace a verbal order "to hold his division in readiness to march at a moment's notice." As soon as he learned that a heavy battle was going on at the front he sent back a written order, which, it is possible, never reached Wallace, "to move up at once by the river road," and growing impatient as the battle deepened, he sent first Rowley and then Rawlins and finally McPherson, to hurry the belated division to the front. By some strange fatality Wallace was slow in moving, and when he did move it was by the road west of the creek instead of the one along the river bank. As a consequence, he was at last forced to countermarch to find a bridge and get on his right road, but failed to arrive on the field in time to take part in the day's fighting. He was severely condemned by Grant at the time and for years afterwards, while Rawlins, from a minute and painstaking study of the case, always contended that this condemnation was fully justified by the facts. He never failed to assert, with the earnest vehemence which characterized him, that no excuse could be found for a division commander, with or without orders, who should march and countermarch all day within sound of a furious battle, less than five miles away, without getting into it. It is true that Wallace was separated from the battle-field, by a creek at flood, but there were both bridges and transports, in sufficient number and proximity, but still the junction was not made.

Lewis "Lew" Wallace (1827–1905) was a lawyer and politician, later the governor of New Mexico Territory. He is most remembered as the author of the novel, Ben Hur.—*Ed. 2015*

Years afterwards Grant took up and reviewed the case and exonerated Wallace from blame, but it should be stated that every fact set forth in the "Official Records" and correspondence, was marshalled and considered by Rawlins, during the preparation of Grant's official reports, while all the important witnesses were living and the incident of the day still fresh in their minds. No important facts not previously known were discovered by Grant, hence it may be inferred that had Rawlins lived, his conclusion in this case would not have been reversed.

It is not necessary to describe in detail the bloody struggle, which resulted in the capture of Prentiss and the greater part of his division, the dispersion of Sherman's raw regiments, the repulse of McClernand, Hurlbut, and W. H. L. Wallace, with the entire national line, the culmination of the struggle in the death of Albert Sidney Johnston, the Confederate generalissimo, and the final rally of Grant's broken but still resolute forces near the steamboat landing. The strength of the opposing armies, even with Lew Wallace absent, was nearly equal. Each had fought the other to a standstill in a battle which was almost constant from daylight till the middle of the afternoon, and which was indubitably the bloodiest of the war up to that time.

Bad as the outlook was for Grant's hard-pressed battalions, as the day was drawing to its close the opportune arrival of the advance-guard of Buell's army put a new phase upon the struggle. Nelson's division was ferried across the river at Pittsburgh Landing and was the first to reach the stricken field. It was followed by Crittenden's and McCook's divisions, which were brought from Savannah by the transports, but did not reach the fighting line till early Monday morning. But the stubborn resistance of Grant's troops, the death of the Confederate generalissimo, and the enfilading fire of the Federal gunboats seem to have paralyzed the Confederate onset before darkness actually ended the conflict. Fortunately, too, Buell's army was united and at hand in time to take the offensive early on

Monday morning, but the actual crisis had passed the evening before and the Confederates had lost their opportunity forever.

Grant and his staff had borne themselves bravely and well. Sherman, McClernand, Prentiss, W. H. L. Wallace, and, indeed, every other general on the Union side, except Lew Wallace, had faced the storm of battle with uncommon courage. Buell arrived on the field in person at about two o'clock Sunday afternoon, when the confusion was the greatest and the hope of victory the lowest. Grant met him on the east side of the river with his headquarters boat, the *Tigress*, and brought him quickly to the scene of battle. On their way through the sickening crowd of stragglers who lined the bank near the landing, Buell asked Grant what preparations he had made for retreating, to which Grant replied with composure and courage: "I haven't despaired of whipping them yet! . . .

Should it come to a defeat," he added, "we can make a bridge of boats across the river and protect it with artillery. But in that event," he continued, "there won't be many men to retreat."

This ended the colloquy. Grant went about his business, while Buell, with soldierly promptitude, made haste to place the oncoming veterans of Nelson's division in line of battle. Their appearance was timely and their advance, which was begun at once, turned the tide which had already begun to ebb, recaptured the guns which had been lost, reoccupied a part of the camps and advanced positions which had been abandoned, and pushed back the worn out and discouraged Confederates all along the front. But it was too late to convert defeat into an overwhelming and complete victory. Night put an end to the battle, with the opposing armies confronting each other substantially as they had been before the battle began in the morning.

It is useless to consider whether Buell could have reached the field earlier, or whether his leading division could have driven the broken and dispirited enemy further that night.

It is equally foreign to this narrative to consider whether either commander was at fault for the incompleteness of the result. Both had done their best, and the first day's fighting with its frightful losses and its varying fortunes was at an end. The whole of Buell's army was at hand though greatly fatigued by its closing march, and hence it was perhaps wisely decided that nothing more could be done till dawn the next morning. Even then it was too late to bring the enemy to a decided stand, for having lost his greatest general and already been foiled in his main object, he had begun the night before to withdraw his main body towards Corinth, leaving only a strong rear guard to delay the pursuit.

This summary of events is based largely upon Richardson's *Personal History*, in the preparation of which Rawlins was freely consulted and upon reports from other sources gathered after the end of the War. It is besides in strict accord with the accounts which Rawlins repeatedly gave me afterwards. He shared all the hardships and dangers of his Chief, wrote and transmitted all the orders, carried several of the most important ones and took the keenest interest in every incident. Fortunately he availed himself of the first lull in the campaign to write to his mother, and as his letter tells how the battle appeared to him at that time, I give it in full as follows:

Pittsburgh Landing, April 8, 1862.

. . . Yesterday's sun went down on one of the hottest contests [that ever took place] on this continent, rivaling any in the numbers engaged and equaling any in its importance. The enemy had fortified himself since the breaking out of the rebellion. The capture of Forts Henry and Donelson opened their eyes to the fact that no fortifications could be built so as not to be taken, and a new order of things was to be inaugurated. They were to bring the "Northern Hessians" into an engagement in the open field and there Southern chivalry would surely triumph.

On Sunday morning, clear, bright and beautiful, they began the attack, and during the entire day the battle raged with varying fortune. They had 110,000 men; we not half that number, who could be brought into the fight. About 5 o'clock P M. they had driven our forces from all our outer camps, and then we looked (as Napoleon did for Grouchy or night) for Buell or Wallace or night, each of whom had notice and was ordered forward to reinforce us.

Just when they were needed, and not a moment too soon, Buell's advanced forces, ten thousand strong, arrived on the opposite side of the river, were quickly crossed to the side of conflict, and checked the enemy. Night setting in they fell back and occupied many of the camps of our men, to renew the fight that had evidently closed favorably to the South. During the afternoon and night General McCook's, Crittenden's and Wood's divisions arrived, and Wallace's division also, giving us 40,000 reinforcements in fresh troops.

Instead of waiting for an attack on Monday morning, we attacked the enemy and fought until night, regaining all our old positions and utterly routing the enemy who left their dead and wounded on the field, burned many of their tents, and destroyed and scattered their arms along their line of retreat. We followed them today some seven miles, capturing some prisoners. In prisoners they have got more than we have. They captured General Prentiss and a part of his division on Sunday.

The number killed and wounded on each side is very great, not less than 5,000. Among their killed is the celebrated Albert Sidney Johnston, who with Beauregard, Bragg and Breckenridge commanded their forces.

The army of the West has thus far borne itself nobly and victoriously. I was on more than one occasion in the thickest of the fight, but remained unharmed.

Barring the overstatement of the enemy's numbers and the understatement of the killed and wounded, which was common at that time, this letter is a correct summary of the principal events as they took place.

It was a great and bloody action followed by far-reaching results, but I have dwelt upon it rather for the purpose of pointing out certain consequences of a personal nature to Grant than for drawing from it the lessons of strategy and military policy which it teaches.

The first reports of victory sent North caused great rejoicing throughout the loyal States. The President appointed a day of thanksgiving and new praise was freely bestowed upon the hero of Donelson. But a flood of injurious rumors and reports as well as of false inferences drawn from the events as they occurred, were sent out by the reporters, by the army contractors, and even by disappointed officers. Many of Buell's intelligent soldiers of all ranks who had passed through the crowds of stragglers near the landing and felt that they had saved the day without having received proper credit for it, added the weight of their criticism to that of the newspaper men. Grant was again charged with being drunk, with having arrived late on the battle field, with being- incompetent and with having neglected the ordinary precautions for the protection of his encampment and base of supplies. The country, and what is worse, Halleck the chief commander in the West, were swift to believe these reports, and although Grant was entirely guiltless of anything to his discredit, except perhaps overconfidence and failure to see that his troops were properly posted and entrenched, he took no public notice of the hue and cry against him, though Rawlins and other officers of the staff publicly denied and denounced the charge of drunkenness as wicked and unfounded; but the mischief had been done.

Halleck hastened to the field, and, as was his right by seniority, assumed chief command of the united armies. His confidence in Grant had been again severely shaken. In distributing the command and giving the forces a working organization, he transferred the bulk of Grant's troops to the right wing under Thomas, assigned Buell to the command of the center, Pope to the command of the left wing, and McClernand, one of Grant's subordinates, to the command of the reserve. He left Grant in titular charge of his own territorial district, but actually relieved him from all responsibility by announcing him as "second in command," and taking special care that he should neither be consulted in reference to plans, nor be permitted to exercise any authority whatever over their execution. Indeed Grant was actually for the most part kept in ignorance of what was going on. He often told me that he was not consulted in reference to the disposition of his own troops and that whenever the commander of either grand division of the army came to headquarters for conference, if he chanced to be near, Halleck would lead the visitor apart and talk with him in tones which could not be overheard. Or if Grant, who really knew the country, ventured upon a suggestion, it was generally rejected with the plain intimation that when his advice was needed it would be asked for.

It was a period of national as well as personal humiliation to Grant, during which the army grew to a hundred and twenty thousand men or nearly three times that of the enemy, and notwithstanding its preponderance of strength, became accustomed, when it moved at all, to move with the torpidity and circumspection of a tortoise. It fortified itself by night and dug its way forward by day, even when the enemy was not in sight. By these means it advanced just fifteen miles in six weeks. In the end it confronted the enemy at Corinth, and by the mere weight of numbers compelled him to evacuate that place, but fortunately Grant could not be regarded as in the slightest degree responsible for the timid policy which controlled the movements of the national forces. He held his peace, studiously abstaining from criticism and recrimination, with the confident hope that patience and reticence would save him in the end if anything could. He however remonstrated with Halleck by letter and as he often said afterwards, seriously thought of asking to be relieved with a view to seeking employment elsewhere, but Rawlins and Sherman both sympathizing deeply with him, strongly advised against this course! and fortunately their advice prevailed. This support in adversity necessarily drew still closer the bond of friendship and interest between Grant and Rawlins, while it laid the foundation of lifelong friendship and confidence between Grant and Sherman. The latter, it will be recalled, had also suffered greatly in the public estimation not only because he had been inconsiderately charged with being "crazy," but because of the insignificant resistance his raw troops had made in the battle of Pittsburgh Landing. It was both natural and creditable that these great officers should stand together under the load of obloquy heaped upon them by unsparing criticism. Their friendship, which was strengthened by Sherman's unselfish support from the rear during the Donelson campaign, was in the highest degree beneficial to the country as well as to themselves. Neither Grant nor Rawlins ever forgot or became indifferent to it, but this is not all. They never forgot or entirely forgave those who supplanted Grant, or those who failed to show their sympathy for him during this trying period. And the significance of this will be better understood when it is remembered that even so lofty a character as George H. Thomas was never included among their closest friends. Conscious of his own merit, that officer had accepted the superior position assigned him by Halleck, without question or protest. He knew Grant but slightly, and doubtless felt under no special obligation to him. Besides he was far too proud to solicit preferment at all, and far too fair-minded to accept it at the cost of a brother officer, if he knew it, but austere and reticent by nature, he was one of the last men in the army to court the confidence, or to participate in the controversies and grievances of others.

Be all this as it may, it is well known to many that no great intimacy ever grew up between Grant and Thomas, or between their respective followers. The armies of the Tennessee and the Cumberland, as they afterwards came to be called, and especially the officers thereof, never became particularly friendly. They supported one another loyally and well, both in the Shiloh campaign and in that of Chattanooga. Finally they became intermingled and welded together in the campaign of Atlanta and in the March to the Sea, but neither ever lost its identity with the other. There always remained a difference, and a distinct plane of cleavage between them. Moreover each shared to the end in some degree the characteristics of the men who organized them. As Grant, Sherman and McPherson, on the one side, differed from Buell, Rosecrans and Thomas on the other, so the Army of the Tennessee differed and remained separate from the Army of the Cumberland to the last day of their existence.

While it was the duty of Rawlins as adjutant general to share the fortunes of Grant, it later became his duty as chief of staff to hold the scales of justice between the officers and the armies with which he was serving. Although a man of extraordinary earnestness and firmness of conviction, it will be shown hereafter that he never permitted any influence or prejudice to run away with his sense of fairness or to warp his judgment in the performance of duty. Acting always from the highest motives, it seldom occurred to him to question the motives of others. An unselfish patriot from the first, he naturally believed every other officer to be as self- sacrificing and disinterested as himself, and in this spirit he upheld the fortunes of his Chief and performed the duty of his position.

During the operations which followed the dispersion of the great army Halleck had gathered for the capture of Corinth, Grant played an important but subordinate part. When Halleck in recognition of his great services was shortly afterwards ordered to Washington as General-in-Chief, he first offered the command of the great army on the Tennessee to Colonel Robert Allen, a graduate of West Point, an old army quartermaster, and a man of merit, but one who had had no field experience in the war, and not until Allen declined the honor did it settle upon Grant. Even then it came by seniority and was limited to the District of West Tennessee and to the troops originally serving under him. Buell's army was maintained intact and directed to the eastward on Chattanooga. The enemy seizing the opportunity, made an offensive return, and the bloody but inconclusive battles of Iuka and Corinth were fought by Grant's subordinates, with the general result that West Tennessee was permanently freed from Confederate occupation and control. The Mississippi having been cleared from Cairo to Island Number Ten by the National gunboats cooperating with the land forces under Pope, Memphis was permanently occupied, and the arrangements for the advance into Central Mississippi and for the capture of Vicksburg gradually took shape. Much time was however lost after the occupation of Corinth because of the so-called "Pepper Box strategy," which scattered the great army gathered there, but withal Grant's patience and modesty had strengthened him with his command and raised him in the public confidence. The newspapers had apparently become less inimical to him. The trade regulations drawn up by Rawlins were vigorously enforced, order was restored, and the supremacy of the Union was acknowledged throughout the district, but withal it is certain that Grant had not yet gained the entire confidence of the Administration. The advent of Halleck as General-in-Chief in Washington neither relieved his lieutenant from distrust nor protected him from the intrigues of political and professional rivals, as it must have done had he given Grant unqualified commendation and support.

It was during this period that Grant issued his drastic order expelling all Jews from the limits of his command, but it is worthy of note that this was done against the advice of Rawlins, who pointed out its objectionable features and called attention to the fact that only two weeks before a similar order issued by one of his post commanders had been countermanded. Grant, who was perhaps unduly incensed by the fact that his own father was interested at the time in carrying on trade within the limits of his department, said with unusual firmness: "Well, they can countermand this from Washington if they like, but we will issue it anyhow." Great excitement was aroused by it throughout the country. The newspapers denounced it in unmeasured terms. Congress took notice of it and a long debate followed, but the ever-watchful Washburne headed off a vote of censure by a motion to lay the subject on the table, which was carried. Meanwhile the President in the exercise of his own prerogative as Commander-in-Chief countermanded the order, but without expressing any direct censure of Grant. It may be assumed, however, that the incident did not strengthen Grant either with the Administration or with Congress, but rather tended to prolong the suspension of judgment which had previously shown itself in reference to him.

Before passing to the consideration of the Vicksburg campaign, it is proper to call attention to the fact that Grant, on April 7 and 8, 1862, reported to Halleck at St. Louis by telegraph and on April 9 by letter the result of the battle which had taken place near Pittsburgh Landing. These communications were both crude and incomplete. They were evidently the work of Grant's hand alone, unaided by his adjutant general, or any other member of his staff. They were not followed, as afterwards became customary, by a careful and exhaustive report, based upon the reports of the subordinate commanders, for the reason stated by Grant himself as follows:

> ... Although I was in command of all the troops engaged at Shiloh, I was not permitted to see one of the reports of General Buell or his subordinates in that battle, until they were published by the War Department long after the event. For this reason I never made a full report of this engagement.

In this connection it should be noted that no battle of the war gave rise to so many controversies, nor to so much professional criticism and discussion as did the battle of Shiloh. The case of Lew Wallace, who failed to reach the battle field in time to take part in the first day's fighting, gave rise to a long and bitter discussion, in which McPherson, Rawlins and Rowley all filed statements in compliance with Grant's instructions.

These statements are fully set forth in the "Official Records," and were carefully summarized by Rawlins in a communication dated April 1, 1863. The controversy has long since ceased to be interesting and need not be further considered, except by the student of military history, but no one can read Rawlins's clear and convincing account of the efforts made to get Wallace into that battle, without reaching the conclusion that Wallace was not only inexcusable for taking the wrong road, but was culpably slow in all his movements that day. It seems to be equally clear that if he had moved with the rapidity that his men, who were "marching light," and were besides in "buoyant spirits" and "eager to get forward," were capable of marching, after they got on to the right road, which was "in good condition," they would certainly have reached the field "in time to engage the enemy before the close of Sunday's fight." Rawlins gave clear and unequivocal testimony to support this conclusion, and sets it forth in a way which shows that he perfectly understood every military consideration involved in the controversy. In spite of all that was afterwards said in behalf of Wallace, it is to be observed that Rawlins, whatever others may have done, never changed his statement of the facts nor the conclusions based upon them, but stood by both to the day of his death. As he and McPherson actually joined Wallace at 3:30 P M. and accompanied him during the march au cannon, it is not to be presumed that they were mistaken as to the facts which they reported, or as to the inferences to be drawn therefrom.

OPERATIONS IN THE WEST, 1862

IN pursuance of orders issued by the War Department, I reported for duty at Grant's headquarters at LaGrange, West Tennessee, November 8, 1862. I had come straight through from temporary service on the staff of McClellan during the Antietam campaign. Although I was at the time only a first lieutenant, I had received flattering overtures for service and promotion and had knowledge of certain important plans which had been adopted by the Administration for raising additional troops in the Northwestern States, to be used in opening the Mississippi through to the Gulf of Mexico.

On reaching headquarters I was shown into the adjutant general's office, where I met for the first time John A. Rawlins, the subject of this narrative. He was seated at his desk with his back to the door, with no one else in the room. As I entered he swung around with a look of inquiry upon his dark and serious face. I told him who I was, and, handing him a copy of my orders, said I had come to report to General Grant for duty. He replied at once that the general was absent at Memphis, but would be back shortly, that I had been expected for several days, and that I would probably be sent temporarily to McPherson, with whom I was intimate, and who would lead the advance with the right wing of the army towards Central Mississippi. After adding that he knew all about me and my people, that I was from Illinois, as he was, that regular engineer officers were much needed in that army, and that I should be fully employed, he explained the situation at headquarters with startling frankness, disguising nothing and extenuating nothing.

He said in substance that Grant had been more or less justly criticised at one time or another, and emphasized this by handing me a written pledge in Grant's own handwriting, which he had received some time before. He dwelt upon the danger which this pledge was intended to guard against, and marked his apprehensions in a most dramatic manner by referring to the sword of Damocles. Having thus revealed the worst aspect of the case, he turned swiftly to the other side, and with words equally frank, he assured me that he regarded Grant as a good man, an experienced and courageous officer, who did his whole duty loyally and well, and always told about it plainly and truthfully; that he was cool, level-headed and sensible, of sound judgment, singular modesty, loyalty, and patriotism, and could certainly lead us to victory, if his friends could "stay him from falling." Rawlins then added that there were some good officers on the staff, but more bad ones, and that he wanted me to help clean them out. With this done he concluded by declaring that he wanted to form an alliance, offensive and defensive, with me for the purpose of weeding out worthless officers, guarding the general against temptation and sustaining him in the performance of the great duties which he would be called on to perform.

The entire conversation was a serious and unusual one, but I was by no means surprised at its tenor. The newspapers and the officers I had met on the way had partly prepared me for it. What Rawlins said not only gave the key to the actual situation, but put me on the alert for additional facts.

We naturally renewed our conversation as occasion offered, and I was soon thoroughly informed not only as to Grant's personal habits but as to his very great and substantial merits as well. The character of his staff officers and leading generals, together with the inner history of the army and of its campaigns, speedily became as familiar to me as if I had served with it from the beginning of the war. I need not add that the acquaintance thus begun with Rawlins grew day by day and month by month into the closest intimacy, which existed unbroken to the day of his death, seven years later. From this time forth I shall naturally speak largely from my own knowledge of events as they took place, and from personal observation of Grant and the officers who served under him.

Aided as I was by the clear head and vigorous character of Rawlins, I was not long in arriving at a full understanding of the problems confronting Grant as well as the army which he commanded. He was expected by the Government to march through Holly Springs and Oxford to Grenada, and to operate from the latter place in such manner as to cause the evacuation of Vicksburg, or to bring about its capture.

Immediately after I joined, movements were begun to that end, but the winter, with its frequent rains, was too near at hand, the roads which were of the most primitive kind were in bad condition and the streams much swollen. To make matters worse, the Confederate cavalry under Van Dorn promptly swept around our flank, threw itself on our rear, captured our depot at Holly Springs, destroyed our reserve supplies and broke our railway to the rear. The result was that the overland campaign became paralyzed before it was fairly under way, and it was apparent to all that the line on which we were operating was not only impracticable but would have to be abandoned, and the sooner the better.

About this time a personal incident occurred which deeply aroused the feelings of Rawlins. On entering the army he left his professional, business with his partner David Sheean, a friend from boyhood, who had studied law in his office, whose brother married his sister, and, like himself, was a Democrat of decided views. It was a period of arbitrary practices. The writ of Habeas Corpus had been suspended even in the North, and those having influence with the Federal authorities not infrequently paid off personal scores by procuring the arrest and incarceration of peaceable citizens whom they could not otherwise silence. An outrage of this sort was inflicted upon Mr. Sheean in the fall of 1862. While in the peaceful pursuit of his profession he was arrested on the charge of disloyalty, carried to New York and imprisoned in Fort Lafayette. This arbitrary act led to much local excitement, during which Rawlins took a short leave of absence and made an investigation of the circumstances. On his return to the army, he drew up a full statement of the case, and sent it to the Secretary of War with letters from Grant, Hurlbut, and Logan, and also from his fellow-townsmen, Maltby and Rowley, asking for the release of his friend. Impatient at the delay of the Secretary in acknowledging his communication, and taking favorable action, he wrote urgently to Washburne, asking for his intercession. Late in December, Mr. Sheean was released and a statement of the fact was published in the newspapers, whereupon

Rawlins wrote to Sheean, assuring him with genuine feeling that nothing had occurred since the outbreak of the war which had pleased him more than to learn that his friend from childhood had been restored to liberty and to the rights that every American citizen is entitled to enjoy. As this manly letter glows not only with patriotism but with the feeling of determination which characterized the best officers of the time, its conclusion is given in full:

> ... I am as firm today in the support of my Government and yours as ever. I believe if the war is properly conducted it must finally end in the triumph of the Government established by our fathers, and whether it ends in one year or ten, I am for its vigorous prosecution; but to the arrest and imprisonment of loyal citizens without trial, I am opposed and shall be opposed to the end of my life. For the maintenance of my country's honor and the upholding of the Constitution, I am willing to take my chances on the field of battle, but for the destruction of individual liberty, never. We can have but one Government on this Continent north of Mexico and south of the St. Lawrence and that must be the United States of America. There is little if any difference of opinion in the army. All are for the success of our flag, and but little is said of Proclamations.

Soon after arriving at Grant's headquarters, I made it known to Rawlins, as I had been informed at Washington, that the President had directed McClernand to proceed to the Northwest with orders to recruit and organize an independent force to be commanded by himself for the purpose of capturing Vicksburg and opening the Mississippi, so that "it might flow unvexed to the sea." This was the first authentic information received at Grant's headquarters in regard to the scope of McClernand's instructions, although the newspapers had already mentioned them as foreshadowing what they designated with unseemly levity "the Castor Oil Expedition." Evidence was leaking out through the politicians that the Administration regarded it as one of the first importance.

Immediately after our railroad supply line was broken at Holly Springs, the superiority of the great river as a line of operations against the Confederacy became evident to me, as well as to others whose duty it was to consider such matters. It was perceived that although the river might be commanded by strong fortifications, as at Island Number Ten, and on the bluffs at Vicksburg, it could not, like a common railroad, be permanently cut or successfully obstructed. I pointed out and emphasized this important fact to both Rawlins and Grant, contending that the Overland Campaign should be abandoned, and that the entire army should be transferred to Memphis, embarked upon transports, and sent by water as far as possible towards Vicksburg. I also contended that it would not be sufficient to send the raw levies, which McClernand was raising, or even a strong detachment of the seasoned troops against Vicksburg by water. I dwelt upon the fact that this strongly fortified city was conceded by all to be the chief strategic point in that theatre of operations, that therefore its capture should be made certain by sending all the available forces against it, and that Grant himself, as the senior general of the department, should of right go in chief command. Rawlins became the earnest advocate of this policy from the first. Grant fully concurred, and as soon as he could lay the matter before Halleck, and get the Government's consent, set vigorously about the task of carrying it into effect. Had he delayed or hesitated, it is obvious that the honor of playing the principal part in that great undertaking would have fallen to the lot of a subordinate, not only because he was next in rank, but because both the Secretary of War and the President had virtually promised it to him.

In face of the President's promise to McClernand, Grant designated Sherman, in whom he had greater confidence, to lead the movement and sent him forward with a strong force to Chickasaw Bayou, near the mouth of the Yazoo River, where he effected a landing, made an attack through the swamp against the enemy's strongly fortified position on the bluffs overlooking the river valley, and was repulsed with heavy loss. Before he could make further dispositions there, he was joined and superseded by McClernand, who had learned from the press or from Washington what was going on below, and had hastened to the front. The united force was then transferred, under Sherman's advice, by McClernand to Arkansas Post on the Arkansas River, and, by the aid of the gunboats under Admiral Porter, captured that place with several thousand prisoners. As might have been expected, these movements and the formidable difficulties to be overcome, arrested the attention of the country and made it apparent that Grant's entire army must be transferred to the scene of active operations.

Admiral David Dixon Porter (1813–1891) played an important role in the western campaign and again when Grant moved east. He wrote a delightful memoir titled, <u>Incidents and Anecdotes of the Civil War</u>.*—Ed. 2015*

Grant, having meanwhile obtained Halleck's permission, hastened to the front himself, joined the army at Milliken's Bend, some twenty miles above Vicksburg, and took the direction of further operations under his own control. This was clearly within his right as the department commander, but McClernand, an ambitious, high-strung man, who had done gallant and effective service at Belmont, Donelson, and Shiloh, resented it as a direct violation of the President's promises to him. He had not concealed the fact that he had but a poor opinion of Grant at best and regarded his assumption of command as an act of special injustice. This was followed during the campaign by such open ill-feeling and such disregard of military amenities as finally made it necessary for Grant to relieve him from the command of the Thirteenth Army Corps, to which he had been assigned by the President, after it had taken a leading part in driving back the enemy and in shutting him up within the fortifications of Vicksburg. Rawlins was of course an active and watchful spectator and adviser in all this. Like McClernand, he was a War-Democrat and naturally wanted to promote harmonious relations between Grant and his subordinates, especially those from his own State. Recognizing its wisdom, I did what I could to encourage him in that course. Although McClernand was a native of Kentucky and a much older man than I, I had known him from my boyhood. He had lived in my native county and he had been a private soldier in my father's company in the Black Hawk War. He was besides a lawyer and politician of national character, a distinguished member of Congress, and candidate for Speaker, who had much influence at home, and hence I found a double pleasure in making it my special mission to smooth over the rough spots, and do all in my power to promote friendly relations between him and Grant. In recognition of this disposition on my part I was frequently entrusted with verbal instructions for him and did what I could to mitigate the smart of his wounds as well as to present him and his services in a favorable light at headquarters. I had encouraging success for a while, but McClernand, with all his merit, was a man of hasty and violent temper, with whom it was difficult for one of even Grant's self-control to get on smoothly. The end came at last under circumstances which will be more fully explained in its appropriate place.

As the only regular officer then present with the staff, I left Memphis by special boat with Grant and Rawlins, January 16, 1863, for the purpose of visiting the army which had been operating against Vicksburg. The trip down the Mississippi and back lasted four days, during which every question connected with the campaign, its magnitude and importance, the organization and efficiency of the army, and the policy of the Government in connection with the war in that theatre of operations, was fully discussed. Grant, without the slightest show of reserve, took the lead in the conversation and showed an active interest in all that was said. Without showing the slightest reserve he treated Rawlins and myself as equals, and encouraged us to express ourselves with the utmost freedom. It was during this trip that I commented specially upon the geographical unity of the Mississippi Valley, the interdependence of the States lying within it, and the necessity for a single military command to cover and include them all. Both Grant and Rawlins were favorably impressed with my views and asked me to draft a letter on the subject, which I did, and which Grant shortly afterwards embodied in a letter to Halleck. It is worthy of note that the suggestion finally received Halleck's official approval and was in substance embodied in the order promulgated by the War Department, after the battle of Chickamauga, establishing the Military Division of the Mississippi.

In consequence of the conference on this trip, I was, shortly after getting back to Memphis, sent ahead of Grant and the rest of the staff to rejoin the army in the field. Fortunately, it had meanwhile captured the Confederate Post of Arkansas, which, so long as it was held by the enemy in force, was a menace to the navigation of the river between Memphis and Vicksburg. Having captured that post and its garrison of nearly five thousand men, McClernand and Sherman returned with their troops by transport to Milliken's Bend. My instructions were to look over the ground about Vicksburg and to study the question of capturing that important place as fully as circumstances would permit, in order that I might be prepared to advise with the general on his arrival. I reached the front January 27, and at once made a reconnaissance of Vicksburg and the heights upon which it is situated, from the lowlands in front of it. I made a careful study of the surrounding country and conditions, and became deeply impressed with the strength of the enemy's position, of its inaccessibility directly from the lowlands, and of the almost insuperable difficulty of carrying on military operations through the bottoms and swamps, cut up on both sides of the great river by a network of bayous, creeks, and tributary streams. Without roads, or bridges, this country with its unfordable water courses, even if undefended, could hardly be traversed by an army with its impedimenta. None but the larger bayous was navigable, except in times of flood, and at such times the country was widely submerged on both sides. The problem was to get a footing on the uplands of Mississippi, so that the army could maneuver against the enemy, maintain a base on the river, and keep up an unbroken connection with the upper country from which it must draw its supplies and reinforcements.

Grant arrived the next day at Young's Point, and, accompanied by Sherman, McPherson, Blair, and Steele, and several staff officers, rode across the point in front of Vicksburg along the line of the proposed cut-off, or canal, to the bank of the river below the town. While he and they were discussing the problem before them for solution, Rawlins and I sat down on the trunk of a cottonwood tree which had been undercut and had fallen into the river. In response to a question as to what I thought of the situation, I pointed out that we could not defeat the enemy unless we could get at and engage him on fair terms at close quarters, and that we could not do that unless we could secure a footing with freedom to maneuver on the uplands. To that end we must either turn the enemy's position on the Yazoo at Hains's Bluff, effect a surprise by landing under cover of darkness on the waterfront of the city, or pass below Vicksburg and move into the interior against its rear from the first place on the east side of the river, at which a landing could be made.

During the conversation I called attention to the fact that another great army was about ready to advance from Middle Tennessee, under Rosecrans, that it would be almost impossible to time its movement with ours, or to make either army support the other; that they were separated by some three hundred miles, as the crow flies, and that it ought to be the policy of the Central Government to unite these armies and make their success certain, rather than to keep them separated and to risk the defeat of either. With the river transports at hand, it was evident that this might be done by using the lower Ohio and Tennessee rivers. But as Grant was operating on a line he had chosen himself, and was not over-strong in the confidence of the Government, it was thought that such a suggestion coming from him would be looked upon as evidence that his own campaign had failed, and might therefore result in his removal. Manifestly he must confine himself to the solution of the problem in his own front, and in view of all the difficulties to be overcome by moving to the left, or trying to capture Vicksburg by a *coup-de-main,* the best way to solve the complicated problem, according to my judgment, was to march the troops across the point in front of Vicksburg, and run the batteries with the gunboats and transports under the cover of darkness. Once below the city, they could take the troops on board and ferry them to such landing place on the enemy's side as might be chosen further down the river.

Rawlins showed the deepest interest in my views as thus expressed and fully agreed with me at once in reference to the difficulties and dangers of carrying out either of the other plans. He recognized the practicability of the land march across the Peninsula west of the river, where there were open fields and no enemy to oppose, but expressed serious doubt as to the feasibility of running the batteries with the gunboats and transports. Fortunately he did not reject the idea as impracticable, but asked me to explain why I thought it could be carried into effect. Whereupon I told him I had come recently from Port Royal, where I had served as chief topographical engineer with Hunter and T. W. Sherman, that I had seen the earthen fortifications at Hilton Head made untenable by the fire of the wooden ships and gunboats, which had maneuvered nearly all day up one side and down the other between them without losing a single vessel or suffering material damage, and that I had become thoroughly convinced from what I had seen in person that our Mississippi fleet, although composed of comparatively light river steamers, could run by the Vicksburg batteries under cover of darkness without serious loss. I emphasized my opinion by dwelling upon the fact that the operations at Port Royal were conducted in a narrow harbor in open daylight, and lasted several hours, during which each ship passed three or four times between sea-coast batteries on either side under the fire of heavy guns, and that in the case under consideration, the passage would be made at night, under fire from one side only. So confident was I of the result that I ventured the prediction that we should not lose more than one boat out of five. The sequel afterwards showed that no gunboats were lost or injured, that only one transport was burned, and one disabled so she could not use her own machinery. She was, however, afterwards lashed to another, and served with entire efficiency as a transport. The actual loss was only one in nine.

Rawlins became convinced, and before we got back to the headquarters' steamboat *Magnolia* assured me that he should advocate that plan without doubt or hesitation. After a visit the same afternoon to Admiral Porter, who was on his flagship in the mouth of the Yazoo River nearby, I started by a swift steamboat, under orders from Grant, to Helena, with instructions to take charge of such engineering operations as might be connected with cutting the Mississippi levee across the entrance to Moon Lake, the Yazoo Pass, the Coldwater, and the Tallahatchie rivers. It was hoped that a strong detachment of the army might be conducted by that intricate and crooked route of several hundred miles into the Yazoo and thereby to a footing on the Mississippi uplands above Hains's Bluff. The route was found to be practicable for gunboats and transports to the junction of the Tallahatchie and Yallabusha rivers, which form the Yazoo, and two divisions of infantry reached that place without material delay; but further progress was barred by fortifications and obstructions which could neither be battered down nor turned.

During my absence I kept Rawlins fully informed, both personally and officially, in reference to the needs and progress of the expedition, and in return received his most earnest encouragement and support. On February 16 he sent me a letter, from which I quote as follows:

> . . . Your letters have been duly received. I am delighted with your success but chagrined that we had not things in readiness to have taken an earlier advantage of it. By that probably the enemy's obstruction of the Pass might have been prevented. I have taken the liberty to show our General your private letters. Knowing his appreciation of your abilities, alone induced me to do this. It has done immense good I assure you. He has ordered Ross with ten regiments of infantry, in addition to the force now with you, for the Yazoo Expedition, and is bending every energy for an early move. Orders have been given for collecting a sufficient number of steamers, etc., and they have the right ring. All may yet be well. Some great success must be soon had or everything may be lost to us. This growing opposition to the war at home (judging from the papers) is much to be regretted. "Old Brains" says you are to remain for active duty. I rather think you are, on that. I have great hopes of the "Canal" here. In ten days it ought to be completed. Lake Providence looks well and they are guarding against the misfortune that befell you in your enterprise. Another gun-boat ran the batteries at Vicksburg on Friday night last. We now have two below here, one of which, however, is a ram. They will communicate with General Banks if possible. Only twenty-two shots were fired as the last boat passed. . . .

Nathaniel Banks (1816–1894) was a politician from Massachusetts and a Union general.—Ed. 2015

Notwithstanding the slow progress of the Yazoo Pass expedition, due mainly to the obstruction of the Coldwater, which the enemy ahead of us caused by felling forest trees from its banks into the streams, Rawlins continued to have faith in our ultimate success. But while this route for a time seemed to be the only one holding out substantial hope of leading us through the enemy's outer defenses, it is evident from the quotations given above that Rawlins had not lost sight of the turning movement across the peninsula in front of Vicksburg. But that the interest and anxiety felt at headquarters in the expedition through the Yazoo Pass were unabated is well shown by another letter from Rawlins, written at Young's Point, February 28, as follows:

. . . Yours of the 26th instant came duly to hand, official as well as private. Everyone here is delighted with your success, in getting into the Coldwater, for whatever light we may hope for in the movement against Vicksburg comes from that direction. I send you the instructions to General Ross and to the naval officers, which should have been done before, but supposed as a matter of course General Ross would communicate them to you, as you were one of the principal parties mentioned in them. I also send you a report from General Dodge, received through General Hurlbut. Your report was forwarded to Old Brains who will discover from it that you are on active duty. A despatch boat, according to your suggestion, is ordered to report to General Prentiss by which I send this. General Grant will use every means necessary to make your expedition a success, rest assured of that. Your views on the subject strike me as the most feasible of any I have yet heard, and I assure you it is with much anxiety I look after you and pray for your success. I wish to God I were with you. I could at least sympathize with your plans and views.

We have had a terrible misfortune below, lost both the ram *Queen of the West* and the splendid gun boat *Indianola*, the result of positive disobedience of orders in each case. Had they kept together they must have kept the Mississippi River below here clear and each protected the other. The ram fell into the hands of the rebels with her armament complete, and with her and their other boats, they went down and sunk the *Indianola*. I say sunk the *Indianola,* but of this latter we are not positively certain. We know she is captured and only from rebel sources have we heard that she is sunk. You know, Wilson, they are smart and would like to deceive us into the belief that she is sunk whether she is or not.

The river has risen very much and impeded the work on the Canal here considerably, but we shall be able to resume it tomorrow. It is bound to succeed as a canal. You know I have taken large stock in its success.

I am glad to know that General Washburne pleases you so well. I have every confidence in his energy and ability, for energy is generally the introduction to ability and success.

McPherson's corps is or will be soon at Lake Providence. A more enthusiastic little army is nowhere to be found. Logan, God bless him, maintains the honor of our glorious state of Illinois. A truer patriot lives nowhere on the earth. Bowers is well and enthusiastic over your success. He is one of the diamonds. I send you copy of Brains's despatch. Let us hear from you often. Napoleon sends your letters. Good-bye old friend.

"Old Brains" was a derogatory nickname for General Henry Halleck.— Ed. 2015

Notwithstanding the failure of the expedition through Yazoo Pass, as became certain in a few days, Sherman and Admiral Porter undertook to conduct a cooperating expedition of naval and land forces into the Yazoo below Fort Pemberton by the bayous further south, but after incredible labor, they were also compelled to turn back. Renewed and more strenuous efforts were then made to dig a canal across the point in front of Vicksburg, while still another into Lake Providence was begun some seventy-five miles above, with the hope of reaching a navigable bayou further inland, and connecting with the river further down; but these plans failed one after the other, and, what was worse, took up so much time that the country began to cry out that the movement down the river was a failure and that Grant should be removed for incompetency. The old charges were renewed against him with increased violence, and although without foundation the situation was fast becoming desperate. Every possible route through the bayous, creeks and lateral rivers had been tried and failed. Swamp fevers and smallpox broke out, and while the army was growing in strength by virtue of the reinforcements coming forward, its progress seemed to be stayed by obstacles that could not be overcome.

On the statement of Rawlins to me, it is known that on the evening of Grant's first reconnaissance across the point in front of Vicksburg, he invited the generals, who had gone with him, to dinner on board the *Magnolia*, after which they naturally fell into a discussion of the important problem before them. It was not a formal council, but a long and anxious conversation followed, during which various routes to the highlands north of Vicksburg were considered, without developing great confidence that any of them would prove practicable. It was agreed that the certainty of the spring rise in the great river and the difficulties which must result from the overflow sure to follow would necessarily add to the difficulties to be overcome. While the flood would make the bayous navigable, it would also make the adjacent lowlands impassable. It could hardly be hoped that the season between high and low water would be of just the right length nor that the water would come just high enough to serve without crippling the necessary movements. It was conceded that every possible route presented too many difficulties to permit accurate calculations or to justify certain hopes, and yet every route and plan must be fully tried.

After listening patiently to the discussion and noting carefully the difficulties to be overcome, Rawlins broke in with the remark that there was another and a more promising plan than any yet mentioned, but as it involved the boldest movement that could possibly be made, he hesitated to bring it forward. He was, however, encouraged by both Sherman and McPherson to give his views, and did so clearly and distinctly, in favor of marching the army across the peninsula and running the batteries with the gunboats and transports to a common meeting place below. He gave the reasons which had been developed in our conversation for believing that the movement could be successfully carried out; but, as he expected, the plan received but slight consideration from those present.

At the time Grant expressed no opinion in regard to it, but Sherman was particularly outspoken against it. He pronounced it clearly impracticable, and declared that neither the gunboats nor transports could live under the fire that would certainly be turned against them by the Confederate batteries on the bluffs. Rawlins strenuously adhered to his views and contended that they would prevail in the end, but the non-professional volunteer staff officer was overborne for the time being. Each of the other possible plans received the preference over his; but as each in turn proved abortive, it strengthened him correspondingly in the advocacy of and the ultimate success of the one which he brought forward. He lost no opportunity thereafter of advocating it, and finally, when every other plan had been tried and failed, he had the satisfaction of seeing

Grant openly adopt this one and carry it to a brilliant conclusion. Notwithstanding Grant's silence about the matter while it was under discussion, he tells us many years afterwards that he favored it from the first. While he does not explain his reticence, he doubtless felt that the very boldness of the plan and the success with which two gunboats afterwards ran the batteries imposed upon him the necessity of trying every other plan before venturing upon one so full of danger, but which, as it turned out, led to a series of extraordinary victories and secured for him a place among the greatest captains of modern times.

There can be no doubt that the foregoing gives correctly the origin and history of this plan, nor is there any reasonable doubt that Rawlins's persistent advocacy of it was finally one of the most important factors in its adoption and execution. The responsibility, however, was entirely Grant's. He was the chief commander and must have realized that if the plan failed it would ruin him, bring disaster upon the army, and jeopardize the Union cause. He doubtless understood from the first that he could not turn his back on Vicksburg, or withdraw his army from the advanced position it had maintained so long, without sealing his own doom. With unerring instinct, he realized that ruin was still more certain behind him than in his front, and like a brave and imperturbable man whose fate and fame were at stake, he resolved at the right moment "to put it to the touch, and win or lose it all!"

When it was certain that the expedition through Yazoo Pass had failed, and orders were sent for the troops and gunboats to withdraw from that line, I returned to headquarters. Arriving there April 7, I found the army still working patiently, but making no satisfactory progress in any direction. The deadlock was complete, and how to break it was the question. After careful inspection and still more careful consideration, followed by nightly conferences with both Rawlins and Grant, the conclusion was reached that none of the canal projects could succeed, and that there was no alternative but to run the batteries and march the army below, or to confess ourselves beaten and the campaign at an end. Grant, in face of all the facts and of the continual pressure upon him, fully concurred in the conclusion, but Sherman, in whom Grant's confidence was unshaken, opposed it strongly from the first, and could not be brought to give it his approval till it was successfully under way. He thought the risks were too great, and paid me the compliment of asking me to join him in a final effort to convince Grant that he should not venture upon it, because, as he alleged, it would result in severing our communications with the North and might end in the destruction of the army in case of defeat.

After an earnest discussion in which the actual situation of the army, the state of the campaign, and the pressing necessity for success, together with all the dangers, were recounted, Sherman, without the slightest encouragement from me, remained firm against the plan, till after it was well under way. Shortly after we parted he wrote his celebrated letter against the plan, but fortunately he did not succeed in shaking Grant's resolution, though it may now be stated that it was mainly because of Sherman's opposition to the plan that he was left behind to protect the communications and to bring up the rear with his army corps when the success of the turning movement should no longer be in doubt.

McClernand, although never consulted by Grant, had in a general way favored the idea from the first. Indeed, he had informed me before I left Washington to join Grant that he thought the true plan of operation would prove to be a turning movement to the south of Vicksburg, followed by a march eastward into the heart of Mississippi, and thence against the enemy's fortifications commanding the river and covering the town of Vicksburg. But this was obviously a speculation without details, based upon inadequate knowledge of the enemy's position, or means of defence, or even of the natural obstacles to be overcome. He had no accurate information of the facts as they were gradually developed by the successive steps of the campaign. As has been shown, those steps seem to have been necessary to convert what might have occurred to any experienced officer into a definite and distinct plan as well as to fully justify its adoption. The preliminary movements, resulting one after the other as they did in failure, were doubtless important factors in throwing the enemy off his guard and preventing that concentration of resources necessary to a successful defence.

As it turned out, the plan finally adopted was carried into effect without a single important mishap, but, strangely enough, the newspapers could hardly believe that the modest and discredited Grant had worked it out himself, but concurred with singular unanimity in suggesting that McPherson, the distinguished engineer, must have done it. This view was strengthened by the commendation that the professors at West Point persisted in bestowing upon that rising officer, as the one of all others most capable of conceiving such a plan and arranging its details, when in fact he had nothing whatever to do with either beforehand. He was present at the conference when Rawlins first brought it forward, but expressed no opinion nor was he ever consulted about it separately, and so far as known he neither favored nor opposed it till it was under way. His attitude up to that time was one of neutrality, but as was his custom, when the time came for action, he threw himself into it with all his might. Although he did, at one time and another, some grumbling at the amount of work falling to his lot, especially after the affair at Raymond, he generally put forth his best efforts to make the campaign a success. Quite contrary to the estimation in which he was commonly held, he was in fact a cautious leader who regarded it as no part of his duty as a subordinate commander to work out general plans for the army. While he always gave prompt and willing obedience to those in authority over him, it should be observed that his high intelligence, his cheerful demeanor, aided by engaging personality, made him not only one of the best and most popular corps commanders in the army, but won for him the ardent and unvarying friendship of Grant, Rawlins, and Sherman, as well as of his own division and brigade commanders.

It is an interesting circumstance that, while the army was still floundering among the bayous and lowlands of Mississippi, several of the officers, who had more time than work on hand, were using their influence to secure promotion before they had earned it. Among them was one whose case is fully set forth in a letter without date from Rawlins to Mr. Washburne. As it illustrates the writer's independence as well as his sense of justice and his ideas of good policy, it is given in full as follows:

Headquarters Dept, of the Tenn.,

Before Vicksburg.

DEAR SIR:

I see by the papers the name of Napoleon Bonaparte Buford before the Senate for confirmation as Major General, which confirmation would be so unjust to the many brave and deserving men and officers of the "Army of the Tennessee" that I feel it my duty to call your attention, "as the friend of the Army" and the one to whom it owes so much for proper representation at Washington, to the fact that if possible so great a calamity, if it has not already fallen, may be prevented.

General Buford is a kind hearted and affectionate old gentle man, entertaining views at variance with our republican institutions, and believing the Government of England, because of its titled nobility, much preferable, and further, that the final result of this war will be the overthrow of our present system and give us dukes and lords and titled castes, and that his family will be among the nobility. This may seem idle talk and unmeaning declamation, but nevertheless he urged it with great vehemence and earnestness to General Richard Oglesby and myself as long ago as 1861 at Cairo, Illinois. General Oglesby will remember it, I have no doubt, just as I have stated it. To me, however, it evinced a diseased and addled brain, a weak and foolish old man.

His disobedience of positive orders given him on the field of battle at Belmont came near losing to the country his entire regiment, which was only saved from such fate by the fire from our gunboats driving him off of the main road, and thereby avoided meeting the enemy. Had he obeyed the orders given him by both Generals Grant and McClernand he would have helped defeat the enemy in the fight coming out of Belmont, saved the lives of many gallant men and embarked his regiment with the other troops, before reinforcements for the enemy could have crossed from Columbus. As it was, it was the merest accident by which he was saved. For his conduct at Belmont he was never afterwards trusted by Generals Grant or McClernand.

He was left behind on the expedition into Kentucky, and also against Forts Henry and Donelson. How he demeaned himself under General Pope I am unable to say, but know that since he returned to this command he has been absent from one cause or another most of the time, and when here is continuously insisting on the command of some post not in the field, and has at last succeeded in getting himself assigned by order from Washington to the command of Cairo, displacing General Tuttle, an officer who by his bravery and good conduct while leading the 2nd Iowa to the assault of the enemy's works at Donelson won the admiration of that best soldier of the Republic, the late lamented Major General C. F. Smith. From physical infirmities consequent upon exposure in the field, General Tuttle is unable for active field duty, but might well command the post of Cairo. Besides, the promotion of such men as General Buford is establishing too high a rate of pensions for the Government long to stand. But the greatest calamity to the army is the dissatisfaction it creates among men who remain in the field and do their duty under all circumstances. He is placed over such men as Logan, Oglesby, Lauman and Dodge, and others too numerous to mention, all his superiors in everything that constitutes the soldier.

Logan deserves promotion for his unflinching patriotism and desire to whip the enemy by any route or means practicable. He should be made a Major General by all means, and if Buford is promoted, should be dated back to rank him. The same can be said of Oglesby and Dodge of Iowa by every officer or soldier in the army.

General Grant has written the President on the subject of promotions today. I am glad to see John E. Smith's appointment confirmed. His star will never lighten a coward's path or be disgraced by the one whose shoulder it adorns.

Everything here is as favorable as could be expected considering the high water. Work on the canal is progressing. Jones is here, making himself generally useful.

Trusting that that which is for the best interests of the country may prevail, I remain, etc.

That this letter was known to, if not inspired, by Grant there can be but little doubt.

During the final stages of the Vicksburg Campaign, and after the tentative movements through the bayous had been abandoned, because of the insuperable difficulties encountered or the vigilance and enterprise of the enemy, a most important person appeared upon the scene and became one of Grant's most earnest supporters.

I refer to Charles A. Dana, who had been sent to Grant's headquarters as the confidential representative of the War Department. He afterwards became Assistant Secretary of War. He joined headquarters on April 9, by which time aggressive operations had come to a temporary standstill. The conviction was growing throughout the country that Vicksburg could not be taken by the route upon which the army was operating and that both Grant and his plans were a failure. The temperance men, encouraged by his lack of success, were renewing their efforts to secure his removal. The newspapers were criticising him again severely. The situation was a critical one. Rawlins was deeply concerned, and on my return to headquarters, April 11, at once acquainted me with the basis of his anxiety and of his hopes. He was one of the few men acquainted with the actual condition of affairs who had not been altogether cast down by the failure of the various operations which had been tried, but rather regarded them as necessary preliminaries to the great turning movement which he had brought forward and strenuously supported from the first. He fully concurred in my suggestion that we should take Dana into our confidence, not only in reference to the plan of operations which must now be carried into effect, but in regard to the real state of affairs at headquarters and to the basis of our own unshaken faith in Grant's capacity to lead the army to victory. We had early reached the conclusion that, if Grant should be relieved, the President would appoint McClernand or Sherman as his successor, and that neither of these generals, however patriotic or capable, would bring superior judgment, steadiness, or leadership to the great task which would thus devolve upon him.

Accordingly we made Dana our messmate, took him into our offices and tents, or had his own tent pitched adjacent to ours.

We invited Dana to ride with us on every occasion, and long before the campaign ended he became our constant companion. We confided in him without reservation, and he in turn confided fully in us. At that time he was suffering from weak or overworked eyes and found it difficult to write by the light of the usual camp candle, or lantern. Hence, it soon became customary for me to act at night as his amanuensis, a service which for obvious reasons I was always glad to render. He had met Grant first at Cairo, and later at Memphis, whither he had gone before entering the service for the purpose of buying cotton, but as yet no intimacy had grown up between them. His position had now become both official and influential, and, although he was regarded by some with disfavor, it is but just to add that Grant, who fully shared our views, at once recognized their soundness, expressed his full concurrence in them, and thenceforth treated Dana with all the respect and confidence that his official position and personal qualities entitled him to expect. A genuine friendship, free from concealment or reservation, grew up between them and lasted without a break or cloud till after Grant became President, when he in a measure cut loose from his military counsellors and friends and entered upon the troubled sea of political and personal government.

In this connection it should be observed that Dana proved himself to be in every way worthy of the confidence reposed in him, and at no time ever modified his views as to Grant's real and substantial merit as a virtuous, competent and successful general, or ever permitted his campaigns and battles to be unjustly criticised or condemned in the columns of the journals he controlled. He had learned from personal observation the real facts about Grant and his fitness for command, and became a firm and efficient supporter of his plans, of his continuance in office, and of his final promotion to the chief command of our armies with the rank of lieutenant general.

As the correspondent and intimate associate of Secretary Stanton and the President at Washington, there can be no doubt that Dana did all in his power to remove the prejudice against Grant from the minds of those high officials, and to build up in its place a feeling of respect and confidence. It is as praiseworthy as it is remarkable that he did this without concealing or minimizing the peculiarities of the general, or of his staff, or of his subordinate commanders. His position was a delicate one, but he filled it with such tact and ability as to satisfy the Government, to strengthen the hands of Grant, and at the same time to win his personal friendship. Rawlins from the first recognized this even more fully than did Grant. He honored and respected Dana to the last, and when Grant became President, exerted his influence, as he thought, successfully in behalf of Dana's appointment to the principal government office at New York. Indeed, on the strength of what must have passed between the President and himself, he authorized me in a personal interview to notify Dana that his appointment as Collector of Customs would be made. But unfortunately Washburne, who was called temporarily to the Cabinet as Secretary of State, for some reason, never explained, interfered with the arrangements, and, either on his own account or by direction of the President, caused the appointment to be given to Moses Grinnell, a far less able and efficient man.

Thirty years afterwards, Dana published his *Recollections of the Civil War*, giving many interesting details of his relations with Grant and many graphic sketches of the general and staff officers he met during the various campaigns in which he took part, but as these sketches are not germane to this narrative, I confine myself to the following quotations:

> After Grant, I spent more time at Vicksburg with his assistant adjutant general, Colonel John A. Rawlins, and with Lieutenant-Colonel Wilson, than with anybody else. Rawlins was one of the most valuable men in the army, in my judgment. He had but a limited education, which he had picked up at the neighboring school and in Galena, Illinois, near which place he was born and where he had worked himself into the law; but he had a very able mind, clear, strong, and not subject to hysterics. He bossed everything at Grant's headquarters. He had very little respect for persons, and a rough style of conversation. I have heard him curse at Grant when, according to his judgment, the general was doing something that he thought he had better not do. But he was entirely devoted to his duty, with the clearest judgment, and perfectly fearless. Without him Grant would not have been the same man. Rawlins was essentially a good man, though he was one of the most profane men I ever knew; there was no guile in him—he was as upright and as genuine a character as I ever came across.

> James H. Wilson I had first met at Milliken's Bend, when he was serving as chief topographical engineer and assistant inspector general of the Army of the Tennessee. He was a brilliant man intellectually, highly educated, and thoroughly companionable. We became warm

friends at once and were together a great deal throughout the war. Rarely did Wilson go out on a specially interesting tour of inspection that he did not invite me to accompany him, and I never failed, if I were at liberty, to accept his invitations. Much of the exact information about the condition of the works which I was able to send to Mr. Stanton, Wilson put in my way.

Shortly after the capture of Vicksburg, Dana returned to Washington; but on the way North sent Stanton two notable letters, from the second of which, dated at Cairo, Illinois, July 13, 1863, I quote as follows:

> . . . Lieutenant-Colonel Rawlins, Grant's assistant adjutant general, is a very industrious, conscientious man, who never loses a moment, and never gives himself any indulgence except swearing and scolding. He is a lawyer by profession, a townsman of Grant's, and has a great influence over him, especially because he watches him day and night, and whenever he commits the folly of tasting liquor hastens to remind him that at the beginning of the war he gave him (Rawlins) his word of honor not to touch a drop as long as it lasted. Grant thinks Rawlins a first-rate adjutant, but I think this is a mistake. He is too slow, and can't write the English language correctly without a great deal of careful consideration. Indeed, illiterateness is a general characteristic of Grant's staff, and in fact of Grant's generals and regimental officers of all ranks.
>
> Major Bowers, judge-advocate of Grant's staff, is an excellent man, and always finds work to do.
>
> Lieutenant-Colonel Wilson, inspector general, is a person of similar disposition. He is a captain of engineers in the regular army, and has rendered valuable services in that capacity. The fortifications of Hains's Bluff were designed by him and executed under his direction. His leading idea is the idea of duty, and he applies it vigorously and often impatiently to others. In consequence he is unpopular among all who like to live with little work. But he has remarkable talents and uncommon executive powers, and will be heard from hereafter.

I now return to the Vicksburg campaign which Rawlins had done so much to get started in the right direction. In addition to supervising the duties of the Adjutant General's office, he had succeeded Webster as ex-officio Chief of Staff, and as such took an active interest in everything connected with the campaign, as well as with the relations between Grant and his subordinates.

At the battle of Port Gibson, fought mainly by McClernand and the Thirteenth Army Corps, Rawlins made a special effort to bring about a reconciliation between Grant and that ambitious but irascible general, but failed. McClernand, although slow in getting across the river and starting to the front, had behaved with his usual gallantry from the time he got in reach of the enemy. Without waiting for orders or for reinforcements he attacked vigorously and gained a substantial victory, which was specially important at that stage of the campaign. It not only made good our advanced position on the Mississippi Uplands, and resulted in driving the enemy back, but gave increased confidence to McPherson's corps, and to the invading army. Rawlins naturally agreed with me that it was a good occasion to establish a better feeling between Grant and his next in rank, but the breach was too great to be bridged over in that manner. Grant, who arrived on the field after the action was practically at an end, refused with an unusual show of feeling to make any advance towards a reconciliation, and in the meeting which soon occurred with McClernand displayed no cordiality whatever, but contented himself with formally extending his thanks and directing him to push forward at once in pursuit. This was done, but the advance halted for the night at the South Fork of the Bayou Pierre, where the retreating enemy had destroyed the highway bridge. McClernand, who was expected to repair it and move on, also halted, because, as he claimed, his troops were worn out with marching and fighting. On receiving information of this fact, I hastened to the front as acting chief engineer, and took the repair of the bridge in hand.

As soon as the repairs were finished, which was before dawn the next morning, the troops advanced to the north fork of the bayou, some five miles further on. Here they found that a second but still more important bridge had been burned, and again halted till it could be repaired. This was done during the night while the generals and the troops were sleeping. As before, Rawlins gave his active assistance and support, both in helping at the work and in detailing and bringing forward the necessary detachments to carry it on.

Having been reared as a woodsman, he was quick to see what could be done with simple tools and the rude materials at hand. He neither rested nor slept till the breaches in the bridge were repaired, and the troops were again in motion. No man knew better than he that under such circumstances time was of the utmost value. Hence he made it his personal business to see that not a minute should be lost, either in the repair of the bridges or in sending the troops across them in pursuit of the enemy. Most adjutants would have contented themselves with issuing the necessary orders and leaving others to see that they were carried out, but this was not Rawlins's way of doing business. He had committed himself too earnestly in favor of the plan of campaign and had labored too long to get it adopted to rest supinely while others were working out the details upon which its success depended. Besides, he had the true instincts of a soldier, and lost no opportunity to learn from others how the practical work of an army should be done. At this time he was as robust and hardy as any man in the service, and while he was not and perhaps never became a model adjutant general or "paper man," he was fast learning the higher duties which were to devolve upon him thereafter as chief of staff.

During the advance to Hankinson's Ferry, and the concentration of the army near that place, Rawlins shared all the anxieties and labors of his chief. Every order, whether verbal or written, passed through his hands and was delivered on time. Not one went astray, was badly expressed, or was in any degree uncertain in tenor or obscure in meaning. In the advance through Raymond to Jackson, which resulted in the capture of the latter place, with its military depots and railroad crossing, as well as in the splendid countermarch by which the united army threw itself upon the enemy at Champion's Hill, drove him from the field, forced him across the Big Black, and finally shut him up in Vicksburg, Rawlins was the inseparable companion and counsellor of the commanding general. Realizing, as before, the value of time, after the victory at Champion's Hill and the pursuit of the enemy to the Big Black, he assisted in repairing the railroad bridge and in locating and constructing three floating bridges across which the troops were pushed without delay, to close in upon the fortifications of

Vicksburg. As at Bayou Pierre, these bridges were laid under cover of darkness while the generals and the troops were resting from the exhausting work of the day. But again Rawlins helped the engineers without taking the slightest rest till the bridges were completed and the troops were again on the march to the scene of their final victory.

Like his chief, Rawlins was making tremendous strides in the art of war. Both had learned lessons and gained experience of extraordinary value, not the least of which was that each was in a measure necessary to the other. Perfect confidence existed between them. Rawlins's fears for his friend had become measurably allayed and, so long as active operations were going on, there seemed to be neither temptation nor danger in the way. But when communication had been reestablished with the river, and the chance of ultimate failure was at an end, although the tentative assaults upon the enemy's fortifications at Vicksburg had failed, the army necessarily settled down into the toilsome occupations of a regular siege. The exhilaration of victory gradually disappeared. The hot weather of a Southern summer came on and a feeling of lassitude, if not of exhaustion, took possession of both officers and men. One day was like another, where all were hot, depressing, and disagreeable. The surrounding country had been cleared of its green food supplies, and all were compelled to live entirely on soldier's rations.

Early in June, Grant, like the rest, began to feel the relaxing effects of hard work and exposure, and while on an expedition by steamer up the Yazoo River to visit an outlying detachment in the neighborhood of Satartia, "fell sick," whereupon Dana, who had been invited to go, took charge of the boat and turned it about, to its starting point. The trip was abandoned and the party returned to headquarters about midnight. An hour or more later Rawlins, who had learned the details of the excursion from those who had participated in it, and having made discoveries of his own, wrote Grant a remarkable letter, which has passed into history. As it produced a profound impression on all who knew about it, and was fraught with the greatest consequences to the country besides, it is given here in full:

DEAR GENERAL:

The great solicitude I feel for the safety of this army leads me to mention, what I had hoped never again to do, the subject of your drinking. This may surprise you, for I may be, and trust I am, doing you an injustice by unfounded suspicion, but if in error, it had better be on the side of the country's safety than in fear of offending a friend.

I have heard that Dr. McMillan at General Sherman's a few days ago induced you, notwithstanding your pledge to me, to take a glass of wine, and today when I found a box of wine in front of your tent, and proposed to move it, which I did, I was told you had forbid its being taken away, for you intended to keep it until you entered Vicksburg, that you might have it for your friends; and tonight, when you should, because of the condition of your health, if nothing else, have been in bed, I find you where the wine bottle has just been emptied, in company with those who drink and urge you to do likewise; and the lack of your usual promptness and decision, and clearness of expressing yourself in writing, conduces to confirm my suspicion.

You have the full control over your appetite, and can let drinking alone. Had you not pledged me the sincerity of your honor early last March, that you would drink no more during the war, and kept that pledge during your recent campaign, you would not today have stood first in the world's history as a successful military leader. Your only salvation depends upon your strict adherence to that pledge. You cannot succeed in any other way. . . .

As I have before stated, I may be wrong in my suspicions, but if one sees that which leads him to suppose a sentinel is falling asleep on his post, it is his duty to arouse him; and if one sees that which leads him to fear the General commanding a great army is being seduced to that step which he knows will bring disgrace upon that General and defeat upon his command, if he fails to sound the proper note of warning, the friends, wives and children of those brave men whose lives he permits to remain thus in peril, will accuse him while he lives, and stand swift witnesses of wrath against him in the day when all shall be tried.

If my suspicions are unfounded, let my friendship for you and my zeal for my country be my excuse for this letter; and if they are correctly founded, and you determine not to heed the admonitions and prayers of this hasty note, by immediately ceasing to touch a single drop of any kind of liquor, no matter by whom asked or under what circumstances, let my immediate relief from duty in this department be the result. I am, General, Yours respectfully,

JOHN A. RAWLINS.

Rawlins, who was deeply moved, at once made the action he had taken known to Dana and myself, as well as to Bowers, who was his inseparable companion and principal assistant throughout the war. He later told McPherson and Sherman about the letter and the occasion for it. They were Grant's closest friends, and deeply interested in every circumstance which could in any way affect his success. But the context of the letter was not made public till after the death of both Rawlins and Grant, when it was given to the newspapers and received the widest circulation. Its authenticity is undoubted. It has since been frequently cited by writers and orators as reflecting equal credit upon the courage of the man who wrote it and the good sense of the man who received it.

It appears from an endorsement which Rawlins placed on his retained copy of the letter, in the possession of his family, that his admonitions were not resented, but were heeded for a season. This was certainly the case till after the capture of Vicksburg, but it is well known that his apprehensions were never entirely dismissed. Through succeeding campaigns and to the last day of his life he was haunted by the fear that the appetite might at any time break loose again and endanger Grant's military plans or bring discredit upon his civil administration.

Lincoln, who doubtless received from Dana in due time a correct understanding of Grant's real merits, as well as of the influences which were constantly at work to undermine and overthrow him, seems to have dismissed all serious apprehensions after Vicksburg, and to have given unquestioning confidence and support to him till the end of the war. Rumors of irregularities at New Orleans, and at rare intervals during the final campaign in Virginia, did not fail to reach Washington. It is known, besides, that McClernand, as did others later, prepared a statement immediately after he was relieved from duty in the field, reflecting upon Grant's personal habits, and threatened more than once to publish it. But this was not done, and whatever may have been the underlying facts, it is certain that both the Government and the country at large concurred in ignoring them, and in giving the General a free hand with increased rank and unlimited means for the overthrow of the Confederate armies.

After his courageous letter, the part played by Rawlins had still more to do with Grant's personal fortunes and policies than with the adjutant general's office or with the details of army administration. Ably seconded by Bowers in preparing and issuing orders and in keeping the records, he devoted himself unceasingly to building up and maintaining harmonious relations between his chief and his subordinate commanders, as well as with the Government at Washington.

As has been seen, McClernand and his attitude towards the army commander, as well as towards the other corps commanders, had been a subject of solicitude from the first. His intimate relations with the President, his fellow-townsman, had doubtless laid him under suspicion of being one of the channels of communication through which information prejudicial to Grant reached the Government as well as the newspapers from time to time, and this suspicion was in a certain degree strengthened by his congratulatory order to the Thirteenth Army Corps, and its publication in a St. Louis newspaper before it was received at army headquarters. As it seemed to claim undue credit for the Thirteenth, and to reflect unfairly upon the Fourteenth and Seventeenth corps, both Sherman and McPherson protested officially against it. The case was a serious one on its merits, but it had been preceded by an outburst of anger and threatened disobedience of orders on the part of McClernand, which precipitated a crisis that Rawlins neither desired to stay nor could have stayed had he tried.

Shortly after the investment of Vicksburg I carried a verbal order from Grant to McClernand, directing him to send more troops to the crossings of the Big Black, for the purpose of strengthening the defenses in that direction; but instead of yielding cheerful compliance with the order, the choleric general declared emphatically that he would not obey it, and would not be dictated to any longer by Grant or anybody else. He intimated that he considered himself in supreme command, and punctuated this with violent language, which appeared to be intended as much for me as for those in higher authority. I expressed my amazement not only at the general's insubordination but at the language in which he had chosen to express it. This was at once followed by a declaration that the oaths he had used were not intended for me, but simply as an expression of his intense vehemence upon the subject-matter. But the impression produced was an unfavorable one, which I felt it my duty not only to resent but to communicate to Rawlins, and which he in turn communicated to Grant.

The effect of this incident was further to heighten the discontent at headquarters with McClernand. It convinced Rawlins at least that an open rupture would soon take place, which would necessarily result in the relief of the subordinate, no matter what might be his claims upon the Government or his relations with the President. Grant had already shown himself to be a patient and prudent man, of unusual reserve and self-possession, with whom a more impulsive man was always at a disadvantage. His modesty and self-control were at times considered as an indication of weakness, whereas they were really the cover of a firm and resolute will. He was naturally kind and conciliatory, without being effusive. He was, above all, considerate towards both subordinates and equals. Indeed, he was the last man to blame those under his command inconsiderately or unjustly or to look for a purpose, on the part of any one to treat him personally with disrespect or officially with insubordination, but when his suspicion was once aroused, he was quite as slow to forget or to forgive an offence as he was to perceive it.

As before intimated, McClernand was not only under suspicion but was regarded by many as a rival whose pretentions might under certain conditions receive the backing of the Government. Grant therefore appealed to Halleck to know how far he could count upon the support of his official superiors. Dana, who had become fully informed as to the merits of the case, about the same time sounded the Secretary of War. Both received the assurance that Grant was in full authority and must exercise his own judgment in reference to every question arising within the limits of his command.

Strengthened and reassured in this way, Grant was swift to act upon McClernand's congratulatory order as soon as he could satisfy himself of its authenticity and of the reasonableness of the protests which had been made against it. The frank avowal of McClernand that it was genuine, and that he was prepared to maintain every statement it contained, gave Rawlins, who had become much more impatient than his chief, a sound basis upon which to urge instant action. Grant, now thoroughly aroused, needed but little pushing, and at once directed the issuance of an order relieving McClernand from the command of the Thirteenth Army Corps, instructing him to proceed to such point in Illinois as he might select, and to report thence to the Secretary of War for further orders. The order was written on the night of June 17, with the intention that I should deliver it the first thing the next morning. It so happened that my duties had kept me out that day till about midnight, but on my return to camp I found Rawlins up and waiting for me. As this was a somewhat unusual circumstance, I made haste to ask what it meant, and was informed of the general's order relieving McClernand and his wish that I should deliver it as soon after daylight as possible. As I was in full accord with its purposes, and felt that delay might be fatal, I asked permission to take it to McClernand that night, late as it was, and to notify the general next in command, on my way, of its import.

We were at that time expecting a sortie of the beleaguered garrison, for the purpose of breaking through our lines and forming a junction with Johnston, who was maneuvering in the open country with a view to compelling us to raise the siege. It was thought that the sortie, if made, would probably be directed against the front held by the Thirteenth Corps, which covered the two principal roads leading to the interior of the State, and it was regarded as certain that, whatever might be his infirmities of temper or of character, McClernand would make a gallant resistance. His troops were veterans and, although somewhat loose in discipline, had never been beaten. They were justly regarded as among the best in the army and sure to hold their lines of circumvallation even against a night sortie in force, if any soldiers could. It was also regarded as certain that McClernand, who with all his shortcomings was an officer of undaunted courage, would be in the thick of the fight; in which event Grant would probably overlook his past offences and withhold the order, which would merely defer the trouble to another day. This statement of the case seemed to be conclusive, and without referring the matter again to Grant, Rawlins authorized me to deliver the order of relief at once.

McClernand's headquarters were four miles to the south, the night was dark, and the roads both crooked and obscure, but accompanied by the provost marshal, Colonel Marsh, with a detachment of four mounted men and a non-commissioned officer, I reached there at 1 A. M., and after a few minutes' interview, attended by all the formalities appropriate to the occasion, I received an acknowledgment from the general that he understood that the order went into effect immediately, and that under no circumstances which could arise was he to exercise any further command in that army. It was supposed that his confidence in the support of the President and Secretary of War might cause him to contest the order or even to resist it, but fortunately this supposition was unfounded. It was, however, an occasion of grave importance, which filled Rawlins with anxiety and kept him up till I returned at half-past two in the morning with the report that the order had been delivered, and that the general had given proper assurances that he understood it, and would observe its provisions in accordance with the verbal instructions which I had given in explanation thereof.

From that time till the surrender of Vicksburg, which occurred on the 4th of July, perfect harmony prevailed in the investing army. Indeed, harsh as it may seem at this time, the example which had been made of McClernand, the aggressive and ambitious leader, the powerful and popular politician, the friend of the President, and by no means without friends in the army, had a good effect upon the discipline of the higher officers, and did much towards making the Army of the Tennessee, composed as it was entirely of volunteers, many of whom were politicians, ever afterwards one of the most subordinate, cheerful and effective organizations that ever upheld the national cause.

While Grant's great but hazardous campaign had resulted in defeating the enemy in detail at Port Gibson, Raymond, Jackson, Champion's Hill, and the Big Black; in the capture of a strongly fortified city with its defending army of over thirty thousand men; in the opening of the Mississippi River from Cairo to the Gulf; and in effectually severing the Confederacy into two great parts, neither of which could cooperate with or support the other, that of Rosecrans, after a most brilliant opening, followed by the expulsion of the enemy from Tennessee, finally came to an unfortunate end a few weeks later at Chickamauga.

In looking back upon the events of this year, we can now see, however, that they did not yield all the advantages that should have flowed from them. The national Government was strangely negligent of its opportunities and of the dangers by which it was beset. Grant's victory, resulting first and last in the destruction and capture of an army of sixty thousand men, was in itself both Napoleonic and complete. Coming as it did on the heels of the great disappointment felt by the country at the escape of Lee's army, with its organizations and trains intact, from the field of Gettysburg, it was received without question as ending the war in the Southwest, and yet the victory was seriously marred by the lenient terms of the surrender by which the captured garrison of Vicksburg was paroled and allowed to march back into the Confederacy with its haversacks filled and its regimental, brigade and division organizations unbroken.

It will be recalled by those familiar with the history of the War that in consequence of the deadlock, which had taken place in the East between the National and Confederate authorities in regard to the exchange of prisoners, the Confederate Government made haste to ignore and repudiate this capitulation and to order the entire force covered by it back to their colors. Consequently it was but a few weeks till every Confederate regiment paroled by Grant at Vicksburg was rearmed and again doing duty in garrison, or on detachment in Eastern Mississippi and Alabama, in place of troops drawn from those regions and sent to reinforce Bragg in Northeastern Georgia. On the other hand, it is apparent that if the Vicksburg prisoners had been sent to the prison camps of the North, as Rawlins and others advised, and nearly everybody expected, or had two corps of Grant's army been sent at once, as could easily have been done, to reinforce Rosecrans, as Longstreet was sent to reinforce Bragg, the overwhelming disaster of Chickamauga would have certainly been avoided.

When it is remembered that Vicksburg surrendered July 4, that the battle of Chickamauga was fought September 19, or fully six weeks later, and that the distance between those two important points by water and rail could have been easily covered in ten or twelve days, as was the much greater distance from Washington to Chattanooga a couple of months afterwards, it will be seen that the Government at Richmond greatly outgeneraled the Government at Washington during that eventful summer. Grant and Rosecrans, commanding independent armies, did their part well enough with the means at their disposal, but neither had discretion to go to the assistance of the other. To make such a concentration of force pertains to the higher functions of the General-in-Chief or of the War Department, and that neither had the sagacity to order it is one of the most unaccountable facts of the war. Grant was allowed to visit Banks at New Orleans, entirely outside the field of active military operations, while Sherman, with the bulk of Grant's army, was sent on a wild-goose chase via Demopolis in the direction of Montgomery.

The Confederates meanwhile were making war on more scientific principles. Longstreet had been detached from Lee's army and was on the way to reinforce Bragg on the Chickamauga, in Northwestern Georgia, in consequence of which a desperate battle was fought, and a great defeat was inflicted upon the over-confident Rosecrans and his army at Chickamauga.

This calamity thoroughly aroused the authorities at Washington, and convinced them that they must concentrate without delay at Chattanooga, a few miles to the rear, an overwhelming force with which to stay the Confederate advance and make good the hold of the Union army upon that great strategic centre.

It was also seen at once that, if the Confederates could send Longstreet's corps from Virginia by their poorly constructed and poorly equipped railroads, the Union administration could send a corresponding force from the same theatre of operations without any greater risk than their opponents had taken.

Accordingly they sent Hooker with the Eleventh and Twelfth Corps, an aggregate force of twenty-three thousand men, by rail from Bristow Station, Virginia, to Stevenson, Alabama, near Chattanooga, a distance of twelve hundred and thirty miles, in eleven and a half days. It was now seen that Grant's army, resting at or near Vicksburg, could also be drawn upon, and after the loss of much time, the greater part of it under Sherman was ordered by the way of Memphis to reinforce Rosecrans at Chattanooga.

Meanwhile the enemy had closed in upon Chattanooga and broken its railway connection with the North. Winter was approaching, the rainy season had begun, the roads to the rear were rough and muddy, food and supplies were becoming scarce, the horses of the artillery and the mules of the wagon trains were starving, and the necessity of a further retreat had already been conceded, unless a way could be found to regain possession of the railway to the rear, and to reopen "the cracker line." But what was most important of all was that it had at last become apparent that a supreme commander was necessary on the ground to give direction and unity to the operations which must at once be undertaken. Under these circumstances the hero of Vicksburg was naturally assigned to the chief command. The departments of the Ohio, the Cumberland, and the Tennessee were now united into the Military Division of the Mississippi, as Grant had recommended in the opening days of the Vicksburg campaign. The modest general had played his part with consummate ability and success, but, as has been shown, his friend and adjutant general had contributed a full and unusual share not only towards the adoption of the plan which had led to such splendid results but to the maintenance of that authority over his subordinates, and to the establishment of that discipline among the rank and file without which neither tactics, however good, nor strategy, however brilliant, could prevail.

For particulars, see the very interesting <u>Lincoln in the Telegraph Office,</u> *by David Homer Bates.—Ed. 2015*

That Grant harbored no ill-feeling on account of Rawlins's manly letter of June 6 is conclusively shown by the fact that he not only continued Rawlins in the confidential position of adjutant general but recommended him, on July 27, for promotion, along with a number of others whom he also praised for "gallant and meritorious services," and for "extreme fitness for higher command." It was no slight honor for anyone to find his name coupled with those of Dodge and William Sooy Smith, who were selected for promotion to the rank of Major General, or with those of such fighting colonels as Gresham, Corse, and Force, who were designated for the rank of Brigadier General. Much to his surprise and gratification, Rawlins found his name in this distinguished list, and it is worthy of notice that, although he was only a staff officer, he was singled out of the entire lot for special mention in the concluding paragraph of the General's letter, as follows:

> . . . Lieutenant Colonel Rawlins has been my assistant adjutant general from the beginning of the Rebellion. No officer has now a more honorable reputation than he has; and I think I can safely say that he would make a good corps commander. This promotion I would particularly ask as a reward of merit. . . .

The appointment of Brigadier General was promptly made, but notwithstanding the unusual terms in which it had been asked for, the Senate was slow to give its consent. Indeed, it did not do so until the middle of the next year, and then only in response to a personal appeal made by Grant, April 4, 1864, after his own appointment as Lieutenant General, to the chairman of the Senate Committee on Military Affairs, as follows:

> ... I would most respectfully but earnestly ask for the confirmation of Brigadier General John A. Rawlins by your honorable body. General Rawlins has served with me from the beginning of the Rebellion. I know he has most richly earned his present position. He comes the nearest being indispensable to me of any officer in the service. But if

his confirmation is dependent on his commanding troops, he shall command troops at once. There is no department commander, near where he has served, that would not most gladly give him the very largest and most responsible command his rank would entitle him to.

Believing a short letter on this subject more acceptable than a long one, I will only add that it is my earnest desire that General Rawlins should be confirmed; . . .

In conclusion Grant ventured to express the fear that the Senate's failure to confirm this worthy officer would work injury to him as well as to the service, because it might fairly be considered as due to the fact that the officer had made himself too valuable in a lower position. But this is not all. When the news that the President had acted favorably in regard to Rawlins's promotion was received at Vicksburg, where Rawlins remained with the headquarters of the Department during the summer after the capture of Vicksburg, Grant made haste, August 13, 1863, to write to their fellow-townsman and representative in Congress, E. B. Washburne, as follows:

. . . Rawlins and Maltby have been appointed brigadier generals. These are richly deserved promotions. Rawlins especially is no ordinary man. The fact is, had he started in this war in the line instead of the staff, there is every probability that he would be today one of our shining lights. As it is he is better and more favorably known than any other officer in the army who has filled only staff appointments. Some men—too many of them—are only made by their staff appointments, while others give respectability to their position. Rawlins is of the latter class.

These letters show beyond question that Grant had the highest regard for the fidelity and usefulness of Rawlins, and while it may be contended that they overestimate his fitness in point of technical knowledge and experience at that time for the command of an army corps, there can be no doubt that they bear the best possible testimony to his military aptitude, as well as to the soundness of his judgment and the elevation of his character. They bear equally conclusive testimony both to Grant's own magnanimity and to the delicacy with which he expressed his appreciation of the services which his friend had rendered to him, and which his adjutant general had rendered to the country at large.

That the letter last quoted put the ever-vigilant Washburne on his mettle to procure the favorable action of the Senate on Rawlins's promotion is well known to their common acquaintances. He had been from the first the devoted friend of both Grant and Rawlins. They were his neighbors and constituents at Galena, where their advancement was regarded as his advancement. He had seen them at work in the field, and had heard in what estimation they were held by those who served with and under them. He had especially come to know how necessary Rawlins was, not only to Grant's self-control but to his military career as well. They stood absolutely together in his mind, and the success of one was the success of the other. It was for this reason that he worked at all times willingly and cheerfully for the promotion of Rawlins, by the same steps, if not to the same degree, that Grant was promoted or showed himself to be worthy of it.

We may now pause to consider more fully what sort of man Rawlins, the charcoal burner, had become. Attending the neighborhood school for eight terms, transferring to the town High School for a single term, working alternately at the charcoal pits and the farm, and gradually saving money enough, he entered the Rock River Seminary. Here he studied the higher branches for two academic years and hoped to graduate, but as his money gave out, he was forced to return to charcoal burning for a season. But in doing so he was conscious that his education, though not complete, was as good as that of the average young man of the period.

We have seen how he lighted his pits again, how his team gave out as he was hauling his charcoal to market, how he sold his load, his wagon, and his oxen to the railroad contractors, and then how he pushed on to Galena, where he studied law and in due time was admitted to the bar, became city attorney, and made himself known as a good lawyer and a rising man. He had already developed a strong taste and considerable skill in public speaking. Although lacking in city polish and refinement, he was far from being rough or illiterate. He had a genuine taste for good books, and had read such as were within reach. He sought good company, as became a sober, serious, and ambitious youth, and, like many of his friends at the Seminary, he early developed a decided taste for public affairs.

As the times were stormy and "the noble controversies of politics" uppermost in everybody's mind, he soon began to take a leading part in the community of which he was a citizen. A Democrat by conviction as well as by inheritance, he became an ardent supporter of Douglas and his doctrine of "popular sovereignty" and when the Presidential election of 1860 came on he was chosen by his party in the Galena district as its candidate for the honorable position of Presidential elector. Challenged by his opponent to a joint debate, he accepted the challenge and stumped the district, with the result that his eloquence and moderation certified him to the State at large as one of its most promising young men.

After all efforts to prevent civil war had failed, and the South Carolinians had precipitated the conflict by firing upon the flag at Fort Sumter, Rawlins's patriotic speech at the Galena mass meeting had produced a genuine surprise and a genuine sensation. It aroused the faint-hearted, dissipated the fears of the doubtful and stirred a raging fever in the minds of every loyal citizen who was fortunate enough to hear him. It made Grant his friend, and brought them both to the threshold of a new career, in which one became the leading general of his time, and the other his adjutant and finally his chief of staff.

We have seen how Rawlins, without military knowledge or experience but with a full sense of his own unfitness, took up the duties of his new position, patiently and persistently learning them one by one, till all were creditably performed. We have seen how at the threshold of his military life he was brought face to face with serious charges against his chief; how he refuted them, and made himself responsible for his good behavior; how he became his monitor and watchful guardian, the enemy of those who pandered to his weakness, and the friend of all who helped to stay him from falling.

No one can read the narrative, from Belmont to Vicksburg, in which Grant's star was rising to its zenith, without perceiving that

Rawlins's task was scarcely less difficult than Grant's, or without acknowledging that he performed it with such tact, cleverness, firmness, and patriotism as to merit not only all that Grant could do for him but to entitle him to all the rank and consideration his country finally bestowed upon him. When it is remembered that the staff officer who played this important but unusual part never put himself forward to claim credit, reward, or promotion, but silently and firmly effaced himself, while doing all he could to shield his friend from criticism, to advance his fortunes, and to ensure his final triumph, it must be admitted that Rawlins had grown to a noble and fearless manhood, in every way worthy of the admiration of all who read this simple story.

The part played by him in bringing forward and advocating the plan by which Johnston's army was defeated and Vicksburg with its garrison were captured lifted him to another sphere and to another altitude. Hitherto, he had concerned himself mainly with the routine duties of his office and with the personal interests of his chief, but this raised him to the rank of military adviser and strategist, in which, as this narrative will show, he was destined to the end of the war to exert a powerful influence over the plans and policies by which it was brought to a fortunate conclusion.

Finally it must be admitted that the emergency which was signalized by Rawlins's letter of June 6, 1863, was one which called for courage of a different sort from that of the soldier in the fighting line. To such as are familiar with military hierarchy and its rules, it will appear almost incredible that an adjutant should have taken such a liberty as he did; and when it is recalled that he did this entirely without advice from anyone and on his own responsibility, it must be conceded, in the words of Grant's letter of August 13, that "Rawlins especially was no ordinary man." When it is recalled in addition that Grant, the next year, in asking for Rawlins's confirmation as brigadier general, strengthened his former recommendation by the statement that "he comes nearest being indispensable to me of any officer in the service," it becomes certain that the admonitions of a friend had not only given no offence in his case but had rather drawn closer the bonds of interest and respect between the parties to the incident. Indeed, Grant's written declarations in favor of Rawlins receive a peculiar significance from the remonstrance and the circumstances which called it forth. Happily, so far as known, they stand alone in our annals and may well be regarded as reflecting unusual credit upon both of the men connected with them.

When Vicksburg surrendered and filled the country with the fame of General Grant and the Army of the Tennessee, Rawlins had reached the rank of Lieutenant Colonel. He was in his thirty-third year, a man of medium size and weight, about five feet seven inches high, with black hair, dark, almost black, eyes, and swarthy complexion. His features were regular, without being noticeably handsome. He had no color in his cheeks, and made no pretension to elegance of deportment or military bearing. He was just a plain, blunt man, full of purpose and vigor, of austere habits, severe morals, inflexible will, resolution and courage, and of most aggressive temper. He had no thought but for the success of our arms and the preservation of the Union under the Constitution and laws. American to the innermost recesses of his heart, and alive to the drift of public opinion, with a mind alert and responsive to every noble sentiment, he reached conclusions of his own upon all subjects, both military and civil, and never for a moment hesitated to express them with independence and vigor, whether they were asked for or not. His very ignorance of military customs and ceremonies was a source of strength rather than of weakness, as it caused him to go straight to the highest authority without fear and without hesitation. Conscious of his own rectitude and unselfish devotion to duty, he expected every officer, however high, and every man, however low, to give all there was in him to the cause of the Union.

As a rule, his voice was low and well-modulated, but withal he was capable of the most vehement flights of eloquence when occasion called for them. Direct in purpose and deliberate in manner, his ordinary speech was firm, straightforward, and convincing, but in the face of opposition or delay he did not hesitate to raise his voice to emphasize what he was saying or, all unconsciously perhaps, to punctuate it with epithets and even oaths that were sure to arouse and stimulate rather than to shock or offend. He was altogether the most earnest and impressive man of his rank the army had in it. With an absolute unconsciousness of self, his thoughts were naturally direct, coherent and logical. Never hesitating for a word, and never uttering one indistinctly or hurriedly, his sentences were short, crisp, and convincing. Nor do I recall a single instance in which they failed to carry through the recommendation or measure in behalf of which they were uttered.

Profoundly impressed by the responsibilities resting upon his Chief, and indirectly upon himself, he took neither rest nor respite from his work, but stood by night and day to see that no weakness was displayed, no duty was neglected, no effort was misdirected and no opportunity was allowed to pass by unimproved. With such a mind as this, its possessor needed nothing except technical training to become not only a model chief of staff but a model corps or army commander. Situated as he was, however, there was no such destiny in store for him. Fate or circumstances had cast his lot in another sphere, and while there is no evidence extant that he had any other ambition, or ever indulged in vain repinings, it is certain from the foregoing narrative that he was fully conscious of the dangers which lay in the path of the easygoing and sociably inclined chief with whom he was associated. While it cannot be said that Rawlins ever presumed upon the slightest familiarity with Grant, they were the best of friends, though it must be confessed that Grant, in their daily intercourse, showed more bonhomie towards his staff officer than his staff officer showed towards him. In this they were not unlike Lincoln and Stanton. Grant, who was always kind and considerate, loved to chat with those about him, by the campfire or on the march, but Rawlins was more serious and apparently more preoccupied. He of course had the orders and staff details to look after and these necessarily absorbed his time and attention while others were at rest. But the close of the Vicksburg campaign, which was not only the most brilliant but the most complete in all our annals, inaugurated a new era in his career. It had inflicted the first mortal blow upon the Confederacy. It had raised the hopes of the Union men everywhere to the certainty of a complete triumph in the end, and not only they but the world at large were calling for the details by which the army's rapid marches had been made, and its splendid battles had been won.

It has long since come to be well known that Grant had up to this time made no elaborate reports, and had apparently forgotten that he had sent in one of seven closely-written pages, in regard to the battle of Shiloh. The fact is that he was looked upon by the War Department as a poor correspondent and at best but an indifferent reporter of his own deeds. But now all this was to be changed, and the complete story was to be told. As was his habit, Grant wrote with his own hand an outline of what had taken place from first to last as far as he could recall it, and then turned that over to Rawlins as a basis for the final and complete report, in which every date and figure should be verified and every essential detail should be fully given. Henceforth this was the rule and practice, and the duty of carrying them into effect fell upon Rawlins and his assistant, Major, afterwards Lieutenant Colonel, Bowers. As the former was a methodical lawyer and the latter an experienced newspaper man and ready writer, the work was thoroughly done, and as a consequence Grant's reports from that day forth are justly regarded as models of clearness and completeness.

Department headquarters remained at Vicksburg during the summer, and while Grant had gone to New Orleans on a trip which Rawlins did not approve, the report of the Vicksburg Campaign was finished. As will be more fully set forth hereafter, Rawlins was at the same time in virtual command of the army, attending to all branches of its administration, and making all the necessary orders, in the name of its absent commander.

It is specially worthy of note that Grant's recommendations were now received at Washington with full credit and due respect. The authorities could not do too much for him.

Even Halleck wrote him complimentary letters and treated him with marked consideration, and what was still more to the point, the promotions he had asked for were made without delay. Rawlins shared the good fortune of the army and was gazetted Brigadier General of Volunteers on August 11, 1863. Naturally he felt that this new rank was intended in a measure to relieve him from the drudgery of paper work, which he naturally disliked, and to impose upon him the larger and more important duties appropriate to the peculiar and very unusual personal and official relations which had grown up between him and his Chief.

In his relations with his brothers of the staff, and with the general and other officers having business at headquarters, Rawlins was singularly cordial and approachable. While he liked to see all official papers framed and submitted as required by the army regulations, he had no patience with mere red tape as such. Far from being a martinet or caring for formalities and ceremonies, he made every officer and enlisted man feel that it was a pleasure as well as a great privilege to meet him. Every leading officer of the army knew and appreciated him as a modest, unselfish, and able man, who could not be swerved from his duty, nor induced to look leniently upon the vices and shortcomings of military life. Kindly and considerate towards all, civilians as well as soldiers, no man could know him or hear him converse without marking him in his memory as a man of the highest character and patriotism. While he was cheerful and friendly towards all, he was never light or trivial in speech or behavior. As though conscious of his lack of the lighter accomplishments, he never sought the society of ladies, but was painfully shy in the presence of such as called upon him on business or met him by chance. Altogether and everywhere, though clad with the rank and power of office, he never forgot that he was one of the plain people. While he never became a communicant or a regular church member, he had a profound respect for religion and all who regulated their lives by its precepts. Throughout life he revered the ways of the godly, and looked with contempt upon the idler and the drunkard. He drank neither beer, wine, nor liquor, played no cards, and spent no time in idle ways or light and profligate behavior. In the times of the Commonwealth he would have been a Puritan of the straightest sect, if not a Covenanter and an Ironsides. And when his sturdy English name is considered along with the austere ways of his life, who can say that he was not descended from the very loins of the New Model Army, which was the crowning glory of the immortal Cromwell?

It is not certain that Rawlins ever read the story of that most heroic organization of our race, but if the officers and men who upheld the Union cause with him had all been as simple, steady, orderly, and inflexible in character, behavior, and courage as he was, there can be but little doubt that we should have had the greatest army the world had ever seen up to that time.

AFFAIRS AT VICKSBURG

IMMEDIATELY after the capture and occupation of Vicksburg, army headquarters were established at the house of a well-to-do planter in the lower part of the city, and in due time both Grant and his staff made the acquaintance of the ladies of the family. Among them was the governess, a charming and accomplished young woman from Connecticut, named Miss Hurlbut. Rawlins was at that time in the prime of life and apparently in perfect health, but he was singularly shy and restrained in the presence of ladies, and always avoided their society when he could do so without rudeness. Others, however, less backward at once discovered the beauty and attractiveness of the fair Yankee and made her the object of attentions which, although intended to be flattering, soon became embarrassing. This led to the presentation of Rawlins to the ladies as a measure of protection during the absence of Grant, and was soon followed by the development of an interest which no one, and Rawlins least of all, expected. He was far from being a beau but he was full of chivalry, which needed only a proper occasion to make itself known. This he found in the protection he was called upon to give to innocence and beauty. He had been a widower nearly two years, and although a man of sedate manners, his reserve was soon relaxed, and in the course of a few weeks, he asked for and obtained the hand of Miss Hurlbut, who was at that time a most attractive picture of health and beauty [see cover photo taken at City Point in 1864]. They were married shortly after the great victory of Missionary Ridge, on December 23, 1863, at Danbury, Connecticut, and became a devoted and contented couple; but, quite unconscious of the danger that menaced them, they were destined to close their lives in turn, after a few short years of sorrow and suffering, as victims of that most dreadful of diseases, pulmonary consumption.

As has been previously stated, Rawlins's first wife died of that disease at the outbreak of the Civil War, and it is now certain that she communicated it to her husband. It first showed itself in him at Chattanooga in the winter of 1863-64, but the victim, with delusive hope, regarded it not only then, but for several years afterwards, as merely a cold, or at worst a slight bronchial affliction, which would soon pass away. Its progress was slow, but certain and irresistible; and finally, after seven years of alternate hope and despair, it proved fatal. The fair young wife took the disease in due course, and although every aid known at that time to the science of medicine was tried, she succumbed to it a few years after her husband's death. These three cases afford most pathetic but indubitable evidence both of the communicability and the fatality of the dread disease. The microbe or bacillus theory had not yet been announced, and the modern tests of the disease were still unknown. The doctors repeatedly assured Rawlins that he was free from consumption, but the fear of it was with him from his first persistent cold at Chattanooga to the end of his life, and this, together with his anxiety and suffering, had a modifying influence upon his temperament and career.

But to return to the consideration of current events. It will be remembered that the surrender of Vicksburg was concluded by Grant's decision to parole Pemberton and his army and allow the officers and men to proceed to their homes, there to remain till properly exchanged. Rawlins, as before stated, felt that this was mistaken liberality, and that it would lead to complications, if not to the immediate reenrollment of the surrendered army in the fighting force of the Confederacy. He suggested that it would be better to send the prisoners to the North for detention and safe-keeping, but unfortunately Grant upon this important occasion adhered to his own views, and after disarming and enrolling his prisoners and putting them on parole not to take further part in the war till duly exchanged, allowed them, after stacking arms and colors, to march back again into the Confederacy, under the command of their own officers, with their various organizations intact.

It is only necessary here to call attention anew to the fact that a month had not passed before the Confederate authorities repudiated the validity of the capitulation as not complying with the terms of the formal agreement between the two governments, and ordered the paroled troops to take up arms and resume hostilities against the United States.

Shortly after the surrender Sherman was ordered towards Jackson and beyond with a strong force of cavalry, infantry, and artillery for the purpose of clearing the State of Mississippi of the enemy. Ord, with another corps, was sent to take part in the operations in Louisiana, and almost immediately after these dispositions were made, Grant himself, accompanied by that portion of the staff which neither Dana nor Rawlins valued very highly, went to New Orleans for the purpose of conferring with Banks. The result of these measures, which originated mostly with Grant and were approved in Washington, was to scatter and practically neutralize Grant's splendid army, not far from eighty thousand strong, and to place its nucleus practically on the defensive.

Of course these dispositions could not have been made or carried into effect but for Halleck's consent. Although the author of a standard work on the art of war, he seemed to be utterly unable to understand the policy of concentration, or how to use the overwhelming forces at his disposal so as to follow the enemy to his real points of defence and make his overthrow certain. Rosecrans was about crossing the Tennessee River for the purpose of maneuvering Bragg out of Chattanooga. To thwart this purpose and to prevent the Confederacy from being again cut in two by an advance of the national forces to Atlanta, the Confederate Government detached Longstreet's splendid corps of veterans from Lee's army in Virginia, and ordered it to report to Bragg in Northern Georgia. Instead of acting on the timely discovery of this important movement, which had been made by Meade's provost marshal and confirmed by spies operating in East Tennessee and Virginia, under orders issued from Dodge's headquarters at Corinth, neither Rosecrans nor the Washington authorities made any adequate preparations to anticipate or counteract it. As elsewhere stated, it was feasible to send at least two army corps, or 50,000 men, from Grant's army on the Mississippi, and a like number from Meade's army, at any time after the fall of Vicksburg, to reinforce Rosecrans; but this was not done till more than ten weeks had been wasted in secondary operations, or, what was still worse, in idleness at sickly encampments, or in futile and fragmentary operations in the field.

My duties as Inspector General of Grant's army required me to visit the posts and detachments scattered throughout the widely extended Department during the lull of operations, and as the northernmost post was at Paducah, and there was much work to be done at that place as well as at Cairo, Columbus, Jackson, Memphis, and Helena, I was necessarily absent for several weeks. During the summer months and especially while Grant was absent, Rawlins remained at Vicksburg in charge of headquarters, in virtual command of the army. Strangely enough, although both Sherman and McPherson as next in rank were entitled in turn to succeed, they concurred in waiving their right under the Army Regulations, in favor of Rawlins. It was a compliment which he fully appreciated and yet he was far from satisfied with the arrangement. He not only strongly disapproved Grant's trip to New Orleans but chafed under the arrangements, which he could plainly see were neutralizing such an important part of the national army.

During my absence I wrote him freely and received several characteristic letters in reply. From one, dated September 15, 1863, I make the following extract:

... I am sorry that General Asboth's Columbus improvements cannot be justified on sound military principles, for it will make him feel badly, but an officer in the discharge of a duty must perform it strictly no matter whom it may place in an unpleasant situation. Of course he will not go outside of his proper path to injure one's feelings.

I anticipate a large amount of valuable information from the result of your present inspection, not heretofore had at Department Headquarters; information of utility as well as interest. General Grant returned from Memphis to this place on Saturday the 29th ultimo, and left here on the 31st for New Orleans accompanied by General Lorenzo Thomas and staff, General T. Kilby Smith, Colonels Riggin and Duff, Captains Jaynes and Ross, and has not yet returned though I am looking for him hourly. I hear a rumor that on Friday of the first week in this month, on returning in company with General Banks from a grand review they were riding quite rapidly when General Grant's horse fell and injured him very badly. I have no other knowledge than that which rumor has put afloat. No one of his highly intelligent staff has deemed the matter of sufficient importance to write me one word nor even as much as send a verbal message. The General I understand is at Carrollton and I suppose his staff are in New Orleans enjoying hugely the time the General's indisposition from injuries gives them.

In the meantime, however, matters here move on as smoothly as could be desired. Sherman and McPherson are both content that I should carry on the current business of the Department the same as if the General were here. All General Hurlbut's requisitions for troops with which to reinforce Steele have been filled and he informed that if necessary more could be spared. I have also written to Colonel Kelton the satisfactory status of things here. The expedition of General Crocker to Harrisburg, Louisiana, was a complete success. The enemy evacuated the place leaving four field pieces in our possession. I hope Steele may get up a fight and entirely rout the rebels at Little Rock. I have high regards for Steele but would like to see Hurlbut with the expedition himself.

In the omitted part of this letter Rawlins disclosed for the first time the great interest which Miss Hurlbut had excited in him, and on my return to headquarters he confessed that he hoped to make her his wife. As she was in every way worthy of him, he had the best wishes of his family and friends, and especially of both General and Mrs. Grant. It was a pleasure to all to see this strong and rugged man softened and humanized by the smiles of a beautiful and interesting woman. It was a still greater pleasure to see him finally made happy a few months later, by the union of her lot with his for life.

During this interesting period, and just before Grant left for New Orleans, an incident took place which well illustrates the relations existing between him and his adjutant. Under the trade regulations then in force throughout the Department, citizens were still forbidden to buy or ship cotton to the North, but in violation of standing orders a connection of Grant's by marriage, who had come ostensibly to visit him, bought and undertook to ship North a lot of cotton from a landing nearby. The circumstance was at once reported to Rawlins, and as a matter of routine, without even consulting his chief, he issued an order expelling the offender from the department. This shortly became known to the General, who at once most modestly asked Rawlins to recall or suspend the order. Thinking that the request foreshadowed a weakening on the part of the General in behalf of his kinsman, which would not be extended to an ordinary citizen, Rawlins broke forth in a flood of violent language, concluding with the declaration that if he were a general commanding an army of a hundred thousand men and a relation of his came down into it and violated one of his important standing orders, he would march him out under guard and hang him to the highest tree within five miles of camp. Grant was naturally amazed at this outburst, but with admirable self-control made no reply whatever, whereupon Rawlins retired to his office, pale with rage. The scene was an embarrassing one violating in every way the rules of official propriety. It was the first time I had ever seen Rawlins lose his temper with the General, and feeling sure he had acted under a hasty and ungovernable impulse, I followed him out, and after remonstrating with him on the impropriety of his violent outburst, pointed out the necessity for the withdrawal of his words and an immediate apology therefor. Without a moment's hesitation he acknowledged his fault, and returning at once to the General's room, said with a full and sonorous voice:

"General, I owe you an humble apology for my exhibition of temper and for the rude and profane language I have just used in your presence. I sincerely beg your pardon, and hope you will grant it. I thought I had mastered both my tongue and my temper, for when I made the acquaintance of the ladies here, I resolved to quit cursing and flattered myself that I had succeeded."

But by force of habit he unconsciously closed even this manly declaration with the unconscious utterance of a few emphatic words, which brought a smile of forgiveness to Grant's face, with the remark:

"Of course you were not cursing, Rawlins, but like Wilson's friend merely expressing your 'intense vehemence on the subject matter.' Don't think of it again, but now that the storm is over, you can destroy that order, and tell the gentleman to whom it refers that his health requires him to take the first steamer back to Cairo."

The reconciliation was instantaneous and complete, and Grant never referred to the incident again except playfully, to illustrate how Rawlins, who had early in the war become somewhat famous for the habit of expressing his "intense vehemence on the subject matter," but ultimately gave it up after marrying the lady in whose honor he had made the worthy resolution.

The summer, which was both hot and dry, wore away without further friction though not without unhappiness. Rawlins employed himself for the first few weeks after the occupation of Vicksburg in editing the General's rough report of operations, and in looking after the routine business of the army and the Department. Affairs were conducted at headquarters with great simplicity and modesty. No display nor dissipation of any sort was allowed, and but little social intercourse was held with the people. Even the uniforms of the officers were dull, and the camp equipage and office furniture were plain and primitive to a degree that the neediest of the Confederates would have regarded as mean, if not niggardly. Rawlins, with his simple and inexpensive habits, was apparently unconscious of all this, and when Bowers remonstrated with him against using wooden blocks for candlesticks and asked for better ones, he replied with a grave shake of the head:

"Oh, no, Bowers! Those wooden candlesticks are good enough. They fill a very important purpose. They are the connecting link between silver candlesticks and no candlesticks at all!"

During the hot weather of July, Rawlins was perplexed by a lot of petty annoyances. The work of preparing the official reports and of watching over the ladies at headquarters, was incongruous if not exacting, and had it not been for the alternate consolation and uncertainties of love making they would have made him very unhappy. Grant was away, the army was more or less idle, and altogether official matters were not going to suit him. But when Grant returned and found the reports ready for signature, he concluded to give Rawlins an outing by sending him to Washington as bearer of despatches. This was most honorable and acceptable duty and as it was intended as a special compliment to Rawlins it pleased him greatly. He arrived in Washington July 30, and the next day had an interview with the President and cabinet lasting two hours. On his return to the army he of course made a full report to General Grant, but told the rest of us but little about it. Fortunately, however, Gideon Welles, the Secretary of the Navy, made an interesting entry in his diary, and as it not only shows the favorable impression Rawlins made but confirms other statements of this narrative, I quote from the *Atlantic Monthly* as follows:

Friday, July 31, 1863.

I met at the President's, and was introduced by him to, Colonel Rawlins, of General Grant's staff. He arrived yesterday with the official report of the taking of Vicksburg and capture of Pemberton's army. [I] was much pleased with him, his frank, intelligent and interesting description of men and account of army operations. His interview with the President and Cabinet was of nearly two hours duration, and all, I think, were entertained by him. His honest, unpretending, and unassuming manners pleased me, the absence of pretension, and I may say the unpolished and unrefined deportment of this earnest and sincere man, patriot and soldier pleased me more than that of almost any officer whom I have met. He was never at West Point, and has had but few educational advantages, yet he is a soldier, and has a mind which has served his general and his country well. He is a sincere and earnest friend of Grant, who has evidently sent him here for a purpose.

It was the intention of the President last fall that General McClernand, an old neighbor and friend of his, should have been associated with Admiral Porter in active operations before Vicksburg. It was the expressed and earnest wish of Porter to have a citizen general, and he made it a special point to be relieved from associations with a West Pointer; all West Pointers, he said, were egotistical and assuming, and never willing to consider and treat naval officers as equals.

The President thought the opportunity a good one to bring forward his friend McClernand in whom he has confidence, and who is a volunteer officer of ability, and possesses moreover a good deal of political influence in Illinois. Stanton and Halleck entered into his views, for Grant was not a special favorite with either.

Rawlins now comes from Vicksburg with statements in regard to McClernand which show him an impracticable and unfit man. He has not been subordinate and intelligent, but has been an embarrassment, and, instead of directing or assisting, has been really an obstruction to any movements and operations. In Rawlins's statements there is undoubtedly prejudice, but with such appearance of candor, and earnest and intelligent conviction, that there can be hardly a doubt McClernand is in fault; and Rawlins has been sent here by Grant in order to enlist the President rather than bring despatches. In this I think he has succeeded, though the President feels kindly toward McClernand, Grant evidently hates him, and Rawlins is imbued with the feelings of his chief.

For more, see Diary of Gideon Welles Volumes I & II.—*Ed. 2015*

Meanwhile the course of the war in the neighboring Department of the Cumberland was preparing work of a more serious character for all the troops which could be drawn from far and near. The battle of Chickamauga took place on September 19-20, and followed as it was by the withdrawal of the Union army into the fortified lines about Chattanooga, and the investment of that place south of the river, it became necessary for the Government to bestir itself and to utilize all its resources to make good its hold and to restore its supremacy in that quarter. As before stated, the union of the three departments of the Mississippi Valley into one Military Division, under one supreme head, was now recognized as an important measure which must be carried into effect without further delay. An order to that effect was issued, Grant was by common consent assigned to the chief command, and as soon as he was informed and the necessary arrangements could be completed, he proceeded with his staff to the new field of duty and glory which the fortunes of war had prepared for him.

Rawlins had in the meantime received his commission as Brigadier General, and had been announced as chief of staff. He was relieved at once by Bowers from the routine work of the adjutant general's department, and was thus enabled to devote himself exclusively to the more important duties of his new position. He had grown steadily with his commander in knowledge and experience, and was regarded by those who knew him best as fully entitled to the increased rank which had been bestowed upon him. If he had been necessary to the General in the formative period of their military life, he was still more necessary now that they were about to enter upon a broader stage and to undertake a task of far greater magnitude than any which had yet engaged their attention.

EVENTS IN TENNESSEE

THE disastrous battle of Chickamauga took place about twelve weeks after the surrender of Pemberton's army at Vicksburg. It was long contended that inasmuch as Rosecrans had occupied and made good his hold on Chattanooga he had gained a substantial victory; but as he retreated from the field of battle it must in fairness be admitted that he suffered an actual defeat, although, as is frequently the case, the victorious army was almost as much exhausted as the one it had beaten. It had put forth its very last effort, and if Thomas, who had succeeded to the command of the Union army and resisted every attack, had not voluntarily concluded, after darkness had closed in, on receipt of special authority from Rosecrans, to retire, the struggle would probably have gone down to history as at most a drawn battle. But night found neither army in condition to strike another blow. Longstreet's arrival from Virginia with his splendid corps, in time to take part in the second day's battle, made the contending hosts nearly equal in strength. Had it not been for Longstreet's weighty reinforcement of his antagonist, Rosecrans could doubtless have held his position intact, and might have gained a substantial advantage. On the other hand, had the Government sent Grant's disposable force promptly from Vicksburg to reinforce Rosecrans, that general would have had a tremendous preponderance of strength and this would have given him every reasonable assurance of a complete victory.

But, unfortunately, the authorities at Washington were late in discovering the detachment of Longstreet from Lee's army, and never seemed to realize that while superior genius might give us the victory, nothing short of a great superiority of strength on the actual field of battle could give absolute assurance of it. No general ever had a better knowledge of the strategical principles involved than had Halleck, the General-in-Chief, and yet no one ever failed more egregiously than did he to profit by their application. With the introduction of improved firearms, the open formation for battle and the rapid construction of rifle trenches and breastworks, the dangers of the direct attack had already become greatly increased. It is now recognized among military men that rapid marching and an overpowering superiority in numbers, particularly in mounted troops, which are specially fitted to operate effectively against the enemy's flanks and rear, are more than ever necessary to insure success in warfare; but simple as it is, this lesson never became properly understood in Washington.

News of the disaster of Chickamauga reached Grant late in September, and immediately afterwards he sent me to Cairo by steamboat with despatches for Halleck. I arrived there on Saturday, October 2, sent off my despatches at once, received the replies the same night, and returned to headquarters as rapidly as a swift steamer could carry me. On the 10th Grant gave orders to break up at Vicksburg, and on the 16th arrived at Cairo with his staff. The next day he continued his journey by rail, met Stanton, the Secretary of War, at Indianapolis, and accompanied him without delay to Louisville.

Neither Grant nor any member of his staff except Rawlins had ever seen the great Secretary, and naturally enough, they were all anxious to meet him. When the train stopped at Indianapolis he was at the station and came at once into the General's special car. Overlooking or not seeing Rawlins, he walked directly up to Dr. Kittoe, the chief surgeon, who was wearing a flowing beard and an army hat; he held out his hand and said:

"How are you, General Grant? I knew you at sight from your pictures."

Of course the error was discovered instantly, but the incident was not without embarrassment to the Secretary, and trivial as it was, seems to have produced an unpleasant impression, if not a positive prejudice, in his mind. He evidently expected to meet a more impressive man than the quiet and modest General, and acted throughout the ride to Louisville as though he was disappointed. They, however, dined and spent the evening together and Stanton doubtless bore himself with perfect frankness in giving the General his instructions in reference to the new command and the new campaign, but it was no secret to any of us that neither of these great persons was greatly taken with the other. They cooperated henceforth loyally and effectively in the cause, till the struggle was closed, and so long as Stanton remained Secretary of War their relations were friendly, but they never became intimate or particularly sympathetic with each other.

It is not to be supposed that the trivial mistake at the beginning of their acquaintance had any appreciable effect upon the feelings of these great but dissimilar characters. Grant was shy, diffident and reserved with strangers, and knowing that ill reports had been sent to Washington about him, he may have been more or less under restraint, in the Secretary's presence. Stanton, who was a man of extraordinary severity of manner, was profoundly conscious of his own importance, and may have desired to impress Grant with his personal as well as with his official power. Whatever may have been the inward feelings with which they regarded each other, it was evident from Grant's conduct not only the next day but always afterwards that he felt no great interest either in the man or in the Secretary.

Dana, who met the party on the way south from Louisville, returned with us by the same train to Stevenson and Bridgeport, and gave us full particulars of the great battle and of the behavior of the leading generals. As is well known, he had not brought from the field of Chickamauga a favorable opinion of Rosecrans, and Grant, who was at best not over-partial to that general, during the conversation with the Secretary signified his wish that the unfortunate general should be relieved from command and that Thomas should be assigned to the vacancy. It has long been believed by some that this change was partly due to political intrigue, but so far as I have been able to ascertain, there is no contemporaneous evidence to sustain this belief. It was shown by the Official Records years afterwards that during the interview at Louisville the Secretary of War wisely placed the choice of subordinate commanders entirely at the discretion of Grant, and Grant, who up to that time had never been governed in the performance of his duty by considerations of a political nature, did not hesitate to decide in favor of the change. Rawlins and I were informed of all the facts so far as they were then known, and fully concurred in the wisdom of the decision. I am sure that neither of us then knew or cared what Rosecrans's politics were nor was influenced in the slightest degree by any other consideration than the good of the public service.

Pausing on the way to the front to confer with Rosecrans, who met the party at Stevenson, and with Hooker and Howard, who had been stopped at Bridgeport, Grant and his staff went forward by horseback over the rough and roundabout road through Jasper, over Walden's Ridge to Chattanooga. As Dana and I were anxious to get on we took a shorter cut from the same point over the Ridge and along the north bank of the river within range of the Confederate pickets, and under the cover of darkness rode into the beleaguered town just before midnight. Grant and the rest of the staff reached the town wet and weary after dark the next night. But the road was so rough and slippery that Grant's horse had fallen upon him, severely bruising the leg which had been so badly injured at New Orleans. The wagons with the baggage and camp equipage could not keep up and were consequently left far behind. As there were no hotels open at Chattanooga, Grant necessarily became the guest of Thomas, while his staff officers were bestowed wherever room could be found for them.

It will be recalled that Grant and Thomas had last met during the Shiloh-Corinth Campaign, in which Thomas had virtually superseded Grant and that this or some other circumstance had prevented the establishment of cordial relations between those distinguished officers. The tables were now turned. Grant was in supreme command. He was the hero of the most successful campaign which had been made on either side during the war, and twelve weeks later, without the suspicion of personal influence or intrigue, had been placed in authority over both Rosecrans and Thomas. He had without the slightest hesitation turned down the former and exalted the latter, and yet Thomas, whom he had preferred, did not receive him cordially.

I had been busy during the entire day calling upon the leading officers, inspecting the army, and studying the situation at Chattanooga, so as to be prepared to make an intelligent report to General Grant on his arrival. Grant, wet and weary, reached town between eight and nine o'clock at night, and of course went directly to Thomas's headquarters. I got in from my work a little later and found the two generals seated on the opposite sides of a blazing wood fire, a little puddle of water under Grant's chair and his clothes steaming from the heat. They were both silent and grave. Rawlins, whom I had shaken hands with as I was going in, was white with anger at the cool reception the general and staff had received. They had made a long and tiresome ride and were soaking wet, but as yet nothing had been done to relieve their discomfort. They had found shelter but apparently nothing more. Taking in the situation at a glance, I pushed my way into the room and after the usual salutations and a few questions, I spoke substantially as follows:

"General Thomas, General Grant has been on the road two days. His wagons are behind; he is wet and suffering from a bruised leg; besides, he is tired and hungry. Can't you get him some dry clothes from one of your staff and order some supper to be provided for him?"

This broke the restraint and recalled Thomas, who was ordinarily one of the most thoughtful and considerate of men, to the duties of hospitality, as well as to the requirements of official courtesy. He replied promptly:

"Of course, I can."

And calling Willard, his senior aid-de-camp, he gave the necessary orders, which, it is needless to add, were cheerfully obeyed. Grant was soon clad in dry clothes and called to a plain but bountiful supper, during which he listened to my report, which was by no means encouraging. As soon as his meal was finished he discussed the situation with Thomas as quietly as if he had received the heartiest welcome; but it is a fact worth recording that neither he nor Rawlins ever quite forgot the frigidity of their reception. Rawlins referred to it more than once during the subsequent operations about Chattanooga. He regarded it as entirely inexcusable, if not intentional, and cited the captious conduct of Thomas's adjutant general, an old regular officer, perfectly posted in all official courtesies, as positive proof that an unjustifiable state of irritation and resentment prevailed at Thomas's headquarters towards Grant and his staff. I was particularly struck by the evidences of it from time to time and have referred to it frequently since for the purpose of finding a satisfactory explanation of its origin, and of pointing out its baneful influence over the subsequent relations of those distinguished men. It is admitted by all who knew them at that period that they were not sympathetic with each other. Perhaps they never became so. They were alike in their taciturnity and reserve. Neither was ever effusive or demonstrative towards even his intimates, and yet both were warmhearted and considerate to their closer friends. That they were not so towards each other was doubtless due to circumstances over which neither had entire control, but which concerned them both, and exerted a great influence over events in which they were deeply interested.

Between Grant, Sherman, and McPherson a warm friendship, characterized by perfect cordiality, prevailed from the first days of their association. Grant could not do too much for either of them. He preferred them over all others for honors and command. He considered them as more prompt and probably more trustworthy than Thomas, and yet in many respects Thomas was the superior of either. He was a man of greater deliberation and solidity of judgment, as well as a better and more experienced practical soldier, organizer, and administrator, than either of them. Indeed, in these respects it may well be questioned if he had his superior on either side of the Great Conflict. I have elsewhere undertaken to point out how personal pride, the consciousness of a blameless life, of unfailing success, and of duty always well performed, on the one side, in unconscious contrast with careless habits, hard luck, and ill report, even in the face of unusual victories, on the other side, may have had a tendency to arouse a spirit of rivalry and distrust between these great men. After all they were only human, and it was but natural that they should not understand each other as well as they understood those with whom they were more frequently and more favorably brought in contact.

Rawlins recognized the full significance of these facts and exerted all his influence to bring about greater intimacy and a more cordial feeling; but while his convictions urged him in that direction, the daily intercourse between the Military Division and Department headquarters was never placed upon an entirely satisfactory basis. There was always friction, which Rawlins finally resented with such energy as to put an end to its open exhibition thereafter. His relations with Thomas were always most punctilious, but never intimate. Dana and I were the means most depended upon to cultivate friendly relations and to bridge over difficulties. Our success was only partial. We succeeded in preventing an open breach, but failed to bring about a cordial understanding.

The plan of operations, the concentration of forces and the battle of Missionary Ridge have been so frequently and so fully described that further reference to them may well be omitted from the life of a subordinate. Rawlins was of course at the very focus of information and events. Every letter and order sent, as well as every communication received, was necessarily known to him, if it did not actually pass through his hands. Grant consulted him more fully than ever, and the chief of staff did not hesitate to express his views whenever he thought it necessary. He did his best from the start to hurry up reinforcements, to open shorter lines of communication, and to bring forward an adequate amount of supplies. Grant and Rawlins had during previous campaigns met all the leading officers except W. F. Smith, the chief engineer, who had recently come to the Army of the Cumberland from the Army of the Potomac. He had been at Chattanooga long enough to become familiar with the topographical features of the surrounding country, and to evolve a plan for opening a direct line of supplies between the beleaguered town and the railroad terminus at Bridgeport, 30 miles away. That accomplished, he was duly transferred to Grant's staff as chief engineer, and turned his attention at once to the development of a plan of attack against Bragg's position. In this he found himself daily in contact with Rawlins, and soon learned to confide fully in him, and to depend confidently upon his cooperation. A warm friendship, based upon mutual respect, grew up between them, and when the plan of operation was ready for execution, every feature of it had the approval not only of Grant but of Rawlins.

The features of the country and the condition of the army, at the time Grant took command, as well as the preliminary movements ordered by him are well described by Rawlins in a letter dated Chattanooga, Tenn., November 6, 1863:

... Much of the country between here and Nashville is the hardest in appearance and the worst for military operations I have ever seen. The fact is, when we reached here the fate of this army was suspended by a single thread and that the line of its supplies, which was a road leading from Bridgeport through the Sequatchie Valley and over the mountains to Chattanooga, a distance of sixty miles, the valley road almost without bottom, and the mountain road the roughest and steepest of ascent and descent ever traversed by army wagons and mules. One riding over the road if he did not see with his own eyes that they did get over it, would not believe it possible for them to do so.

Since General Grant's arrival here the distance for wagon transportation has been reduced to eight miles, by the moving of forces across to the South side of the Tennessee River and fortifying all the mountain passes leading to it from below Lookout Mountain to Bridgeport and through which the enemy had been enabled to pass to the river and cut off its use for transportation purposes to us and even prevent our soldiers passing along its bank on the North side. This movement of ours was to the enemy's perfect surprise, and the next night after it was effected, he attempted by a night attack to regain the advantages we had wrested from him, but after a severe battle in which we lost in killed and wounded full four hundred, he was repulsed, leaving on the battle-field one hundred and fifty of his dead, many of his bad and dangerously wounded and seventy-five well prisoners, and full one thousand good Enfield rifles. The necessity of this movement had been considered here for weeks prior to General Grant's arrival, but until General Rosecrans was relieved and General Thomas succeeded him in command, no steps had been taken to carry it into execution that I am aware of. General Thomas immediately on being placed in command had issued orders for this purpose which were concurred in by General Grant and the necessity of their prompt execution urged. The advantages of this new line of communication and supplies to us, is no less than enabling us to hold Chattanooga, for I have no hesitancy in saying that it would have been during the winter almost if not quite out of the question to have supplied the army here by the old line. The mules were so poor and worn out that they could not in my judgment have made to exceed two more trips. Still man determined to do a thing can accomplish almost impossibilities and frequently does make practicable that which seems utterly impracticable.

The army here under General Thomas is in fine spirits and whatever may be its feelings of love and regret for General Rosecrans, it evinces no regret at his removal, and is united in according to General Thomas the glory of rescuing it from disastrous rout and ruin and saving the honor of our arms at Chickamauga. Had some other generals, brave, double-starred and high in command as he, remained upon the field and rallied their broken divisions, instead of leaving it for Chattanooga at an unseasonably early hour, the Federal and not the rebel army would have cared for the wounded and buried the dead of Chickamauga.

General Gordon Granger shares largely with General Thomas in the glory of that terrible conflict. Between a quarter and half past one o'clock P. M. after the second day's battles of Chickamauga, three divisions or near that, of Crittenden's and McCook's corps were routed by the enemy and our lines broken, and by four o'clock P M., of the same day, Generals Rosecrans, McCook and Crittenden had got safely back to Chattanooga, a distance of full twelve miles from the field of battle.

We are expecting General Sherman's forces here by Monday or Tuesday of next week. On their arrival you may expect to hear news of importance from this section or field of operations. We are now secure or at least in apparent security against getting out of supplies, and if we can so dispose of our troops as to secure General Burnside's in East Tennessee against an attack in overwhelming numbers from the enemy, shall feel we have accomplished a great deal. Every energy is being put forward to this end and I feel certain we will succeed.

General Grant is a quiet, brave and energetic commander, with his eye ever on the foe and watching his movements, with a view to taking advantage of any misstep or weak point he may discover. He is not of those who constantly write letters and issue proclamations and keep their eyes half turned and their ears half listening to see and hear what the people back home are writing or saying of them, and in such predicament lose the successes they otherwise might obtain, and sink out of sight in oblivious waves when they might have been enthroned in fame's temple had the one purpose of defeating the foe only possessed them.

Whether it be called luck or military ability to which is attributed General Grant's successes, I have but little care, so that the same successes that have thus far attended him desert him not in this, his new field of operations. . . .

After Hooker's preliminary movements against Lookout Mountain, and Sherman's across the Tennessee against the end of Missionary Ridge, Grant, Thomas, Granger, Smith, Rawlins, Dana, and many staff officers took post on Orchard Knob to witness the operations of the day. It was expected that Sherman would carry Tunnel Hill and the right of Bragg's army, supported by Howard's corps to his immediate right, by Hooker's movement against Bragg's extreme left at Rossville, and finally by Thomas with the Army of the Cumberland at the centre. But Sherman found the enemy strongly posted, and instead of driving back and doubling up or taking in reverse Bragg's right wing, he suffered a severe repulse, which seemed to paralyze his efforts and to discourage his subordinates. The day was wearing away with but little promise of victory. A feeling of anxiety and doubt began to show itself. Grant's face became overclouded. Thomas was taciturn and silent. Gordon Granger alone was noisy in directing the work of a field battery nearby. Smith, Rawlins, and Wilson, perceiving that a deadlock had been reached, put their heads together in conference as to what should be done. The orders issued the night before contemplated an advance from the centre when it should become apparent that Sherman had carried or turned the enemy's right, and Hooker had turned his left, but by noon, or shortly after, it was painfully evident that the double contingency had not arisen, and that something else must be done. The deadlock was distressingly evident, but neither could suggest anything more promising than a demonstration from the centre against Bragg's advanced entrenchments at the foot of the Ridge; and accordingly it was decided that Rawlins should urge this movement upon Grant. Concurring fully in this conclusion, he stepped up to Grant, and in a low voice made the suggestion; whereupon Grant walked over to Thomas several steps away and in a conversational tone said:

"Don't you think it is about time to order your troops to advance against the enemy's first line of rifle pits?"

To this Thomas made no reply whatever so far as could be heard, but stood silent with uplifted glasses, scanning the enemy's position on the ridge, in plain view, just beyond the range of our artillery, across the intervening fields and open country. He was evidently in doubt. So far as the eye could determine there was nothing to indicate the slightest success in Sherman's front, and so the deadlock continued. Our little group became more and more serious as time passed slowly on. Minutes seemed like hours. Granger kept up the noisy fire of his battery and this added to the annoyance and the embarrassment of the situation. Our group grew still more impatient, and finally at or about three o'clock, Rawlins again pressed Grant to issue a positive order, and this he did with a firmness and decision which brought the desired result. Grant, who had by this time also become thoroughly aroused, turned to Thomas, who was only a few feet away and had doubtless heard all that had passed between the General and his Chief of Staff, and with a blazing face and an expression of unusual determination, said:

"General Thomas, order Granger to turn that battery over to its proper commander and take command of his own corps." After a pause, he added in the same tone of authority: "And now order your troops to advance and take the enemy's first line of rifle pits."

There was no longer room for doubt or hesitation. As was his duty, Grant had taken the entire responsibility and given a positive order which could not be disobeyed. So long as the discretion was left with Thomas, he stood silent. Even now he made no reply, but turning at once to Granger, he ordered him to his corps, and then coolly despatched his aids-de-camp with orders for a general advance. Sheridan, Johnson, Wood and Baird, whose divisions were waiting impatiently for orders, moved out with the promptitude and precision of a parade. Without the slightest hesitation, they rushed against the enemy with irresistible force. In full sight of all the generals they swept over the long line of rifle trench at the foot of the hill, and without halt or pause, pushed on towards the summit. This was more than anyone expected. It was a voluntary impulse of the fighting line, doubtless due largely to the slight resistance it had encountered at the enemy's outlying defenses. It was inexplicable at the time, but it is now known that Bragg made the fatal mistake of dividing his force between the entrenchments at the top and those at the bottom of the Ridge, and in directing the troops at the bottom to deliver their fire, when the Union advance should get within 200 yards, and then to retire to the works above. This order was carried out literally, but the officers standing on Orchard Knob, including Grant and Thomas, all thought that the upward rush of our troops was a mistake which would end in disaster, and there were muttered predictions to that effect in plenty, but as it turned out all fears were groundless. Once under way up the steep hillside, officers and men vied with one another till the summit was reached and the victory won. Grant, seeing that his men had broken the enemy's line and disappeared over the crest, mounted and went forward with his staff to the top and across the ridge, till at nightfall he came up with Sheridan's advance beyond the Chickamauga. His example was followed by Thomas, who took a road to the right, and had Sherman thrown his troops rapidly forward along the ridge or, better still, behind it, Bragg's army should have been taken in flank or rear and captured or destroyed that night. The victory was an overwhelming one, but, as has been seen, while it was gained by movements which had been previously ordered, the vital blow was struck by Thomas and not by Sherman, as was intended, and what is still more singular, the immediate impulse to deliver this blow had its origin with Grant's staff, and was not struck till Grant himself assumed the entire responsibility and gave a positive order to put Thomas's troops in motion. It is but simple justice to add that while another might have given that impulse later, Rawlins actually gave it at the time and in the manner which I have described.

In just fifty-five minutes from the time the national advance began from the centre, both the rifle pits at the foot of the hill and the crest of Missionary Ridge had been carried, the enemy's centre had been broken and swept away and his whole army had been compelled to retreat, leaving many guns and prisoners in the hands of the victors. Bragg, who was unaccountably slow in realizing the extent of the disaster, had scarcely time to make his own escape. It is now certain that if Sherman had been as vigilant and aggressive as was expected of him, this would have been impossible, or if Grant had had an efficient force of cavalry on his left flank, or could have foreseen the certainty and extent of Thomas's success, and the timeliness of Hooker's turning movement by the roundabout way of Rossville, the Confederate General and the greater part of his army must surely have been captured. As it was, the defeat was overwhelming and almost fatal to the Confederate cause.

Grant's fame now became world-wide. All honor and credit were ascribed to him. No one else was considered. He was the one general of the Union army who always triumphed over the enemy, who was charged with no failures, and had nothing but victories to his credit.

By the time he had made the necessary dispositions to drive the enemy further from his front and from East Tennessee, winter was upon him and general operations came to a standstill. After calling for the reports of subordinates, and taking measures for the completion of his own records, Grant decided, about January 1, to visit Knoxville in East Tennessee for the purpose of acquainting himself with the military situation in that quarter. Becoming convinced by the information gathered on the trip that the enemy would not seriously endeavor to hold that region, after tarrying a few days he continued his journey by horseback with his staff through Cumberland Gap to Frankfort and Lexington, and thence by rail to Nashville, where he established his headquarters for the rest of the winter.

Meanwhile Rawlins, who had taken what was at first believed to be nothing worse than a severe cold due to exposure and hardship, availed himself of the lull which followed our victory to take leave of absence for the benefit of his health and for the additional purpose of getting married. On his return to duty, about the middle of January, he began the work of editing and completing Grant's official report of the great campaign. As was his custom the General, relying almost entirely upon his memory, wrote out with his own hand a simple but comprehensive narrative of events, which he then turned over to Rawlins as the frame-work or guide for the full and accurate report which was sent afterwards to the War Department. In such work as this, Rawlins, aided by Bowers, as usual, was singularly capable. He spared no pains to test, reconcile and

141

elaborate every statement and inference. With fidelity to the truth, without prejudice or conscious bias in favor of any one, he strove to get at the facts, and to relate them always just as they occurred. His training as a lawyer and his habit of gathering and stating evidence, so as to bring out the truth and do equal and exact justice to all, gave to his work unusual accuracy and value. Grant relied absolutely upon it; and it is but just to add that never in any instance is he known to have overruled Rawlins, or changed his account of a controverted point. It is for this reason that Grant's official reports, which from Belmont to Appomattox, either as first submitted or afterwards, passed through Rawlins's hands and received the benefit of his investigations, have withstood criticism so successfully. Indeed, it may be safely said that no official reports, whether referring to the American Civil War or to any other war, were ever framed with a more scrupulous regard to the truth, whether resting upon personal statement or embodied in the subordinate reports, than were those of Grant. If any of them contain misleading statements or false inferences, it should be assumed that it was because they were not verified by Rawlins, or because the facts on which they were based were not fully or accurately known at the time.

This is particularly the case in reference to the operations ending with the battle of Missionary Ridge. I pointed out to Rawlins when he was preparing the final report, that Sherman and not Thomas should have won that battle, by doubling up and crushing Bragg's right wing or by falling on his rear. While both Grant and Rawlins claimed that Sherman had met with unexpected resistance, and thought that I was hypercritical, they stoutly maintained that his operations had compelled the enemy on the day of the battle to so weaken his left and center by withdrawing troops from them and sending them to his right for the purpose of resisting Sherman's advance, that it made it correspondingly easy for Thomas to break through the center. As before stated, Grant and Sherman died in that belief, and it may be now asserted with equal confidence, that the same was true of Rawlins. It should be added that this view of the matter is supported by the official reports of such of the Union generals as touched upon that point. All shared in that delusion, and it was not till long after the close of the war that it became certainly known that Stevenson's Confederate division was transferred the day before, and that no troops whatever were moved from any part of Bragg's line on the day of the battle to resist the advance of Sherman's column against the Confederate right. Without these facts, the weight of testimony was all in favor of the Sherman contention and of the conclusion adopted by Grant and Rawlins, as well as by Badeau afterwards, in the *Personal History of Ulysses S. Grant.*

It was apparent to every officer on Orchard Knob, at the time, that Sherman had not carried the enemy's position at Tunnel Hill, but had been repulsed, while Thomas, who was ordered to take the enemy's rifle trench at the foot of Missionary Ridge, rather as a demonstration in Sherman's favor than as a positive attack, had, much to the surprise of everybody, not only carried the rifle trench but had swept up the ridge and over its crest, breaking through the enemy's line and driving him in confusion down the slopes and across the Chickamauga beyond. In spite of all this, Sherman, who really failed, received a larger share of praise than Thomas, who succeeded beyond all expectation, and this fact inevitably tended to intensify, rather than to end, the feeling of estrangement between Thomas and Grant.

There is not the slightest doubt that both Grant and Rawlins believed that they had seen the enemy moving along the crest of Missionary Ridge on the day of battle, to his right towards Sherman, and were entirely honest in their convictions that Sherman, who had promised so much and performed so little, was entitled to greater praise than Thomas, who had promised nothing but performed much. Such is frequently the case in military as well as in civil life, and the lesson to be drawn from it is that a cheerful and confident demeanor is an asset of real value to the soldier as well as to the man of affairs.

To the military reader it will of course occur that Sherman's threatening position on the enemy's right flank, notwithstanding the fact that all his attacks had been repulsed, may have exerted a powerful influence towards weakening Bragg's defence when he saw his centre seriously assailed. Knowing, as he must have known, that the united forces of Sherman and Howard on his right, aided by Hooker on his left, if vigorously handled, must prevail in the end, and would in that case imperil his retreat, it was perhaps natural under the circumstances that he should remain somewhat in doubt and fail to put up as stout a defence against Thomas as he should have done. At all events, his resistance was comparatively feeble, and although he inflicted heavy loss on his gallant assailants and delayed his retreat to the last minute, he succeeded in withdrawing from his entrenchments with insignificant loss except in artillery.

In considering the results of this battle, it should not be forgotten that the weight of numbers and resources, notwithstanding the extraordinary natural strength of Bragg's position, was hopelessly against him, and therefore his retreat, even before the battle, would have been both prudent and justifiable.

The detachment of Longstreet for a campaign against Burnside in East Tennessee in the face of the reinforcements coming from both East and West to strengthen the national forces, was according to all military rules a fatal mistake on the part of the Confederate leader, though it may be doubted that he could have held his advanced position for any great time even with Longstreet's help.

The great national victory won in front of Chattanooga was from every point of view the legitimate outcome of the broad and comprehensive policy which the Government on the heels of a great calamity, had been forced to adopt. The overwhelming concentration of men and materials which followed was a striking tribute not only to the soundness of the policy which Grant had always advocated, but to the success which had always attended his operations. He was the rising man of the Union army. Without pretension or parade, he was making successful campaigns and winning great victories, while both the Administration and the country were wondering how he did it. There was but little in his despatches or his reports throwing light upon the subject. There was no mention of "grand tactics" or of "strategy." They said nothing whatever about "organizing victory," and as for "logistics," it may well be doubted that either Grant or Rawlins ever heard the word or had the slightest conception of its meaning. And yet there was no great mystery in their methods. They were plain, straightforward, earnest, and patriotic men, working together with all their faculties as though they were but one. There was no friction between them, no jealousy, no suspicion, and no misunderstanding. The combination was complete. Grant was the experienced, unpretending, educated soldier, while Rawlins the civilian, was his complement and *ad latus*, rather than "the power behind the throne."

assistant / helper

It added greatly to Grant's strength that he had the habit of absorbing the thoughts and suggestions of others, and incorporating them with his own without showing the slightest false pride or jealousy. There was nothing small or mean in his makeup. Conscious of his own needs and shortcomings and of the inability of any man to think of everything or to do everything, he welcomed assistance from every quarter, and never lost an opportunity to reward or secure promotion for those who had contributed to his success. No general was ever more approachable than he, and neither the records nor the recollections of the times will reveal the slightest evidence that he ever harbored a feeling of resentment towards Rawlins for plain speaking or plain writing.

As for Rawlins, no one can read his letter of June 6, 1863, or his references to the same subject at various other later dates without realizing that he felt himself constantly in the presence of a great danger, and while it is possible that he may have magnified that danger and underestimated the strength of his chief, it is certain that he did not think so and was absolutely faithful and fearless in performing what he conceived to be his duty in respect to it. For this, and for the lofty virtues he always displayed, he enjoyed the respect and confidence of every officer of rank and character who had the good fortune to know him. So long as he remained at his post, no one doubted the success of Grant, or of the army he commanded.

CHANGES IN RANK AND DUTIES

SHORTLY after the Chattanooga and East Tennessee campaigns, and the establishment of headquarters at Nashville, I was relieved from Grant's staff and ordered to Washington for temporary duty, in the War Department as Chief of the Cavalry Bureau. Before leaving, I had participated in all the discussions which took place between Grant, Rawlins, and W. F. Smith in regard to the future conduct of the war in the South and Southwest. I was familiar with every plan that had been considered, and naturally hoped to be permitted to take part in such active operations as might be finally agreed upon. I therefore regarded this detail for duty in the War Department at first as likely to deprive me of further field service, but was reassured by the information that it was understood between General Grant and the Secretary of War that my detail would last not longer than six weeks or two months, and that I should return to the field in time for the spring campaign.

On my arrival at Washington I found that public attention had been so concentrated on Grant and his wonderful successes that his assignment to the chief command of our armies in the field had already become inevitable. The only question open was what rank he should have, and when the assignment should be made. At that time the highest grade known in the army was that of Major General, and although the President was by law authorized to assign officers of that rank to the command of armies or army-corps, without reference to seniority, this proviso was not thought to be sufficient, either as a means of authority or as a reward for such successes as those gained by Grant. It was therefore suggested that the grade of Lieutenant General should be revived, and that it should be bestowed upon Grant along with the command of all our armies, but the measure did not at once receive the approval of the Government. At the instance of an official press agent, then feeling the public pulse for the first time, the newspapers discussed the subject both favorably and unfavorably. Congress was slow to commit itself, but the bill to carry the measure into effect was introduced by Mr. Washburne and received his untiring advocacy from the start. The more it was discussed the more popular it became. Dana, fresh from

Chattanooga and from an intimate association with Grant and his staff, gave it his approval, and when I arrived in Washington early in February, 1864, I found it to be the absorbing theme of every discussion. Although but recently appointed a brigadier general, it was known that I had participated in Grant's greatest campaigns, and had been honored by his confidence. It was therefore thought that my knowledge of his character and methods might be valuable and I was freely consulted both by senators and members of the House of Representatives, as to the advisability of creating the new rank and bestowing it upon Grant. In these consultations, as well as in frequent conferences, both Dana and I took ground in favor of the proposed legislation.

I wrote fully both to Rawlins and W. F. Smith, suggesting among other things that the winter had been spent by the Washington authorities in waiting for something to turn up; that Halleck, who was generally regarded as wise and well informed, was, in fact, selfish and timid; that there was but little hope of a vigorous policy while the General-in-Chief, the Secretary of War, and the President were all pulling in different directions, or while one was pulling forward and the others refusing to pull at all. Notwithstanding Grant's great victory in the West, military operations had everywhere come to a standstill, and each of the great leaders of the Government was apparently trying to shift the responsibility to the other. So long as that condition continued the chances for ultimate victory rested merely upon "main strength and awkwardness," which was the phrase of the day.

A more comprehensive policy was necessary. It was useless for anyone to suggest plans for the reorganization of the army, or for carrying on campaigns till military affairs could be placed under a competent head. Accordingly, I wrote Rawlins in part as follows:

> . . . To be plain—General Grant must be Lieutenant General and General-in-Chief of all our armies. He is the only really successful man the war has brought to the front. Everybody here acknowledges it, and is willing to trust him and the bill creating the grade should be put through as soon as possible. There can be no doubt of this, and if the General has any scruples, he must simply lay them aside. He owes

Halleck nothing, either personally or officially, but the country everything. . . .

When called to the head of the army he can put forward whom he may choose, direct all the armies in unison, and go hereafter as heretofore wherever the danger is greatest. With his honest heart, his clear head and unselfish intentions, there can be no doubt of the ultimate result. He will not be required to remain at Washington. Halleck can be kept there. . . .

In this letter I referred also to the demands which were now coming from the politicians and the public press for Grant's nomination to the Presidency. As these were obviously premature, and for the greater part from men who were out of patience with the Administration, or who distrusted its willingness to allow any subordinate a free hand, I took ground not only against his nomination at that time but against his writing political letters or taking any part in the politics of the country. I felt, besides, that it was unfair that Mr. Lincoln should be confronted by our only successful general in his campaign for reelection, and that it might be well for Grant to let it be known in some authoritative way that he would not allow his name to be used for any such purpose. Fortunately both Rawlins and Smith concurred in the main with these opinions, and after reading my letters to Grant, Rawlins wrote me from Nashville with unusual fullness, on March 3, 1864, as follows:

> . . . While sympathizing with you in the desire for harmony and the greatest attainable unanimity of action possible on the part of the people in the coming Presidential election, I cannot see a better course for us than that we have hitherto pursued, viz., attend strictly to our duties as soldiers, leaving the management and conduct of the canvass for the election of Chief Magistrate and civil officers to the people at home. This will not debar those in the service who desire to do so, from expressing their choice through the ballot box, when from States in which provision has been made for such expression, by law. Unanimity of action on the part of all connected with the military arm of Government, in the one and sole purpose of destroying the armies of the Rebellion and in non-interference with civil matters, will in my judgment tend more to secure the desired harmony and unity of action

in the coming election than all other influences combined. It will give to the masses an earnest of our sincerity, confidence in the ability of the Government to establish and maintain its supremacy throughout the revolted States, and leave powerless the argument of "danger from the military to our Democratic institutions," and by those opposed to coercion, to excite their prejudices.

I cannot conceive how the use of General Grant's name in connection with the Presidency can result in harm to him or our cause, for if there is a man in the United States who is unambitious of such honor, it is certainly he, yet the matter is not in such a shape as to justify him in writing a letter declining to be a candidate for the Presidency. The nomination for the office has not been tendered him by the people; nor has it by either of the great political parties or any portion thereof. ... To write a letter of declination now, would place him much in the position of the old maid who had never had an offer declaring she "would never marry;" besides it would be by many construed into a modest way of getting his name before the country in connection with the office, having, as he always has, avoided public notice or newspaper talk relating to him.

His letter to the Democratic Committee of the State of Ohio, he says was written in the strictest confidence and he wishes it still to be so considered. Any use of it by his friends would, if known—and that it would be known scarcely admits of a doubt—remove from it the curtain of privacy and might give occasion for discussing it in the public press which of all things you know he would most avoid; hence I do not send it.

The Honorable E. B. Washburne I am sure is not in favor of Grant for the Presidency. He is for Mr. Lincoln, and if he has made use of the language imputed to him, it has been to further the passage of his Lieutenant-Generalcy bill; nothing more I am certain. This is my own opinion. That Washburne should seemingly arrogate to himself the exclusive championship of the General, is not at all strange when we reflect upon the fact that two years ago he was the only man in Congress who had a voice of condemnation for the General's maligners. His defence of Grant aided to keep him in his position and enabled him to achieve the successes that have placed him first in the World's History as a military man, and secured for him the gratitude of his countrymen. Grant cannot neglect writing to him, but of course should be guarded in what he writes him as well as in what he writes others. One in the General's position can scarcely write a private letter

149

that in any manner touches upon passing events, because of the eagerness of everyone to give to the public that which they so easily conceive to belong to it, coming as it does from one to whom all look to dispel the dark clouds of war that have drenched our land with blood, and reveal to their longing eyes the bright sky of peace beyond.

I am glad to know you are getting along so well with your new duties. Of one thing we here were certain—that you would bring to the discharge of them an honesty and an energy of purpose that would awe and keep off those who would by undue and corrupt influences, seek advantages against the Government.

The copy of this letter I have never seen.

When we consider the immensity of the cavalry arm of the service and its immediate necessities, then and then only, can we, anything like properly, estimate the importance of your Bureau and the many difficulties to be overcome by you in the successful management of it. All here, Wilson, wish you the greatest success. Department commanders were directed to send names for the inspectors you telegraphed for; all have not yet responded. The suggestions in your letter to W. S. Smith, Chief of Cavalry, are being attended to. As soon as the necessary reports are in from which a correct estimate of the General's cavalry force can be made, and the numbers not mounted or armed ascertained, to the extent of such unmounted and unarmed cavalry, the General proposes to dismount the mounted infantry, armed with cavalry arms, and turn their horses over to the cavalry. In this manner he hopes with what you can do for him to at least secure mounts and arms for all his cavalry.

Sherman's expedition via Meridian towards Central Alabama is the subject of most interest at present. The last information deemed reliable, from him since the rebel papers speak of his being at Quitman, on the railroad South of Meridian, is to the effect that he had reached Demopolis, East of Meridian, which if true removes all apprehensions as to his success and safety. The repairing of the damage he will do the railroads, will be to the enemy the work of months, saying nothing of their losses in negroes, horses, mules and supplies. The expedition under General W. S. Smith, Chief of Cavalry, which started from Memphis with a view to forming a junction at or near Meridian with Sherman, has returned to the neighborhood of Memphis. This we learn by despatch from General Butterfield. No report has yet been received from General Smith. I therefore refrain from comments. He has been ordered South again. Longstreet is evidently abandoning East Tennessee with the greater part of his forces and this is caused in no little degree by the movements of Sherman. He will perhaps, with a few troops, try to hold Holston Valley, from some safe point to cover the salt works in Virginia. Thomas's recent move against Dalton had the effect of making the enemy recall several thousand troops he had started against Sherman.

The Lieutenant-Generalcy bill has I suppose become a law ere this. That General Grant will be appointed to that grade, if any one, I suppose there is no doubt. With his honest patriotism, good common sense, great military ability and experience, and the unexampled success that has thus far attended him we may hope high for the future of our country. To merit by acts, not words, and receive the Lieutenant Generalcy of the armies of the United States, is to be more than President. Let the General but continue to be himself as now and heretofore, giving no public heed although not unmindful of them, to the censures or praises of the press, and there will have lived few men who have secured so bright a fame. Military not civic honors best bedeck the soldier's brow.

The General is very anxious about the confirmation of some of the Generals appointed in his command, among them your own. He has written a letter to General Halleck on the subject and put your name among the first four.

Captain Badeau is here; we welcome him to our military family, appreciate him for his high and gentlemanly bearing and sympathize with him in his misfortune. He is recovering, however, and will I hope soon be able to lay aside his crutches. We expect you to be back with us by the opening of the spring campaign. Your horses are in fine condition. No one uses them except the Engineer Department and that not often I believe. Your boy reports regularly to me pursuant to your directions. He dislikes much to have the horses used and I don't blame him. If you wish it I will let no one have them. Hope of W. F. Smith's promotion seems to be waning. You perhaps know more about this.

General Grant's official report of the battle of Chattanooga has gone forward. It is full and complete, written in his usual happy, narrative style, void of pomposity or parade. . . .

It is known that the President had serious apprehensions in reference to Grant's political affiliations and ambitions from the date of his surprising success at Vicksburg, and shortly afterwards, to satisfy himself, sent for their common friend, J. Russell Jones of Galena, then United States Marshal at Chicago. Jones, who had visited headquarters at Vicksburg, and became convinced that Grant had no political aspirations, was enabled to allay the President's fears for the present, but only to see them aroused again by the extraordinary success of Chattanooga. To an active politician like Lincoln, it was scarcely conceivable that any man, whether soldier or civilian, with such a chance as was now within Grant's reach, should not seize upon it to go up higher. Other politicians shared Lincoln's apprehension; and knowing the intimate relations between Grant and Rawlins, such of them as had the opportunity of seeing the letter from which I have just quoted, did not hesitate to say, they regarded it as conclusive. The clear and explicit declarations which it contained had a tendency to allay apprehension if not to smooth the way for Grant's accession to supreme military power, subject of course to the President as constitutional commander-in-chief.

The Senate passed the bill reviving the grade of Lieutenant General with only six dissenting votes, while the House of Representatives passed it by 96 to 41. It is well known, however, that the President used no influence whatever for or against it, but as soon as its fate became assured and he had given it his approval, he sent for Grant, and the latter, accompanied by Rawlins and one or two other staff officers, started at once for Washington. He arrived there on March 8, 1864, and having received his new commission, three days thereafter began his return trip to complete arrangements for assuming the duties to which the President had assigned him.

Before starting on this trip to the East, Grant wrote, March 4, 1864, to Sherman, then near Memphis, notifying him of his departure for Washington, informing him that he should accept no orders which would require him to make that city his headquarters, and extending his thanks to Sherman and McPherson as "the men to whom above all others" he felt indebted for whatever success he had gained. It is to be observed, however, that the context of this letter shows delicately, but plainly enough, that the thanks it conveyed to his favorite lieutenants were for the energy, skill, and cheerfulness with which they had always executed his orders, rather than for any special advice or valuable suggestions they had contributed to the formation of his plans. Sherman's reply was dated March 10. It heartily praises Grant's "unselfishness, honesty, and simple faith in his success." But with surprising frankness, it indicates the existence of a fear from the first in Sherman's mind that Grant's ignorance of strategy, science, and history, might at any time prove fatal, though this fear is qualified by the confession that an unusual amount of common sense seems to have so far supplied most of Grant's deficiencies.

It is apparent, however, that Sherman still had serious doubts of Grant's strength and stability of character, as well as of his capacity properly to solve the great questions with which he would have to deal in the East. This is indicated by the following extract from his letter:

. . . Now as to the future. Do not stay in Washington. . . . Come out West; take to yourself the whole Mississippi Valley, let us make it dead sure, and I tell you, the Atlantic Slope and Pacific shores will follow its destiny, as sure as the limbs of a tree live or die with the main trunk. . . .

Although the purport of this advice could not be mistaken, Sherman was evidently not satisfied with the way in which he first gave it. Apparently forgetting that the occupation of New Orleans, the capture of Vicksburg and Port Hudson, and the overwhelming defeat of Bragg in front of Chattanooga had practically ended the war in the Mississippi Valley, he changed the form, if not the substance, of his exhortation, as follows:

. . . For God's sake and for your country's sake, come out of Washington. I foretold to General Halleck before he left Corinth the inevitable result to him, and I now exhort you to come out West. Here is the seat of the coming empire, and from the West, when our task is done, we will make short work of Charleston and Richmond and the impoverished coast of the Atlantic.

It is known that most of Grant's trusted subordinates shared Sherman's apprehensions. Indeed such apprehensions were somewhat widespread at the time, but how far they were based upon distrust of Grant's ability to protect himself against jealousy and intrigue, rather than upon a misapprehension of the obligations imposed upon him by his new rank, to meet Lee and the veteran army of Northern Virginia on the field of battle must forever remain a question of doubt. But there can be no doubt that those who favored the courageous course, which Grant actually adopted, did so as much because of their confidence in Rawlins's influence and inflexible character, as in Grant's superior courage, constancy, and generalship.

It will be remembered that Grant had recently recommended W. F. Smith or Sherman for the command of the Army of the Potomac, but this was before the bestowal of the new office of Lieutenant General, and the President's orders placed upon him the actual duty of deciding what should be done in all such cases. The change in his own fortunes and duties was a radical one. His new responsibilities were coextensive with the military operations of the country, and could not be lightly limited to a sectional command. Fortunately neither Grant nor Rawlins was moved by Sherman's earnest appeal to "come out West." They seemed to recognize from the first that the country's greatest danger and consequently its greatest military task lay in the Eastern theatre of war. There was the Confederate Capital, and there was "the foremost Army of the Confederacy under the Confederacy's foremost leader." Lee had beaten McClellan, Hooker, and Burnside. He had baffled Meade, and although he had retreated from Gettysburg, he still barred the way to Richmond, with a confident and almost invincible array of veteran soldiers. Manifestly so long as that army remained unbroken, the country must remain divided against itself. Rawlins saw all this as plainly as any man could see it, and realizing that Congress must have created, and the President must have bestowed the rank of Lieutenant General upon Grant the better to clothe him with power for a trial of prowess and leadership with Lee and his gallant followers, steadily opposed the advice of all who begged him to "come out West" and rightly favored the establishment of headquarters in the field with the Army of the Potomac. So far as can now be ascertained, Grant's only objection to going East was based upon the possible requirement that he should remain in Washington as Halleck had, where he would have been subject to the criticism and intrigue of the politicians. The danger of this course was doubtless in Sherman's mind from the first and may have been the main influence which impelled him to urge Grant so strenuously to return to the West and complete the subjugation of the Mississippi Valley. It is said that when he knew Grant was not to remain in Washington, but was going to make his headquarters in the field and cast his lot in with the Army of the Potomac, he gave this determination his unqualified approval. But it must be observed that this was not till Grant himself had decided the question irrevocably and had made it known that Sherman would succeed to the chief command in the Western theatre of operations.

Where Grant, the Lieutenant General and chief commander of the loyal armies in the field, should place himself for the performance of the new duties devolving upon him, was one of the great questions of the day. Opinions differed widely as to its solution. Many besides Sherman thought that the new General-in-Chief should give his personal supervision to the completion of the campaign in the West. Others thought it would be better for him to remain in Washington to correlate and direct the movement of our widely scattered forces. Even the President himself may have held this view, but Rawlins, whose judgment in regard to such questions acted with the certainty of instinct, was never for a moment in doubt. He held with Washburne, Dana, myself, and other close friends of Grant, that the new commission not only placed him in an independent position, where he was free to act on his own judgment, but carried with it a supreme and imperative duty resting solely upon himself. Manifestly this duty could neither be divided nor delegated to another. Fortunately the two stood together in choosing the right course and when it was crowned with success and the victorious soldier had become a candidate for the Presidency, it was well and forcibly said, and Rawlins approved the saying, that Grant could no more have declined the trial with Lee . . . without injuring his fame and weakening his power to command, than the country could have afforded to allow its lifeblood and treasure to be fruitlessly wasted at the hands of incompetent and irresolute generals. He realized too truly the significance of his new rank and the task imposed upon him by his countrymen to permit himself to be turned from this duty either by the difficulties and dangers attending it or by the solicitations of devoted but misjudging friends.

THE NEW FIELD

ON March 23, 1864, Lieutenant General Grant reached Washington with Rawlins and six members of his Western volunteer staff. There was not one regular officer among them, but the duties of Grant's new position, with all the additional work it imposed upon him, made an increase of his staff absolutely necessary, and, naturally enough, he selected regular officers. Colonel Comstock, a learned, dignified, and experienced officer of the regular engineers, who had served with him as chief engineer of the Army of the Tennessee, and afterwards as inspector general of the Military Division, was naturally assigned to the new staff as senior aid-de-camp. Horace Porter, captain of ordnance, and Orville E. Babcock, captain of engineers, were also selected as aids-de-camp.

See Horace Porter's superb Campaigning with Grant.*—Ed. 2015*

Neither had served on Grant's staff, but largely on my introduction and recommendation, they were both chosen and through the interposition of Dana, who had met them in the field, both were finally allowed to accept the promotion and assignment which had been offered them. These young officers were honor graduates of West Point, of excellent character, and first-class ability each in his own line; but they were to a certain extent new men, unacquainted with Grant or his methods, and without special sympathy for officers from civil life. They had but little acquaintance with Rawlins, or with Grant, for that matter, and were naturally slow to acknowledge the real merit of the former, or to comprehend the reasons for his extraordinary influence over their common chief. They doubtless did whatever work fell to their lot to the very best of their ability, but even in the fiercest campaign the busiest officer finds time for rest and for social intercourse with his fellow officers from the general down.

Grant, it should be remembered, was entirely free from all affectation of superiority, and habitually treated his staff on the regular army theory that "gentlemen are all of the same grade." He regarded them as his companions and social equals, and while he rarely ever consulted them in reference to policies or plans, he never repressed their efforts to help or repelled their informal expression of opinion. He was both kindly and impressionable, and, like other great men, more or less unconsciously absorbed the views and yielded to the influences of such of those about him as he liked and respected.

As has been seen in the course of this narrative, Rawlins, who in a military sense had grown up with the successful general, and knew him better than anyone else, did not hesitate even in the new and greater field to give his views and advice whenever he thought the occasion called for them; but it is not to be denied that with the advent of new officers and new conditions, he grew more reserved. It was both natural and proper that he should be less aggressive and outspoken in counsel, and more considerate of the military proprieties in his new position. On the other hand, it is probable that Grant, in view of his own uniform success, had begun to feel more confidence in himself and less necessity for leaning on others. At all events, to those who knew the inside of their past relations it soon became apparent that the Lieutenant General and his Chief of Staff were measurably drifting apart. There was no rupture, and no public withdrawal of confidence or respect, but Rawlins soon came to understand that there were influences at work which he could not always locate or counteract. During the Overland campaign from the Rapidan to Appomattox, he told me repeatedly that he felt his influence with Grant was not what it used to be, and that neither the policy nor the plans developed themselves with the same absence of friction, or reached the same high level of excellence, that characterized them in the West when the staff was smaller. He recognized, of course, that the problems which confronted them were greater, and that the Confederacy was putting forth its last and best efforts under the command of its ablest leader; but in addition it is certain that as the campaign progressed, he became conscious of complications and difficulties of a more or less intangible character, due partly to the new conditions and partly to the increased complexity of the machinery for military command and administration. The staff was necessarily larger, while the arrangements for supervising the operations of the entire army were in a measure tentative, if not experimental. As it turned out they were also quite defective at times.

When Grant was assigned to duty as Lieutenant General, two courses were open to him in respect to the method of exercising command and arranging his staff for carrying his orders into effect. He might have assumed direct command of the Army of the Potomac and assigned Meade to the command of one of its corps, in which case it would have been necessary for him to issue orders directly to each corps commander; or he might have left department, army and army-corps organizations as he found them, and issued his orders to their immediate commanders, leaving those officers free to regulate and control the details of carrying such orders into effect. Something might have been said in favor of each plan. While the former would have been simpler and more direct, it would have required a larger and much more efficient staff, with much greater experience and knowledge of details and a much closer attention to the various branches of army administration as well as to the strategy of the marches and combinations and to the tactical arrangements of the fighting line in the various contingencies of actual battle. In modern armies the supervision of these duties falls within the province of the general staff. They require not only the highest theoretical knowledge of the art of war, but the greatest aptitude and practical experience in the details of commanding, marching, and fighting troops.

In the consideration of this subject, it is not to be forgotten that the Army of the Potomac was at the time supposed to be the best army we had in the field. It was composed largely of veterans, commanded by regular generals of great experience, with every qualification to meet the actual exigencies of campaign and battle. To tell them how to form their lines or columns, or to bring them effectively into battle might well have been considered as unnecessary, if not presumptuous. Grant himself was never considered a great organizer and still less a great tactician. He was not over-fond of details, and never thought of hampering such officers as Sherman, Thomas, McPherson, or Ord with minute instructions. Still less did he think it necessary with Meade, Hancock, Sedgwick, Warren, Wright, Humphreys, W. F. Smith, or Sheridan. At all events he decided that it was not, and throughout the campaign, till near its close, contented himself with indicating in general terms what he desired to have accomplished, leaving his subordinates to work out the details in such manner as they thought best.

This course not only received Rawlins's approval, but seemed to him, under the circumstances, the best that could be devised. He was conscious, no doubt, of his own lack of technical knowledge and practical experience in the commanding of troops, and while he knew that there were several good officers within easy reach, such as Upton for instance, who were in every way qualified to work out all sorts of military details and to superintend their execution, no such help was called for.

As Chief of Staff, Rawlins could doubtless have obtained permission to detail any other officer he thought necessary, but made no such detail, and the war was fought through to the end without the assistance of anything corresponding to a General Staff. Looking back on the course of operations during the Overland Campaign, it is hard to understand how they were conducted at all without such an organization. Both Grant and Rawlins were to blame for this. Neither seems to have understood the necessity for it, but that the chief responsibility for it should be placed upon Grant, the professional soldier, rather than upon the volunteer Chief of Staff, must be the verdict of the military critic. That Grant was aware of a great defect in the organization of his army is shown by the celebrated simile of the "balky team" by which he typified the difficulty of making the corps commanders work together in harmony, and justified himself for winning "by force of numbers" and "mere attrition," if by no other means. Withal, it is believed by many that if Grant had organized his forces more simply and compactly, and had had a competent general staff for the management of details, he could have ended the war within six months instead of taking nearly a year for it as he did.

It is worthy of note in this connection that while Lee's army was more simply organized, and he had direct command over all the Confederate corps in Virginia, without the interposition of army or department commanders, his staff arrangements were more defective than even Grant's. Lee, the professional soldier, relied entirely upon himself and his corps commanders. He wrote many of his most important orders with his own hand, and, like Grant, refrained from burthening his subordinates with detailed instructions. This did much to mar the result of his operations, especially at Gaines's Mill, White Oak Swamp, Malvern Hill, and perhaps elsewhere. His staff was small and, even to a greater extent than Grant's, was made up of civilians with but little technical knowledge or experience, and therefore capable of performing but little of the complicated technical work usually assigned to the general staff.

But to return to Rawlins. It has been seen that his title was to a certain extent a misnomer. While he was Grant's oldest and most trusted staff officer and had more influence with him than had anyone else, it is evident that the plan under which the national forces in Virginia were then organized had more to do with limiting the nature and extent of the staff, of which he was the chief, than had any lack of knowledge on his part as to the kind of officers it needed, or as to the kind of work they would be called upon to perform. As the army was actually organized, the duties of the staff as well as of its chief were necessarily minimized. Rawlins had therefore more to do with questions of military policy than with details of military operations. He believed in the Overland route to Richmond, and that Lee's army was Grant's true objective. He believed in maneuvering against Lee's flanks and marching rapidly. In the Vicksburg campaign he had seen the futility of assaulting well-defended rifle trenches, however hastily constructed, and of making direct attacks against strong positions. He believed in gathering all the forces that were available, and, above all, he believed in the good sense and the solid qualities of Grant, and in the superiority of his army in numbers and resources. He had no doubt that Grant would win, but after the first few days he became bitterly opposed to the slipshod manner in which many important operations were conducted, and especially to the persistency with which the army was hurled head-on against the enemy's entrenchments on the way to Spotsylvania Court House and beyond. He did not hesitate to declare later that such attacks were a fatal blunder, due mostly to the influence of Colonel Comstock of his staff, a regular engineer, whose advice and constant refrain was, "Smash 'em up! Smash 'em up!" In repeating this refrain, which he did more than once, Rawlins's face grew pale, and his form became almost convulsed with anger. With the fearlessness that characterized the imprudent utterances of W. F. Smith and of that peerless soldier Emory Upton,* he did not hesitate to designate this as "the murderous policy of military incompetents," and there is good reason for believing that his outspoken remonstrance, emphasized as they were by the failure and fearful loss of life which uniformly accompanied the head-on attacks in parallel order against entrenched lines had more to do with their abandonment than anything else, except perhaps the pathetic protest of the enlisted men, who at Cold Harbor, before advancing to the charge, wrote their names on slips of paper and pinned them to their coats in order that their dead bodies might be recognized after the battle was over.

Emory Upton is one of the remarkable but obscure figures of the war. See A Genius for War.—Ed. 2015

Another policy of great wisdom which Rawlins constantly advocated during the campaign in Virginia was in favor of bringing troops from places where they were not needed, or were rendering service of only secondary importance, to the front, where the army was engaged in daily battle and suffering heavy loss. He was doubtless unconscious of the great military principle laid down by the masters in support of this policy, but his own common sense must have told him that it was correct. He had perhaps never heard it stated that the greatest duty of the State in carrying on war is to "keep the road to the front crowded with recruits and reinforcements," to fill the gaps made by sickness and battle, but with a prescience which would have done credit to a great theoretical commander, he not only did his best to carry out this maxim but constantly favored the draft to fill the ranks of the old regiments, instead of organizing new ones, as the quickest and best possible way to make the Union army overwhelming in strength and invincible in battle.

Fortunately Rawlins's attitude in respect to these, as well as other important matters, does not rest upon conjecture, but was made known from day to day in a series of letters to his wife beginning in January, 1864, and continuing almost to the end of the campaign against Lee. The first of these letters is dated January 14, 1864, and the last April 4, 1865. They are without break or intermission, except when his wife was in camp, or he was absent from the field on account of sickness. There is another series, written while absent from her in search of health after the war was over. I shall quote freely from each series as occasion seems to call for it.

It has not been previously emphasized, but it should now be noted, that it was by this time becoming generally known that Rawlins was seriously ill. Soon after establishing headquarters at Chattanooga he began to cough violently and continuously. The weather had become inclement. The rainy season had begun, and his quarters were more or less uncomfortable. Hence we thought at first that his cough was due to a severe cold which would soon pass away; but in spite of every attention, it proved persistent, better one day and worse the next. Finally it aroused the deep anxiety of the patient himself and especially of his home friend, Chief Surgeon Kittoe, who applied all known remedies, but without permanent success. During the whole of his stay at Chattanooga, Nashville, as well as afterwards with the Army of the Potomac, and in the West, to the end of his life his pathetic and baffling fight against the disease was hardly ever absent from his letters. Many another man would have given up the struggle in its earlier stage, but to this noble soul that way out was never seriously considered. For a season his confirmation by the Senate as brigadier general seemed doubtful, and in reply to a question from his wife as to what he should do in case he was not confirmed he expressed both incredulity and indifference; and there can be no doubt that he would have returned to private life with resignation, if not with cheerfulness, had he lost the place to which he had been advanced in the army. While he had frequently expressed the idea that he regarded his services, like those of every other sound man, as obligatory without reference to either rank or pay, and was proud of his success and of the honor in which he was held by his chief as well as by the leading generals who had served with him, he was not without ambition as to what might yet be in store for him. He therefore at no time slackened his work nor relaxed his vigilance over what was going on around him.

During and after the Chattanooga campaign a number of minor operations were carried out: Dodge drove the enemy from Athens towards Florence, in Northern Alabama; Morgan L. Smith, of Logan's command, attacked and defeated a strong force near Lebanon, Kentucky; a third affair took place at Sevierville; a fourth in East Tennessee, and finally Sherman made and relinquished his abortive march eastward from Vicksburg, nominally because Forrest defeated and drove back his cooperating cavalry column under Sooy Smith, but really because he met with greater resistance than he expected. To keep the run of all this, and occasionally to visit an outlying command or to accompany the General to Chattanooga, kept Rawlins fully employed throughout the winter. But fortunately his activity was broken at the Christmas holidays by a leave of absence for the purpose of getting married to the lady whose acquaintance he had made under interesting, if not romantic, circumstances at Vicksburg. The wedding took place at Danbury, Connecticut, on December 24, 1864; but the short honeymoon ended by his return to headquarters at Nashville early in January. Counting on remaining there a few weeks, he sent for his wife and children (by his first wife) whom he installed in a comfortable little house, where he had hardly three weeks of unalloyed happiness, and where the comforts of home checked his disease and encouraged him to hope for an early and complete recovery. The exact length of this period, perhaps the brightest of his life, is fixed by the fact that no letters from him to his wife were found dated between February 16 and March 5, 1864.

It will be recalled that shortly after the victory of Missionary Ridge and the enemy's withdrawal from Northern Georgia and East Tennessee, Congress revived the rank of Lieutenant General, with the evident intention that it should be bestowed upon Grant. Under the old laws the President had full authority to assign any Major General to chief command without reference to relative rank, and had frequently exercised that authority according to his own judgment without let or serious hindrance from any quarter. But it had at last become evident that the new and higher rank would strengthen the hands of the actual commander, whoever he might be. There was some talk, however, at the time that the act of Congress created and was intended to create a military dictatorship, but it cannot be too often repeated that this talk exerted no hurtful influence on either Lincoln or Grant. Both accepted it loyally and modestly, and as soon as it became law Lincoln summoned Grant to receive the higher commission.

Accordingly Grant and Rawlins set out for Washington, but had to wait over at Louisville. That evening, after dining at the Galt House, they went to the theatre, of which Grant was fond. But the play, or his physical condition, or perhaps the important juncture of affairs filled Rawlins's mind with serious reflections, and after returning to his room he wrote to his wife in terms which at least throw a strong light upon his own character. He was evidently depressed by the great responsibility about to be placed on his chief's shoulders, and felt that the latter was yielding more readily and more fully to the applause he received at the theatre than was becoming in one whom he had grown to think both unusually modest and unassuming. He referred, with approval, to a letter on the new promotion, which I had written him from Washington. He was profoundly impressed with the magnitude and weight of the duties which would soon come to the Lieutenant General and himself, and also with his own lack of technical military education for the high position of Chief of Staff. In view of all this, he signified his willingness to withdraw and leave "the place to an educated and finished soldier." But he did not disguise the feeling that having been with Grant throughout his brilliant career, having shared all his perils and "been his stay and support in his darkest hours," without at any time playing the part of an injudicious friend, he had the right to claim the place without subjecting himself to the charge of vanity. It is evident that Grant not only considered the situation fully but reassured him now of his unabated confidence and did what he could to put an end to Rawlins's undue apprehensions and to silence his self-depreciation. The journey to Washington began the next morning, March 8, and of course at the first opportunity Rawlins wrote his wife full particulars of such incidents as attracted his attention. On the whole he was gratified by the modest manner in which Grant received the enthusiastic greetings "which the people, ladies, gentlemen and children" everywhere on the route extended to him. He approved the reticence with which Grant received the congratulations of Halleck and the Secretary of War, and the great modesty with which he accepted his new commission and made haste to return to Nashville for the purpose of turning over to Sherman the next week the Military Division of the Mississippi. He appeared to be particularly pleased that Grant would not even delay a few hours for the purpose of attending a dinner which Mrs. Lincoln, and, doubtless, the President wished to give in his honor at the White House.

The return to Nashville was without incident or delay, and the business connected with the change of station and command was soon despatched. Rawlins sent his wife and children to his parents at Galena, and within ten days had everything ready for the new order of things and was on the way with the Lieutenant General and personal staff back to Washington. It is pleasant to add that Rawlins records with unalloyed satisfaction that the General and Mrs. Grant, who left the party at Harrisburg, were more attentive to him during this trip than ever before, though he naively confessed he was at a loss to account for it, unless it was because his recent separation from his wife entitled him to special sympathy.

IN VIRGINIA

GRANT remained but two days in conference with the President and other authorities at Washington. On March 24 he took post at Culpepper Court House, accompanied by Rawlins and Comstock. He established headquarters in a house large enough for himself, the Chief of Staff, and an office, and at once issued his orders taking command of the Army.

It was rough March weather, with alternate snow and rain, which kept Rawlins, at least, in quarters for several days. Spring, however, was near at hand; but without waiting for sunshine, the work of reorganization, as far as reorganization was necessary, was begun. Two army corps were distributed into the others, thus reducing the organization from five weak corps to three strong ones. Rawlins was apprehensive that this might produce dissatisfaction; but his correspondence with his wife shows that his fears were soon dismissed as unfounded. The most radical changes were in the Cavalry Corps to the command of which Sheridan, from the Army of the Cumberland, fell heir; while Torbert, from the infantry, took the First Division, and Wilson, from Grant's Staff and more recently from the Cavalry Bureau, took the Third Division. The Corps had been overworked and badly needed remounts, therefore it was permitted to reduce the extended front its pickets were covering. While Rawlins was privy to all this, and fully concurred in the orders which brought it about, his routine work was greatly reduced from the first, and this in turn gave him more time to familiarize himself with the country and the great problems which henceforth were to tax his chief to the utmost of his powers.

While it has been stated that Grant had at one time recommended William F. Smith to command the Army of the Potomac, and at another thought of Sherman for that important place, it soon became known that Smith would go to Butler as second in command, and that Meade would continue in the command of the Army of the Potomac, under Grant's immediate supervision. Just how far Rawlins was consulted in this, or in the plans of campaign, cannot be precisely stated, but his correspondence shows that he accompanied Grant to Fortress Monroe, April 1, and necessarily became aware of all measures under consideration. Although Butler was adroit enough to enroll himself in Rawlins's mind, with Sherman and Meade, as a friend whom Grant could thoroughly trust, it is quite certain that both he and Grant thought it wise to supplement that wily politician by sending William F. Smith to him and providing that he should have a large command when the spring campaign began.

Whether Smith ever discussed the plan of operations in person with either Grant or Rawlins does not appear; but it is certain that soon after Grant's return from Fortress Monroe, Smith sent me a letter fully setting forth his views on the forthcoming campaign, and this in turn I sent to Rawlins. It is now known that Rawlins, in laying it before Grant, took strong ground against it, which, it is to be observed, required a good deal of independence of judgment, not only because the plan suggested involved considerations of the highest strategic and administrative importance but because it had the general support of a strong group of older strategists, who had stood behind McClellan in favor of the disastrous Peninsula Campaign. The plan suggested involved all the difficulties of the old one, of which it was a modification; for it required the transfer of a great part of the Army of the Potomac by water and the concentration of an independent and cooperating army on Albemarle Sound, to move from there against the interior of North Carolina and the railway lines connecting Richmond with the interior of the Confederacy.

Rawlins evidently thought that, because I had been made the channel through which this plan was transmitted, it had my approval also; but such was not the case. Recognizing from the first that it was General Grant's exclusive right to make the plans, and that in doing this he should have the help of the best minds in the army, I felt it to be plainly my duty to hand Smith's letter to Rawlins for such disposition and consideration as it ought to receive. The letter itself, although Rawlins sent a copy to his wife, has not been found. Its general character is, however, sufficiently well known. The most important point for present consideration is that it incurred Rawlins's strenuous opposition from the first, mainly because its natural effect would have been to move the army on eccentric lines by sea and further scatter instead of concentrating the national forces. This argument doubtless caused it to be turned down by Grant after the full and careful consideration to which the high rank and great experience of its author entitled it. But Smith's letter derives additional importance from the fact that Rawlins certainly and Grant probably considered it as an evidence of an improper desire on the part of its writer to exert a controlling influence over the plan of campaign in the East as he had over that recently carried out in the West. If this surmise is correct, it necessarily strengthened Grant's decision to attach Smith to Butler's army, which was to move by river from Fortress Monroe towards Petersburg and Richmond, could easily be transferred further south, instead of assigning him to the command of the Army of the Potomac, for which the General had previously recommended him.

Rawlins's letter also shows beyond question that he not only had a correct view of the fundamental principle which should control Grant's plans, but did not fail to use all the arguments he could bring to bear in favor of its observance. Had he been better educated in military history and the art of war, he would not have thought it necessary to ascribe selfish or other improper motives to so distinguished a soldier as W. F. Smith merely because that commander advocated a plan which he thought the Government strong enough at that time to carry safely into effect.

Rawlins, it must not be forgotten, was not only an unusually strong and able man himself, but, as is frequently the case with men of his race and class, he was naturally not above the vice of suspicion. No one can read his letters without seeing that while he was devoted heart and soul to the national cause and to his chief, and was perfectly willing to efface himself as far as necessary in their behalf, he was no more than properly jealous of his personal and official prerogatives. He evidently felt it to be his duty and privilege to express his views or those of others which he made his own, upon both the plans and the motives of those who submitted them. He believed that Grant should know his men "inside as well as outside," and hence he did not hesitate to speak against either men or plans which he did not approve; and when he had condemned either he became quite impatient, and perhaps at times unjust, towards such as continued to stand out against him.

It is to be regretted that Rawlins did not keep a formal diary, and that his letters written as they were from the very centre of the army as it was constantly pressing to the front, were necessarily liable to capture by Confederate raiders or partisans in the rear, and were therefore given up to personal rather than official details. This circumstance will sufficiently account for their lack of vital military interest; yet no one can read them without catching glimpses here and there of how plans were made and great questions were disposed of at headquarters, and how great operations were carried out by subordinate commanders. They show beyond all question that Rawlins, notwithstanding his impaired health and the presence of a number of regular officers on the staff, was the ever vigilant and faithful coadjutor of his chief in the East as he was in the West. They also show conclusively that he threw his entire influence at all times for the success of his chief.

First: he advocated what finally came to be known as the Overland Campaign, or in other words he favored Grant's marching out to find Lee, who was known to be near at hand, and directly in front; instead of transferring the Army of the Potomac several hundred miles by water to the James River, or still further south, to Albemarle Sound, as recommended by Smith and other able strategists.

Second: he favored concentrating the largest possible force on the chosen line of operations in Virginia, by withdrawing troops from other lines and departments where they were not needed, and, above all, by filling up the old regiments through a rigid enforcement of the draft, rather than by calling into the field new volunteer organizations under inexperienced officers. His declaration that he believed more in "the infallibility of numbers than in the infallibility of generals, no matter how great their reputation," is the comprehensive expression of a fundamental principle which should pass into the settled maxims of war.

Third: he strenuously opposed the promotion and employment of political generals over regular officers educated at West Point.

That the Chief of Staff, himself only a citizen soldier, should have formulated and expressed these views at the time and under the circumstances that he did, shows him to have been not only a strong and virile thinker but an extraordinarily, clear and sound one. No professional soldier could have expressed them better, and no soldier, professional or volunteer, could have advocated them with greater force or greater independence.

All arrangements having been completed, Grant's great campaign began at 1 A M., May 4, 1864, with the Third Cavalry Division, under my command, in advance. Grant's headquarters were established that evening near the Old Wilderness Tavern. The army was distributed upon two roads and both columns were well covered by cavalry, but the movements of the infantry from the first were cautious and slow. Had they pushed forward with all the celerity of which they were capable, instead of moving cautiously and slowly, as they did, the first day after crossing the Rapidan they could have passed almost, if not entirely, through the Wilderness and forced the enemy to fight in the open country beyond. From Lee's headquarters at or near Orange Court House, with his front on the Rapidan, which separated him from the Union Army, and his right on Mine Run, he had no means of knowing the direction Grant's columns would take till their movement was well developed. It is of course possible that he might have taken exactly the same roads he did take to strike Grant in flank, and this would have increased the perils of our situation, but competent critics of Lee's methods have generally held that his true policy was to throw himself as directly and quickly as possible across Grant's line of march and thus, with his entire force, impede his foe's progress towards Richmond. That is perhaps what he strove to do in the Wilderness, and although it brought him against the right flank of Grant's columns, instead of in their front, it was perfectly easy for the latter to face to the right and fight on equal terms. It is evident that a flank or rear attack against Grant's probable, or even his real, line of battle formed no part of Lee's actual plan. This is abundantly shown by the "Official Records" and by the light cast upon the course of events by the Reminiscences and Memoirs of various Confederate generals.

It is not my purpose to dwell upon the details of this campaign further than may be necessary to explain the part taken in it by the Chief of Staff. It is here worthy of note, however, that Rawlins, Bowers, Sheridan, Dana, and I were the only officers of high rank in that vast host who had ever been with Grant in battle, and that it was no part of his plan to fight in the dense and almost impenetrable woods of the Wilderness, if he could help it. He was surrounded, as it were, by strangers who were more or less incredulous as to his real capacity as a general, and believed that he had succeeded hitherto by good fortune rather than by good management. As shown by Rawlins's letter of May 2, these critics did not conceal their apprehension that Lee would prove to be too much for Grant. This feeling was widespread and undisguised. It was evidently shared by many of the rank and file as well as by several generals commanding corps and divisions, and doubtless did much towards making the movements of the Union army more cautious and more deliberate than they should have been. As it was, they were inexcusably slow. It was clearly Grant's true policy as well as his plan to force his army as rapidly as possible through the Wilderness to the open country beyond, and all his orders were made to that end; but it is certain that the cavalry was the only part of the fighting force that reached each day the point to which it was directed. The Third Cavalry Division had the advance next to the enemy for five days, and was the only division that ever got into Spotsylvania Court House. It did this early on the morning of May 9; and after driving out Wickham's Confederate cavalry, capturing about fifty prisoners from two divisions of Longstreet's corps, and recapturing a number of our own men, it held the place for several hours, and did not withdraw till after it had received orders not to go there at all.

On the night of May 3, after the orders were issued, the day's work done, and the troops in motion towards the Rapidan, Richardson tells us that Grant, Rawlins, and their anxious friend, Washburne, sat up till two o'clock the next morning "talking about politics, history, and literature." No further record of that conversation is known to exist. It does not appear that Rawlins had time to write to his wife again for several days, but if he wrote, his letters were either captured or have passed out of the possession of his family. It is of course possible that Washburne kept a private account of what took place, and if so it may yet be published. Meanwhile it can be well understood that the conversation must have been one of unusual interest, as it doubtless had first to do with the plans and movements then under way and with the calculations and hopes of those present, before it passed to questions of history and literature, or even to those of current politics.

So far as headquarters were concerned, there was little to be done after the general orders were actually sent out. Under the method of procedure adopted by the Lieutenant General, Meade and his subordinates worked out the details and kept Grant well informed of all that came to them from the front. It will be remembered that Lee was not taken by surprise. He was too able a commander to neglect any precaution along his front, and especially at the crossings of the Rapidan, for obtaining early and exact information of Grant's operations. He was quite as well prepared as Grant was for any movement that might be made, and when the Union columns began their march to pass beyond his right flank, he lost no time in making his dispositions to counteract it. His columns advanced with certainty and confidence, engaging shortly in a two days' death grapple, in which neither commander could see his opponent, nor do much more than face the dangers confronting him.

The fighting on both sides was desperate in the extreme. First one line would gain ground, and then the other, but no decided advantage crowned the efforts of either till late in the evening of the second day, when the Confederates under Gordon turned the right flank of the Sixth Corps under Sedgwick and rolled it back in confusion. Gordon tells in his *Reminiscences* how early on the morning of the sixth he found himself on the extreme right of Grant's line and after satisfying himself by a personal reconnaissance that his presence was unknown, and that no sufficient disposition had been made to stay his onset, asked first his division and then his corps-commander for permission to sally forth, and that this, notwithstanding his urgency and his repeated assurances that he could win, was denied till nearly nightfall, when Lee himself, riding his lines and conferring with his subordinate commanders, listened to his suggestions and gave him permission to carry them into effect.

Gordon's narrative, whether correct or not in all its details, is one of the most graphic and exciting bits of military writing to be found in our history. It is the story of a born soldier who had learned by actual experience one of the great lessons of modern warfare, namely, that an unexpected and well-sustained attack in flank or rear can scarcely fail, if directed against an enemy who has not had ample warning and time to prepare for it.

At all events, Gordon's attack upon the right of the Sixth Corps, after the fighting, front to front, was over for the day, fell upon the Federal line in the nature of a surprise. It was the most important event of the campaign so far, and, like Jackson's flank attack the year before against Howard, was signally successful till darkness put an end to it. It resulted in the capture of Generals Seymour and Shaler, with a considerable part of Seymour's division, but that was not all. It threw the right half of the corps into great confusion and filled with the gravest apprehension the minds of both Grant and Meade, who were encamped together and in constant conference. Fortunately, Sedgwick had all the steadiness that might be expected of a descendant of Major- General Sedgwick of Cromwell's New Model Army. With imperturbable deliberation he gave the necessary orders for an additional change of front, to resist the enemy; but the latter failed to realize the extent of his own success, or perhaps thought further progress was impossible through the darkness, which was made still more impenetrable by the gloom of the surrounding forest. What looked at first like an irremediable disaster to the Union right soon gave place to a cessation of the fight, which was in due time followed by a conviction on the part of Sedgwick and his veterans that the worst had passed.

Shortly after dark I received an order from Sheridan to move, as soon as it was light enough to see, with my division to the Germanna Ford road, for the purpose of ascertaining if the enemy had reached it, or had advanced to the right and rear of the Sixth Corps. The intervening hours were full of anxiety to Sheridan, Forsyth, and myself. We were near Chancellorsville on the Fredericksburg and Orange turnpike, from three to five miles from general headquarters. We had early received the news of Sedgwick's disaster, accompanied by orders to cover the movement of the trains towards Fredericksburg, which we construed as foreshadowing a retrograde march of the army, possibly to the north side of the river. To make matters worse, we thought we could hear the rattle and roar of distant musketry till late at night, but fortunately this turned out to be the noise of the moving trains. Yet withal the night was a gloomy one, long to be remembered.

At early dawn my division turned into the Germanna Ford road and was covering with its skirmishers the entire zone of danger; but happily we soon discovered that the enemy had not fully realized the value of his opportunity and had taken no measures whatever to improve it. Knowing how important it was that both Grant and Meade should be immediately advised as to the exact state of affairs in this quarter, I sent a staff officer to report to the latter, and rode myself rapidly to the former. Naturally I was full of anxiety as to the effect upon Grant of the exciting incidents of the two days previous and especially of the night before, and hence went as fast as my horse could carry me. I reached headquarters on a little wooded knoll in the Wilderness at, or shortly after, seven o'clock, and dismounting at the proper distance, I had started up the hillside when Grant caught sight of me, and before receiving my report, called out cheerily: "It's all right, Wilson; the army is moving towards Richmond!"

This was the first time I had seen the Lieutenant General since he crossed the Rapidan. Of course his hearty reception and confident bearing relieved my mind instantly of all apprehension. An exchange of greetings with Rawlins, Bowers, and the other staff officers followed at once. We congratulated one another on the triumphant manner in which our Chief had met the crisis of his fate. Up to that time the Army of the Potomac had not "fought its battles to a finish"; but it was now certain that it "would fight it out on that line if it took all summer," although this stirring assurance was not made public till Grant sent his memorable letter of May 11 to General Halleck by the hand of Mr. Washburne.

Many misleading accounts have been given to the world in regard to Grant's bearing when the news of Seymour's disaster and capture reached him. He has been reported as having remained unmoved and unshaken throughout the excitement which followed. As the incident was not closed till sometime after dark, it is not to be denied that it constituted a crisis of the most portentous character, calling not only for unusual fortitude but for unusual self-control on the part of the commanding general. As courier after courier dashed up to his headquarters with reports more or less exaggerated, but all most alarming, and as the serious nature and progress of the disaster became better known, it would have been an extraordinary exhibition of stolid insensibility if Grant had actually gone to sleep in the midst of the excitement. Defeat might possibly grow out of this unexpected disaster, and defeat meant more to him than to any other man in that army. Hitherto he had met the enemy but to overwhelm him, and this was, above all, the reason for his being awake and at the head of the army in that field. To suffer a reverse of fortune at the hands of Lee meant in the end a failure that might be fatal to his country's cause, and must be fatal to himself. All this and more may have passed through his mind, and externally composed, as all unite in saying he was, he would have been less than human had it not moved him to the very depths of his soul.

And there is no doubt that such was the case. Rawlins and Bowers united in saying to me aside before I left that the situation the night before for a time seemed appalling, that Grant met it outwardly with calmness and self-possession, but after he had asked such questions and given such orders as the emergency seemed to call for, he withdrew to his tent and, throwing himself face downward on his cot, instead of going to sleep, gave vent to his feelings in a way which left no room to doubt that he was deeply moved. They concurred in assuring me that, while he revealed to others neither uncertainty nor hesitation as to what was to be done, and was equally free from the appearance of indifference and bravado, he made no effort to

176

conceal from them the gravity of the danger by which the army was threatened. They had been with him in every battle from the beginning of his career, and had never before seen him show the slightest apprehension or sense of danger; but on that memorable night in the Wilderness it was much more than personal danger which confronted him. No one knew better than he that he was face to face with destiny, and there was no doubt in their minds that he realized it fully and understood perfectly that retreat from that field meant a great calamity to his country as well as to himself. That he did not show the stolidity that has been attributed to him in that emergency but fully realized its importance is greatly to his credit. It rests upon the concurrent testimony of those two faithful officers that he not only perfectly understood the situation but was the first to declare that the enemy, not having fully improved his advantage, had lost a great opportunity. It was also Grant who was first to see with the clear vision of a great leader that the true way out of the perils which surrounded him was to leave the care of his right flank to the imperturbable Sedgwick, and push his army, as soon as it could see its way, through the Wilderness on its forward march "towards Richmond."

In adopting this heroic course Grant had the earnest support of both Rawlins and Bowers, as well as of those who had yet to learn by actual observation that it was his custom to fight his battles through to the end. I, for one, am free to confess that when he gave me the cheerful assurance that the army was already in motion "towards Richmond," he lifted a great weight from my mind. We who had known him best felt that the crisis was safely passed, and that we were now on the sure road to ultimate victory. I never saw Rawlins in a more resolute nor more encouraging temper, nor Grant in a state of greater confidence. Feeling entirely reassured, I returned to my division, and as soon as possible made known to Sheridan and Forsyth all I had learned. My report, as might have been expected, also lifted a load from their minds and strengthened their faith in Grant and the ultimate success of the campaign in which we were now fully embarked.

Rawlins's first letter to his wife after the army crossed the Rapidan shows that Grant claimed the advantage in the first two days' fighting. It also shows that, when the enemy withdrew, Grant did not know in what direction he had gone. The letter runs as follows:

Battlefield, Old Wilderness Tavern, Va.

May 7, 1864.

... We crossed the Rapidan on the 4th instant with the entire army of the Potomac, without opposition, were met by the enemy at this place on the forenoon of the 5th and after a very sanguinary battle which closed only with the night of the 6th, found ourselves this morning masters of the field, the enemy having withdrawn. Whether within his fortifications at Mine Run, five miles distant from here, or towards Richmond, is not yet clearly ascertained. Our loss in killed, wounded and missing will reach full ten thousand, among them five general officers. On the main road by which the Confederates retired they have left a considerable force to protect their rear. With the pickets of this force our skirmishers are now engaged. The General and staff are all well. I am feeling much better than when I left Culpepper. On my way here I saw Miss Rawlins. She is my cousin and a daughter of Elloi Rawlins. . . .

The next letter runs as follows:

Near Spotsylvania C. H., Va.

May 9, 1864

. . . . Since writing you on the 7th we have progressed about eleven miles nearer Richmond. The enemy beat us to Spotsylvania and now hold the place. By this move they have interposed their whole force, perhaps, between us and Richmond. The feeling of our army is that of great confidence, and with the superiority of numbers on our side, I think we can beat them notwithstanding their advantage of position. In God we trust for continued success. Today the brave and heroic Sedgwick, commanding the Sixth Army Corps, was shot through the head and died instantly. He was a gallant and able officer but thank God his place is well filled by the accomplished General H. G. Wright, who is an able officer and as popular as his predecessor, the lamented Sedgwick.

By a Richmond paper of the 7th we learn that the enemy up to that time had lost in killed and mortally wounded, three general officers;

General Longstreet was also severely wounded in the shoulder. . . I am in very good health. . . .

Two days later Rawlins wrote as follows:

Near Spotsylvania, Va.

May 11, 1864

. . . . We have had six days continuous fighting and heavy losses in killed and wounded, reaching perhaps eighteen thousand, and among them Major General Sedgwick, commanding the Sixth Corps, Brigadier Generals Wadsworth, Hare, Stevenson and Rice. Wounded Brigadier Generals Robinson and Bartlett. Missing Brigadier Generals Seymour and Shaler.

The enemy's loss is perhaps as great as ours, in rank and file, and in general officers; in captures of prisoners, we perhaps have the count considerably in our favor, having already captured near four thousand. In an assault last evening one brigade of ours pierced the enemy's lines, and captured an entire rebel brigade. We have suffered no such loss. In all our losses, we have not yet lost a single regimental organization, much less a brigade. I mention this to show you how complete have been our lines and perfect the discipline of our men, only one brigade having at any time shown evidence of stampeding; this one is the old brigade of General Milroy of Winchester notoriety.

Our progress towards Richmond is slow, but we are on the way, and do not propose, unless some disaster overtakes us, ever taking a step backwards. We have still an abundance of supplies and ammunition . . .

How my heart bleeds to think of the weeping of loved ones, on the receipt of the news from this terrible strife, but those who have been killed, have died in a noble cause, and fallen with their faces towards Richmond, having lost no step taken in that direction. . . .

Again, two days later, he wrote:

Battlefield, Spotsylvania,

May 13, 1864

. . . . Yesterday's battle ended with dark, and during the night the enemy fell back from the position he held stubbornly during the day. Whether they will make a stand for another battle this side of Richmond, is not known, but my opinion is they will fight us again in their present position; a few hours, however, will determine. Our losses have been very heavy, but the advantages in the conflict have been with us most decidedly. It still continues to rain, and the effects of the damp, chilly weather I feel very perceptibly— still I am quite well. . . .

If Rawlins wrote any letters between the fourteenth and the twenty-third of May, they have not come into my possession, nor are they in the hands of his family. It was a period of suspense and uncertainty, during which there was a constant strain, but no great crisis. Sheridan had been detached with the entire cavalry corps to operate against the Confederate cavalry under [J.E.B.] Stuart, and to break up Lee's lines of railway communication with Richmond. Grant was pressing steadily and irresistibly towards Richmond, while his grim determination to win at any cost, which was most popular with the people, was again bringing his name forward for the Presidency. It may be safely assumed that Rawlins was not insensible of this, but it must be recalled that the contingency in which he could favor it, that of complete success over the enemy, had not yet arrived; hence, the inference is safe that he was at that time taking no interest in it, but confining himself rigidly to the duties of his position. It was now evident that Lee could not, as in former days, "command" the Army of the Potomac, as well as his own, and that it had at last passed under a general who did not take orders from his opponent. It may well be doubted if there was ever an army which was held so relentlessly to its work, or which was more bravely confronted by its opponent. The fighting was almost without intermission, and the loss on both sides unprecedented. The necessity for reinforcements, so ably set forth in Rawlins's farsighted letters, was now apparent to all; and after giving a summary of the operations the previous day, on May 25 he wrote:

. . . The entire army was ordered to move out this morning and feel the enemy, and ascertain if he is making a stand here, or falling back still nearer to Richmond. It is now eight o'clock A. M and no firing has been heard. So I infer he has gone south of the South Anna and Pamunkey Rivers. The railroad from Hanover Junction to Gordonsville is in our possession and its systematic and complete destruction has been ordered.

Reinforcements are still coming forward with commendable promptness. I have every confidence, if the Government will keep up this army to its present numbers, all will go well and that before many months, perhaps weeks, Lee's army will be defeated, and the last hopes of the Confederacy extinguished in the bloody storm that called it into existence.

I am in very good health, and stand the campaign finely. In fact it has continued to benefit me. . . .

On May 26 he wrote from Quaile's Ford, on the North Anna, as follows:

. . . Yesterday no changes were made of any moment in the relative positions of the two armies, the reconnaissance on our part having shown us the enemy in strong force immediately in our front and strongly entrenched. You may think the continual mention of the enemy's entrenchments very strange, when you have been constantly hearing of his having been by some movement of ours compelled to abandon first one of his defenses and then another. Now the true statement of this is, that when we crossed the Rapidan the enemy had strong works at Mine Run, some three miles to the right of the road we marched on. He came out of his works and gave us battle at Old Wilderness, after the second day of which he fell back with his main force into his works, and we took up our march by his right flank for Spotsylvania. Discovering our movement, the enemy marched rapidly for the same place, and having the shorter line, arrived there a few hours before us, and commenced at once to entrench his new position. By the time we got up our whole force and had put our trains in a place of safety, he had so far completed his new works as to give him great protection in the battles which were subsequently fought there. So again, when we by a movement similar to that in the Wilderness had started for this point, the enemy broke camp simultaneously with us, and having the Telegraph road to move on, one of the finest in the country, and the direct one to this point, he succeeded in getting here about twelve hours in advance of us and throwing up rifle pits in defence. A few hours always suffice for an army acting purely on the defensive to fortify itself, and the fortifications make up greatly for inferiority of numbers.

I cannot speak of contemplated movements as I would like to do, lest my letters . . . might be captured by the enemy while passing through the country to Washington by courier, or rather to our base on the river. I am in excellent health and spirits, and have full confidence in our final success. The feeling of this army as to its ability to whip that of Lee is good and gives assurance that it can, unless some mistake should be made in movement, which I do not fear. . . .

In spite of the heavy fighting behind field entrenchments, Rawlins wrote confidently as follows:

Hanover Town, Va.

May 28, 1864

. . . . The army of the Potomac is massing here, about fifteen miles from Richmond. So you see the real results of the battles we have fought notwithstanding what may be said by those who do not believe Richmond can be taken. Unless some terrible blunder is committed in the movements of our army, by which the enemy obtains an advantage over us, Richmond must fall. That any such blunder will be committed I do not for a moment believe. General Grant and General Meade are both able and experienced soldiers, either of them the equal and in everything heretofore Lee's superior on the field. Of course our numbers are greater than those of the enemy, but by his fortifications he has made up for inferiority of numbers. You know what I have heretofore written you of General Meade. My opinion which has always been decidedly favorable to him, is much heightened by the soldierly qualities and great ability he has displayed throughout this campaign. He reminds me much of Sherman, and handles his men equally well in battle. If in anything Sherman is superior it is in writing. Of this, I cannot however be sure, for I have seen nothing of General Meade's abilities in this direction. Generals Hancock, Wright, Warren and Burnside are all able and competent soldiers and their subordinate officers and men are equal to any in the world. With such an army of leaders, and such men as fill the ranks of the Army of the Potomac, no nation need fear its triumph, when engaged in the holy cause of liberty and its own existence.

I should never have been fully able to speak impartially of this army of heroes had it not been for the opportunity I now have of serving with and becoming acquainted with them. These soldiers fight as well and bravely as do their comrades in the armies of the West. They are all Americans and why should they not?

Reinforcements are still arriving. A portion of the force from General Butler will be here tomorrow . . .

Our base will hereafter be at the White House, the place made famous as the base of the Army of the Potomac under McClellan in his celebrated Peninsula campaign. How I pray in my heart that God will avert from us the fate that met his attempt to overthrow the rebel army and capital. I have the utmost confidence in success and no fear of failure. I would like to speak particularly of further movements. I know your good sense would appreciate such knowledge, but the danger of the capture of our mails, and prying officials forbid this. . . .

From this time on Rawlins wrote to his wife daily as follows:

Hanover Town, Va.

May 29, 1864

. . . . Today has been delightful. Nothing exciting has taken place. Our reconnoitering forces pushed out in the direction of Richmond and found the enemy in force about seven miles distant from here. The remainder of the army is ordered forward to the support of the forces sent out at noon. The new position of the enemy is on a creek called the Totopotomoy, at the crossing of the Shady Grove and Mechanicsville roads. Whether he intends holding this position against us at the risk of a general engagement is not certainly known. My opinion is that, most likely he will defend his new position as long as he can make it tenable, but the prevalent opinion is that he will give it up and retire behind the Chickahominy. Be this, however, as it may, we shall pursue steadily the original plan of General Grant's to the reduction of Richmond if it is to fall. In this campaign thus far there has been no deviation from it. That which we most desire and what would soonest give us the city, is a battle on something like equal ground, in which I am sure we would defeat and rout the enemy. Sheridan's cavalry corps had hard fighting yesterday evening about three miles in advance of here. It drove the enemy about a mile. Our loss was three hundred and fifty, of whom fifty-four were killed. In the list of casualties were fifty officers, of whom seven were killed. . . .

Near Hawes Shop, Va.

May 30, 1864

. . . . Another delightful day. We are now about three miles nearer Richmond than we were yesterday, but the position of the army is but little changed. Our reconnaissance have, however, developed the enemy in force—perhaps his whole army—in our immediate front with every indication that he will await battle this side the Chickahominy. A

183

few days will solve the question of Richmond, and whether a long siege or a sharp decisive battle is to terminate it. My health is still improving. . . .

Near Hawes Shop, Va.

May 31, 1864

. . . . Another delightful day. The position of this army is the same as last described, save that it has advanced a short distance.

The enemy attacked General Warren's advance forces, on our left, about six o'clock last evening, and after a sharp conflict of perhaps forty minutes, were repulsed with considerable loss. We buried over one hundred of their dead, and captured from one hundred to two hundred prisoners. They removed their wounded from the field. Our loss in killed, wounded and missing was about four hundred.

General Hancock carried a line of the enemy's works in his front this morning and captured about thirty prisoners, the loss on either side not heavy.

General Wilson was sent this morning to destroy railroad bridges. He is a good destructionist, and I have confidence in his rendering the railroads as useless as anyone in the service could. The success of the cavalry expedition under Sheridan in which General Wilson had command of a division, secured his confirmation by the Senate. Of this I am truly glad for Wilson is a brave and energetic officer and I am of the opinion will be popular with his command. His superior officers all think a great deal of him. You remember the letter I wrote him from Nashville. He expressed to me great satisfaction and perfect accordance with its statements.

General William F. Smith has arrived at White House with heavy reinforcements for this army. Another large force is also on the way from Port Royal, and is now near here.

General Breckenridge's and General Buckner's divisions from Western Virginia have reinforced the enemy in our front, but I feel sure they cannot get forward for the grand struggle as large a force as we shall be able to gather.

I enclose you a rosebud from the yard of a beautiful residence just in rear of one of our batteries occupied by the 4th U. S. Artillery, and in front of a battery of the enemy, and from which residence, strange to say, the women folks—a mother, four grown-up daughters and several

184

small children—refuse to go, but sought shelter in the cellar during the cannonading yesterday. The house was struck by canon shot and shell at least twenty times, and is marked much by bullets from the enemy's sharpshooters. These women and children were requested by officers to leave, but they would not, and thought it very hard that the Yankees would put a battery where they did, thereby drawing the fire of the enemy upon them. I mention this to show you that war has not softened in any way its features since you looked it in the face at Vicksburg. . . .

Near Via House, Va.

June 1, 1864

. . . . Today has been beautiful, and closed, or is closing, in a heavy battle. So far as heard from the result is favorable to us. General Smith's troops have arrived and are in position. The only change of the forces from yesterday is that General Wright's Corps (the Sixth) has moved from our right to our left. The cavalry under Sheridan attacked the enemy last evening near Cold Harbor and drove him into and through that place, which holding at one A M. today he was in turn attacked by the enemy, but repulsed the attack and captured about one hundred and fifty prisoners. Neither our loss nor that of the enemy has yet been reported. . . .

Colonel Bowers is in very poor health and goes to Washington tomorrow. I was the only invalid when we started on the campaign, but am, I have no doubt, today in as robust health as any member of the staff, and promise fairly to beat all of them in the end. I am really almost well. . . .

Cold Harbor, Va.

June 2, 1864

. . . . The forenoon was very hot and dusty; this afternoon and tonight it is raining quite heavily.

The enemy yesterday afternoon about five o'clock attacked our lines in front of Warren's, Burnside's and Hancock's corps and were repulsed, the heaviest attack being on General Warren's front. Here they were repulsed three times. At 4.30 p m.

Generals Wright and Smith attacked the enemy in their immediate front, and carried one line of works, which we now hold, excepting, a portion of that carried by General Smith, which, being commanded by

185

another line, was abandoned by us. They captured full eight hundred prisoners. Our entire loss during all this fighting was 2,078 wounded and about 500 killed. The loss of the enemy can only be guessed at, save their loss in prisoners already stated.

Our cavalry under General Wilson succeeded in destroying the railroad bridges across the South Anna yesterday, so altogether yesterday was a day of success for us. Today but little has been done, save that we have made some changes in our lines. During the withdrawal of one of General Warren's divisions the enemy, thinking to take advantage of it, attacked it, but it returned immediately to its old position and forced the enemy back.

Cold Harbor, Va.

June 5, 1864

. . . . Along our lines today there has been comparative quiet. The fighting day before yesterday inclined each of the opposing armies to desist until they could breathe. This very moment heavy firing has commenced in front of General Hancock. It is the enemy, I suppose, trying to drive our working parties from work. It is too late for a serious attack. These days of quiet are long ones, I assure you, but this musketry is growing louder and heavier, and it may be more than I suppose. It still rages with the greatest fury. The artillery has opened, but it sounds not half so terrible and deadly as does the quick and rapid discharge of musketry. . . .

Cold Harbor, Va.

June 6, 1864

. . . . Today has been very warm, a foretaste I suppose of what we are to have during the summer. How I would like to look on this campaign as soon to close successfully. That it will soon be at an end, I scarcely think probable. A people, although in error, will not easily give up that in which they have sacrificed the flower of their youth and impoverished themselves in a bloody war of three years to maintain.

I enclose you a new two-cent coin, the first one received at these headquarters and the first one seen by the Lieutenant General. Please retain it as a keepsake. . . .

Cold Harbor, Va.

June 7, 1864

. . . . This morning was very cold, a great change in the temperature. Everything has been quiet along our lines, except in front of one of Burnside's divisions, where there was a skirmish which resulted in nothing of importance to either side. The *Richmond Examiner* of today states that their forces under the command of General W. E. Jones were defeated twelve miles beyond Stanton; that General Jones was killed on the field, and that his successor retired to Waynesboro in the mountains between Charlottesville and Stanton. This is a triumph which will inure greatly to our interest in this campaign. Hunter is doing what we expected Sigel to do some time since. Hunter and a heavy force, under General Crook, will meet now without doubt at Staunton, if they have not already done so. Their combined forces will be sufficiently strong to enable them to strike a staggering blow against the Confederacy; besides, heavy reinforcements have been ordered to Hunter.

I took dinner today with General Wilson, about four miles from here, in the house of Edmund Ruffin, who fired the first gun at Fort Sumter. His fine plantation is abandoned, and I understand that he is dead. I enclose a lily picked in the yard. . . .

Edmund Ruffin (1794–1865) was a wealthy Virginia planter and a rabidly pro-slavery slaveholder. His plantation still stands and is a National Historic Landmark.—Ed. 2015

After the dinner mentioned above I returned with Rawlins to army headquarters, and during our ride we had an interesting conversation in regard to the policy under which the army had acted so frequently during the campaign, and especially during the last four or five days. I refer of course to its repeated assaults of the enemy's entrenched positions, which assaults generally failed, and always resulted in a number of killed and wounded entirely out of proportion to the advantages gained. Rawlins declared his bitter opposition to such assaults, and to the influences which brought them about, and reiterated that as they were advised by Comstock, a professional soldier, whose specialty on the staff was supposed to be entrenchments and their capture, it was almost impossible to neutralize his influence. He was usually sound enough on most military questions, but his judgment in reference to the conditions under which battle should be delivered, was regarded by Rawlins as faulty in the extreme.

The next day I removed, with my first brigade, to the left of the army and Rawlins repeated his visit; but this time he was accompanied by Dana and Warren. The conversation again turned upon the policy of attacking the enemy behind breastworks and rifle trenches, and again this policy received unsparing condemnation. During the conversation Rawlins and Dana concurred in criticising and disapproving the influence which had come to be paramount at headquarters; and in expressing their regret that I was no longer with them on the staff, but was commanding a division instead, they did not hesitate to declare that their own influence was on the wane and that the new staff was neither so harmonious nor so efficient as the old one used to be.

The next day I received a letter from W. F. Smith, commenting severely upon the "murderous assaults" of Cold Harbor, the demoralizing effect they had had upon the rank and file, and the reflection which they cast upon the generalship of those who had ordered them, or were responsible for their management. I sent this letter at once to Dana at Grant's headquarters, and it is known that he approved its statements; but what use he made of it has never been reported. It is probable, however, that he also showed it to Rawlins, from whom he had no concealments. Be this as it may, a period of gloom and discouragement followed, and the army's feelings were reflected throughout the country. Officers of all ranks participated in it, and the unfortunate controversy between Grant, Smith and Butler ultimately grew out of it; but as I have discussed this controversy with sufficient fullness in *The Life and Services of General Smith*, I return to the letters of Rawlins, which give many interesting details of current events.

On June 8 he wrote from Cold Harbor as follows:

> . . . All quiet today except for occasional firing of artillery and sharp-shooters. The sudden change of the weather from extreme heat to cold night before last was the cause of my taking cold and of a slight return of my cough. . . .

> The papers are filled with eulogies of General Grant and General Sherman, but little is said about General Meade, who is one of the ablest and most accomplished officers. Grant's fame is established as

one of the most successful military men on our side, brought to the notice of history by the Rebellion. Sherman by the success of his campaign thus far against Atlanta has risen and is still rising in the public estimation. You know my opinion of him. General Meade, however, is overlooked by all in the eagerness to see Grant, and let me assure you no one regrets this more than General Grant himself, and when this campaign is ended, whatever may be the result, in his official report he will do justice to the able and patriotic Meade. There has been nothing thus far between Generals Grant and Meade (nor do I have a single apprehension there will be) in their official and personal relations conflicting in the slightest manner with the most cordial cooperation in all movements of the army or marring for one moment their friendship. In no single instance has General Meade shown the slightest indication of indecision. To the contrary he is prompt and decided in everything and at all times. I have never seen the officer who knew more of his army and was more watchful to guard it against surprise by the enemy. He fills my highest expectations of him, some of which, if I remember right, I expressed in a letter from Culpepper C. H. He is of all men in the army of the Potomac the one most fitted to command it. This opinion is not mine only, but is one frequently expressed by General Grant. His modesty and merit will be discovered and made to illuminate the pages of history by searchers after truth and the admirers of worth in the final writing of this rebellion. In your conversations about officers connected with this Army, please give considerable prominence to Meade, for none is more deserving than he. This I particularly desire. . . .

For an intimate look at Meade, see Meade's Headquarters *by his aide, Lt. Colonel Theodore Lyman.—Ed. 2015*

Cold Harbor, Va.,

June 9, 1864

. . . . Greater quiet has prevailed along the lines of the hostile armies today than at any time since our arrival here. An armistice was had on the 7th for the burial of the dead of each army. The number of ours buried was 432. The enemy buried his own and I have no means of knowing the number. These were killed in the battle of the 3rd. General Grant proposed certain arrangements to General Lee on the 4th for the burial of the dead, but they were not agreed to, hence the delay.

General Sheridan left here three days ago with a large cavalry force for Charlottesville or thereabouts. He will, we have great hopes, be able to effect a junction with General Hunter, who after whipping the enemy badly at Mt. Crawford, twelve miles beyond Staunton, on Sunday last, entered Staunton on the Monday following. I mentioned this battle in a previous letter. Hunter and Sheridan will have a force of great strength, able to take care of itself in an open country, and which will, I have no doubt, inflict great injury upon the enemy. . . .

Cold Harbor, Va.,

June 10, 1864

. . . . Today has been more quiet than any day since we crossed the Rapidan. Richmond papers confirm previous reports of the defeat of their forces by General Hunter, and also state that General Crook, in command of a large force of Yankees, was on Monday last at Wilboro, about sixteen miles from Lexington, Va., where the rebels have a military academy, the destruction of which they very much fear. This all looks favorable to us. Sheridan has reached Charlottesville before this and, we have great hopes, has effected a junction with Hunter and Crook, unless they have moved on to Lynchburg, the destruction of which place would be a terrible blow to the rebels. This is, however, almost too much to hope for considering our forces, yet it is not improbable by any means. . . .

Cold Harbor, Va.,

June 11, 1864

. . . . Along our main lines we have had almost perfect quiet since my last writing. Our cavalry on the right this morning drove in the enemy's pickets, and were in turn driven back by the enemy. The loss of the cavalry was fourteen killed and wounded. The enemy's main cavalry force has evidently gone after Sheridan, who started five days ago for Charlottesville.

Our entire loss since the beginning of this campaign, May 4th, 1864, to and including June 9th, as officially reported, is killed 7,289, wounded 37,410, missing 9,862, total 54,561. This statement, however, does not include the losses in the cavalry corps since June 1st. Its loss will be about 600. I send you the exact number of casualties that you may not be in ignorance when you see statements of the same made in the newspapers. The number is great, but the losses of the enemy are also great. We have already captured and sent forward fully 11,000 prisoners, but in killed and wounded their loss must have been considerably less than ours, especially at this place. Our attacks have been against a strongly fortified position. In all other places I should say their loss has been as great as ours.

If any letter was written on the 12th, it has not been found.

Charles City C. H.,

June 13, 1864

. . . . Today has been fine and pleasant. We broke our camp at Cold Harbor yesterday at 3 o'clock P M., encamped near Despatch Station last night and reached here at 4130 P. M. today. The whole army is now virtually across to the west side of the famous Chickahominy. Tomorrow morning we shall commence laying a pontoon bridge across the James River, and also ferrying over troops. Our movement this far has been a splendid success, and the weather most opportune for all our movements. I have no doubt the enemy is also moving to the south side of the James and will meet us, most probably at Petersburg, should we move in that direction. He may possibly make an attack on us in our crossing the river, but I apprehend no such thing. From the commencement of this campaign General Grant has not deviated at all from his written plan, but has steadily pursued the line he then marked out. I shall give it to you in one of my letters hereafter.

A despatch from General Hunter confirms all we heard of the victory he had gained over Jones. He captured 1,500 prisoners, 3,000 stands of arms, three pieces of artillery and large quantities of stores. . . .

I am in excellent health and spirits. . . .

Charles City C. H.,

June 14, 1864

. . . . Another beautiful day has just closed, with a lovely western horizon, giving promise of fair weather tomorrow. Two more such days as this, with no interference on the part of the enemy, will enable us to cross the entire army of the Potomac to the south side of the James River. It seems that thus far we have been especially favored of Heaven. Our last flank movement has been regarded by military men as extra hazardous. General W. F. Smith's corps has already reached Bermuda Hundred, and Hancock's corps is nearly all ferried over to a point nearly opposite here. A pontoon bridge will be laid across the river at Fort Powhattan by tomorrow morning. Our troops are all up, with trains nearby. Everything is progressing finely.

I accompanied the General to Butler's headquarters today. We went by boat. The James River is one of the most majestic of the great rivers of America, and is daily adding to the interest it already possesses in American history. . . .

City Point, Va.,

June 15, 1864

. . . . Beautiful weather. . . . Hancock's corps is across the river and the advance of it near Petersburg. The pontoon bridge was finished this morning, and by tomorrow morning Burnside's corps, which is now crossing on it, will be also well up towards Petersburg. General W. F. Smith, with a force of 15,000 infantry besides cavalry and artillery, has been fighting since about 4:30 A M. at Petersburg. He has carried one line of works, capturing some artillery; was to have assaulted the enemy's line at dark tonight, and there has been heavy firing, which indicates that he did so. We have received no report from him as yet, but are momentarily expecting one. The enemy since about 3:50 P M. have been reinforcing Petersburg by the railroad from Richmond, and we very much fear he will be too strong for Smith. Unless the latter should succeed tonight in conjunction with Hancock in taking Petersburg, we will likely have to commence regular approaches for its reduction.

The news from General Hunter through rebel papers is very encouraging. He captured Lexington, Va., on Saturday, the 11th, and was within 28 miles of Lynchburg and marching in that direction. Great apprehensions are felt by the Confederates for the safety of that place. Should he reach it, a great advantage will be gained by our arms. Nothing could tell more terribly against Richmond unless it were the defeat of Lee's army. Lynchburg is the point where not only two lines of railroad may be cut, but also the James River canal.

Word from Sherman is very cheering, and all looks well, but from Northern Mississippi we have news of another terrible disaster. General Sturgiss [sic] was sent out some days ago with a force of 8,000 men, of whom 3,000 were infantry, from Memphis to drive Forrest, who was assembling his command for a raid against Sherman's communications, out of Northern Mississippi.

He met Forrest near Baldwin on the Ohio & Mobile Railroad, and was defeated with the loss of 4,000 men and all his artillery, and was pursued to Collierville, Tenn.

I cannot understand this, but it seems that we are destined to meet with reverses in that direction and must try the harder to win success in other places. Morgan's raid into Kentucky has been promptly met, and the raiders after the loss of three-fourths of his command is fleeing for safety with the remainder of it. . . .

Samuel Davis Sturgis (1822–1889) was a Mexican War veteran. He was later the nominal commander (as colonel) of George Armstrong Custer's 7th Cavalry, but Custer was the practical commander from 1866–1876. Sturgis lost a son with Custer at the Little Bighorn and publicly criticized the latter for the disaster.—Ed. 2015

City Point, Va.,

June 16, 1864

. ... All the troops except one division of the army are across to the south side of the James River, and four corps are in front of Petersburg. The attack of General W. F. Smith on Petersburg last night was very successful, resulting in the capture of the entire left of its main defenses, 260 prisoners and 16 pieces of artillery. These defenses were very formidable and, had the enemy succeeded in throwing a sufficient number of troops into the place, we would not have been able to carry these works except by siege. They command the city of Petersburg, which lies in a flat below them. The enemy still holds the right of the line around the place, and is busily constructing an interior one. An attack was ordered again this evening, but from it no report has as yet been received.

The colored troops, about 3,000, in the attack last night carried the strongest part of the entrenchments, losing in the assault about 500 killed and wounded. They did nobly, and are entitled to be regarded as among the best of soldiers. You know I have ever had some misgivings of their efficiency, but seeing what they have accomplished, I doubt no longer.

The enemy this afternoon abandoned his works in front of Bermuda Hundred, and General Butler sent out a strong force and now occupies them. He also pushed a force forward to the Petersburg and Richmond Railroad and destroyed considerable of the track. This seems a strange move on their part and would indicate an intention to evacuate

Petersburg. They certainly can't hold it with Butler between it and Richmond. Two divisions of Wright's corps are now passing up the Appomattox to the support of Butler.

A rebel paper of yesterday states that Lieutenant General Polk was killed near Marietta on the 14th instant. He was struck by a shot from Sherman's artillery. Generals Johnston and Hardee were with him at the time. The same paper says that Hampton had attacked and defeated Sheridan at Trevilian Station, capturing 500 prisoners. . . .

City Point

June 17, 1864

. . . . My health is still improving, and you may be assured no one seems less likely to be a subject of consumption than I. The doctors have all assured me that my lungs are not affected, and if you saw me now you would concur in their opinion.

The attack on the enemy at Petersburg made last night and this morning resulted in the further capture of works, six additional guns and four hundred and fifty prisoners. Our loss in killed, wounded and missing was about two thousand two hundred. Petersburg is still firmly held by the enemy. While I write, however, heavy cannonading is going on in that direction. I was out there both yesterday and today.

General Butler has returned to his old lines and the enemy to his old position in Butler's front. Butler has been ordered to drive the enemy back, which he will try to do tonight. His failure to hold and fortify the position they evacuated yesterday morning was a great mistake and may cost us a great deal. The General and all are well. . . .

I have just heard from Petersburg. Burnside attacked the enemy at eight o'clock P M. and has carried, according to report of prisoners taken, the last line of entrenchments between us and Petersburg. The fighting is still progressing. I have great hopes of being able to report the capture of the Cockade City tomorrow night. . . .

City Point, Va.,

June 18, 1864

. . . . We failed to get into Petersburg today, but gained considerable ground in that direction on some portions of our lines, which we are entrenching and will hold. We are within one mile of the main part of the city. Our losses since we arrived before Petersburg have been very

194

heavy. I will be able to state the number in my next letter. I send you a Vicksburg paper, not knowing but in the notices of marriages you might see some name you would recognize.

You ask to know the size of my head and the number of the slipper I wear. My head is seven and a quarter full—my slippers No. 8.

Today, like many preceding it, has been most beautiful. Our headquarters are most delightfully situated on the banks of the James River, overlooking the immense fleet of river and seagoing vessels lying at City Point and Bermuda Hundred. You would be delighted and charmed with the view. . . .

City Point,

June 19, 1864

. ... A despatch from Sheridan, dated 16th instant at Guinea's Bridge, Virginia, states that he had a severe engagement with the enemy at Trevilian Station on the Virginia Central RaiLroad on the 12th, and completely defeated them, capturing 500 prisoners and inflicting on them a heavy loss. He destroyed the road from Trevilian's to Louisa C. H. Among the rebel officers: Colonel McCallister killed, General Rosser* and two colonels wounded. The enemy having sent a heavy force on to the road between him and General Hunter, he commenced his journey back. General Hunter is on the railroad about twenty miles west of Lynchburg, destroying it at a great rate, according to the Richmond papers. . . .

*Thomas Lafayette (Tex) Rosser (1836–1910) was a close friend of George Armstrong Custer from West Point before the war. They had a kind of running rivalry during the war; Custer even once captured Rosser's trunk during a skirmish. In 1873, Custer's 7th Cavalry provided protection to a railroad survey party along the Yellowstone River in Montana Territory. Rosser was the chief engineer.—Ed. 2015

City Point

June 20, 1864

. . . . Today has been clear and fine, with all quiet along our lines. No news from any quarter, except from the White House, which place was attacked by the enemy at daylight this morning, and at 10 A M. the fighting was still going on. Our forces there number about 3,000 men under General Abercrombie. The place is well fortified, and we have every reason to believe will be able to hold out until the arrival of Sheridan, who was near there yesterday.

I am now out of debt and feel independent. If you could exchange your greenbacks for gold, it might possibly be the best investment you could make. Do as you like about it. Don't say to anyone I have advised you thus, but the rapid rise in gold and the great surplus of currency makes me doubt if greenbacks will ever be at par, no matter what may be the result of the war. The trouble in our currency is, in my judgment, the surplus, in excess of the necessities of commerce, and not in the fact that we don't take Richmond. Whatever may be the result of this campaign, the success of which I do not for a moment doubt, our Government is strong and wealthy, and will cancel or put into the course of cancellation all its indebtedness. If you have gold you can always convert it into currency, and I think you had better make the exchange. . . .

City Point, Va.,

June 21, 1864

. . . . Everything quiet on our lines. The attack on White House yesterday was repulsed. Sheridan reached there at 5 P M. and will join us here at once.

The Petersburg papers on the 20th say that General Hunter attacked Lynchburg on Saturday, the 18th, and was repulsed, and that they expected a general battle the next day, which showed that the attack and repulse amounted to no more than a reconnaissance on the part of Hunter.

President Lincoln is here. He arrived about two o'clock p m. today, and in company with the General and staff rode out to the front. We got back to this point about eight o'clock. He goes tomorrow to the pontoon bridge across the James at Deep Bottom. He is greatly pleased with the condition of affairs here, and it was most truly interesting when he was cheered by the negro troops, those who fought so gallantly here on the 16th. Their honest, hearty hurrahs for the man whom they regard as their liberator went up to Heaven I am sure. . . .

City Point, Va.,

June 22, 1864

. ... In moving the corps of Generals Hancock and Wright to the left to circumvallate if possible Petersburg to the river on our left, the enemy attacked Hancock in great force and compelled him to fall back some distance from the intended line, with the loss of four pieces of artillery. We subsequently retook the line, but whether we recaptured the guns or not is not reported. At seven o'clock P M. the advance was to commence again, but we have not heard from it yet. It will most likely result in a heavy fight.

Richmond papers again report the attack of Hunter upon Lynchburg, which attack they say was repulsed with a loss to Hunter of 200 prisoners and three guns, and that they were in pursuit.

President Lincoln left here for Washington this afternoon.

Wilson and Kautz with 7,000 cavalry started this morning for the Danville & Richmond Railroad. They crossed the Petersburg & Weldon road at 10 A M., destroying the track and depot where they crossed. I have great confidence in their success, although cavalry thus far has succeeded but poorly in the destruction of the enemy's communications. The enemy's cavalry are mostly to the north of the river, and hence my belief in the success of this raid.

General Ransom of the old Tennessee Army, who was wounded in the Red River expedition, is here. Also Colonel Hillyer and two French officers. Thus you see we have distinguished visitors. . . .

City Point, Va.,

June 23, 1864

. . . . You say I need give myself no uneasiness about your wearing imported goods. Now, my dear, if you understand me as being uneasy about your doing so, you misunderstand my letter. I simply desire you to give your approval to that movement on the part of the ladies of America and am delighted to know that you do approve it. Everything that looks to rendering our country independent of other countries I desire to favor. Its greatness and glory is the one idea of my heart, after my love and duty to you and our little ones. And all through her greatness and glory I would have her benevolence and generosity shine. . . .

The refusal of Congress to strike out the commutation clause in the conscript law is regarded by many here as very unfortunate. . . .

City Point,

June 24, 1864

. . . . Have just returned from the front. In extending our lines last night we lost very heavily— about 3,000 killed, wounded and missing, at a rough estimate, and four pieces of artillery. We reached the Weldon Railroad and destroyed about one mile of it, and then fell back. We now hold a strong line threatening the road, and cavalry has been at work destroying it today.

This morning the enemy attacked General Smith's line, and were repulsed, leaving in our hands 166 prisoners. Tonight an attack was ordered by General Smith on a hill between ours and the enemy's main line, but the result has not yet been reported. Our entire losses in our operations from the 9th to and including the 19th instant were ten thousand four hundred and fifteen (10,415).

I have made an arrangement with Colonel Hillyer to convert the money on deposit with N. Corwith & Co., that is to say, five hundred dollars, into gold, and have drawn on them for it. . . .

City Point, Va.,

June 25, 1864

. . . . Very dry. Everybody wishing for rain.

General Smith did not make the attack he intended last night. Today all has been quiet. Yesterday afternoon Sheridan had heavy fighting in the protection of his trains, and in getting them to the James River. He succeeded in saving everything and inflicted severe loss on the enemy. His own loss was heavy, say about 400 killed and wounded. . . .

City Point, Va.,

June 26, 1864

. . . . Excessively hot today. So hot indeed as to practically put an end to operations.

Everything on our lines has been quiet except occasional firing of artillery. The extreme heat renders operations exceedingly difficult, but it will enable the army to get that rest which long and continued marching and fighting since May 4th makes necessary. A few days will suffice for this purpose. . . .

I have been urging General Grant to write to the Speaker of the House of Representatives insisting upon the three-hundred-dollar

198

clause being struck out of the conscription act. Whether he will do so or not, I cannot say. It is getting so late that such a letter might not reach the House before action on the bill is had. With the great advantages we now hold on the James River and in Georgia, if we fail to put down the Rebellion, the nations of the world and our own children will arraign us throughout long ages to come for our treason to humanity and liberty. We must succeed. We dare not fail. . . .

City Point,

June 28, 1864

. . . . All quiet along our lines yesterday and today, save the firing of siege guns at intervals into Petersburg and at bridges across the Appomattox.

Richmond papers of yesterday show that General Wilson's cavalry raid is doing great damage upon their railroads. He reached Burkeville Junction on Friday, destroyed the depots, etc., tore up and burnt the ties, bending the rails over the fires. He went on down the Danville road towards Danville, destroying as he went. All communications with Richmond by rail are now out, and I imagine it will take several days, if not weeks, to repair damages so as to get cars through from beyond the breaks in the roads. . . .

They claim to have whipped a detachment of Wilson's cavalry on the Petersburg road about seven miles from Burkeville Junction, but I doubt its truth, as they gave no particulars. General Hunter has reached Gauley, Virginia, after having, as he reports officially, inflicted great injury to the rebels in the destruction of railroads and supplies, and whipped them in every engagement. He says his troops are in good heart and health and ready to move in any direction on getting a fresh supply of ammunition. It was want of ammunition that caused his return.

We have had no rain yet at this point, but yesterday it rained all around us and cooled the atmosphere very considerably. It is now delightfully pleasant. . . .

City Point, Va.,

June 29, 1864

. . . . All quiet along our lines, save artillery firing at intervals. It will be several days, perhaps weeks, before we have another general engagement. We are not idle, however, and should we discover any weakening in the enemy's lines, advantage will be taken of it if possible.

An officer with forty men came through today from Wilson. He is on the Weldon Railroad and confronted by a greatly superior force of the enemy. Sheridan's other two divisions of cavalry have gone to his assistance, supported by Wright's army corps of infantry, which, while they effect the relief of Wilson, will, we trust, effectually finish the work of destruction on the railroads.

News from Washington today says the House has passed the conscription bill without the commutation clause. I hope it will also pass the Senate. It is more like an earnest desire for the end of the war than any act of the House since the fall of Sumter.

The General was at the front today, and I learn from one of his staff he deviated from the only path he should ever travel by taking a glass of liquor. It is the first time I have failed to accompany him to Petersburg, and it was with misgivings I did so. Nothing but indisposition induced me to remain behind. I shall hereafter, under no circumstances, fail to accompany him. . . .

City Point, Va.,

June 30, 1864

. . . . Today has been as dry as any preceding it. In fact it is so dry and dusty that the very river looks like a bed of dust. . . .

News from Wilson is laden with grief. His command was attacked yesterday afternoon this side of Nottoway River and from all the information we have obtained was defeated with heavy loss in men, his train and five pieces of artillery. General Kautz cut his way out, bringing off his own command and a part of Wilson's, while Wilson retreated towards Jarrott's Station on the Weldon road. The cavalry and infantry sent out yesterday to his aid did not reach there in time.

It is hoped that this force will be able to relieve him yet and make up in damage to the enemy all they have inflicted on Wilson. Our reports are vague and unsatisfactory. I have hopes the facts will look better for us when they come to hand.

I have received my commission, which I send you by Express. . . .

City Point, Va.,

July 1, 1864

. . . . Still hot and dry. . . . News from Wilson received this evening confirms the reports of his defeat and loss of train and artillery, all of which he destroyed himself to keep it from falling into the hands of the enemy. His loss in men will not exceed 1,000, I should say, from present information. He destroyed effectually twenty-six miles of the Petersburg & Lynchburg Railroad and thirty miles of the Richmond & Danville Railroad. On the latter road he also destroyed every tie and rail. The Richmond papers say it will take four weeks to repair the damage done. At this time Richmond is entirely isolated from all railroad communications with the South, and we hope to continue the isolation until it falls of its own weight. This, however, will take months. . . .

City Point,

July 2, 1864

. ... No rain yet. All has been quiet today, save artillery firing, which is continued at intervals along a portion of our lines.

Colonel Rowley left for Galena this morning. His health is poor and he talks of resigning, in fact has tendered his resignation, but Bowers and I have persuaded him out of the notion, and urged him to take orders for Chicago, from whence he could go home and stay for a month at least, and at the expiration of the time he could forward his resignation should he still be of that mind. Otherwise he could return to the field.

Colonel Dent* went North yesterday in very low health, and Colonel Babcock is lying sick in camp. I am in very excellent health. My cough, although it still hangs on, is very slight indeed. ... I am better in general health than I have ever been since our acquaintance. . . .

Frederick Tracy Dent (1820–1892) aide to General Grant and brother of Grant's wife, Julia.—Ed. 2015

City Point, Va.,

July 3, 1864

. . . . Another day, dusty, dry and hot, has closed, with no sign of change. Quiet prevails all along the lines of the army. The great giants who have wrestled from the time of their grappling with each other on the 5th of May south of the Rapidan until their feet pressed the soil of Petersburg south of the James, now breathe in each other's face while resting and making ready for another struggle, each looking for the spot to strike at in which he can inflict the greatest injury.

Judging from the newspapers, it would seem that the resignation of [Secretary of the Treasury, Salmon] Chase is creating quite a sensation or, rather, has increased the gloom that has hung over our nation since the breaking out of the Rebellion. I have held Mr. Chase in high esteem as Secretary of the Treasury, but feel that he has shown a want of true patriotism in selecting this time of all others to add to our national embarrassment, and am inclined to the opinion that his withdrawal from the Treasury Department will, after it becomes fully understood, result in good to our cause. Representing as he does the radicalism of the country, he is little less dangerous than Vallandigham.

Salmon Portland Chase (1808–1873) was an ambitious Ohio politician with aspirations to the presidency who caused Lincoln no end of headaches while in the Cabinet, having what the President called "White House Fever." He repeatedly offered his resignation, knowing this would hurt Lincoln with the radical Republicans. Lincoln surprised Chase in 1864 by accepting the resignation. Before the year was out, he appointed Chase Chief Justice of the Supreme Court. Clement Vallandigham was one of the leaders of the Northern Copperheads, anti-war Democrats.—Ed. 2015

Our national currency looks badly, but what of it? Had not the rebellion maintained the war against us from almost the beginning with a depreciated and, for the last eighteen months, an entirely worthless currency? And can we not do what they have with all the advantages and means to boot in our favor? No, a depreciated currency cannot stop the war for national existence. We are too near the goal of triumph now to recede. Give us the conscription bill with the commutation clause stricken out and we will within twelve months stand forth among the nations as a united people, free and powerful for good. Years only can erase the feelings of ill will engendered, but time will heal them in the end. This is the faith of my existence. . . .

City Point, Va.,

July 4, 1864

. . . . Another of our country's anniversaries of independence and the first of the fall of Vicksburg has just closed. Oh, how unlike those before the rebellion, and how my heart aches for the restoration of peace! . . .

Everything quiet along our lines. It is reported that Ewell's force sent from Lee's army to repel Hunter's raid is moving down the Shenandoah Valley, and I fear much excitement will exist throughout the country for the safety of Washington before this reaches you. We suppose Hunter will be able to concentrate his forces at Harper's Ferry in time to prevent the invasion of Maryland. Ewell's command cannot much exceed 15,000, though it may reach 18,000. Should he get into Maryland, however, there will be nothing left undone that can be done to prevent his ever getting back. With our great facilities for the transportation of troops it will take but two days to move from here an army corps if necessary. Besides, we are expecting here the arrival of the 19th Army Corps from Banks's Department within a short time. Vessels to transport them were sent several days since; of this, however, you will please not speak to any one where there would be the least likelihood of its becoming public.

City Point, Va.,

July 6, 1864

. ... I had hoped during the present lull in affairs here to get a few days to myself for the purpose of visiting you in your new home, but all prospects of it vanished yesterday evening, when it became necessary for Colonel Bowers to go and see his mother, who is dangerously ill, and also for the purpose of repairing his own health, which is poor indeed. At present of the General's staff there are absent Colonels Dent, Duff, Rowley and Bowers, and Colonel Babcock is quite poorly and will, I fear, have to go also. I am too well to think of getting off on a plea of sickness; besides, my presence is perhaps more indispensable than that of any staff officer, for in the absence of the assistant adjutant general I know and can perform his duties, which no one else can do so well; and then, too, I look after and care for the personal habits of those who must not be permitted to fall.

All quiet today. Richmond papers say that they have whipped Sherman in Atlanta and that he is in full retreat. This we do not believe. From seven to nine thousand men left here today for Washington to aid in defeating Early. ...

No letter of July 7 has been found.

City Point, Va.,

July 8, 1864

. . . . News from General Sherman is very favorable. He has driven the enemy to the south side of the Chattahoochee. Nothing new along our lines save the firing of artillery by both the enemy and ourselves. But little damage is being done to us, and whether we do any more to them is questionable. . . .

City Point, Va., July 9, 1864. . . . The remainder of the 6th Corps goes to Washington in the morning, and should have gone three days ago but for a despatch from General Halleck stating that they would not be needed. They are now in great trepidation, but I have no doubt we shall get forces forward soon enough to defend the place and at the same time inflict such damage upon the enemy as to make him think he has paid dearly for his whistle. . . .

City Point, Va.,

July 10, 1864

. . . . All quiet along our lines.

Stirring and exciting news from Washington reached us last night and this morning.

The remaining two divisions of Wright's corps left today for Washington—one division had gone forward several days ago. The 19th Corps, on its way from New Orleans to this place, or, rather, its advance, has reached Port Monroe and has gone forward to Washington. All will be well and the rebel movement into Maryland will result, if properly looked to, in great advantage to us. . . .

City Point,

July 11, 1864

. . . . Another hot day, followed by rain after night.

No news here at all. Everything is as quiet as summer. We have a rumor, however, that Hill's corps moved from its position in our front yesterday, Longstreet's corps taking its place, but where it has gone, if gone it has, we do not even conjecture yet. We do not believe it has gone to Maryland for the distance is so great it could not hope to reach Early in time to afford him any material aid. One or two days will determine its whereabouts. If it has gone on any expedition from here we will try and take advantage of its absence to inflict a blow upon the enemy.

The news from Sherman is very encouraging. He has forced Johnston to the south side of the Chattahoochee, and has crossed portions of his own army, and secured the crossings of the river at two different fords.

From Washington we have had no news today. Last night General Grant received a despatch from the President stating that he thought it best for the General to come there. This was a despatch in answer to one the General had sent saying he would go to Washington if it was thought best. I differed with any and all such propositions and told the General that his place was here—that he had started out to defeat Lee and capture Richmond —that his appearance in Washington would be heralded all over the country as an abandonment of his campaign, a faltering at least in his purpose; that he had under orders to Washington full thirty thousand men, with able and efficient officers, besides the troops of Hunter and those already at Washington and Baltimore, and if they could not defeat, rout and capture Early, whose force never could exceed twenty-five thousand, I did not think his presence would help the thing enough to justify his going from here. Falling in with my view, he telegraphed the President in accordance therewith . . .

Colonel Ritter goes to Harrisburg in the morning, for a few days. Colonel Badeau is quite sick and will perhaps have to go North. . . .

City Point,

July 13, 1864

. . . . News from Washington continues exciting but we have no fears for the safety of the place. All the troops necessary for its defence and to follow up and give successful battle have been sent from here. General H. G. Wright, an able and splendid soldier, has the supreme command of the moving forces there, and from the facts as they appear to me, I can see no reason why we should not defeat and destroy Early's whole command and turn into positive success for us this movement of the enemy. What will be done a few days will determine. When this letter will reach you is doubtful. The railroad from Washington north is broken, but I never fail in keeping my word to you in the matter of correspondence.

It would appear that the whole of Lee's army is threatening Washington. It is positively asserted that Longstreet's corps is on the way there, but we have the best of evidence that it remains here, and that it is here I have no doubt. We have deserters from it daily and also make captures of prisoners from it. This latter evidence never has failed us. . . .

City Point,

July 14, 1864

. . . . News from Washington is that the enemy has taken up his return line of march. Whether we will be able to inflict damage upon him is not yet known. Colonel Comstock goes to Washington tonight to try and hasten the return to this place of the troops sent from here, the moment it is ascertained that they are no longer needed there, or that the enemy is beyond their reach. . . .

City Point,

July 15, 1864

. . . . All quiet along our lines here. News from Washington shows the enemy has left Maryland with large amounts of plunder gathered from the Marylanders. Hunter is moving from Harper's Ferry to intercept their retreat.

Sherman has got the enemy south of the Chattahoochee and will himself move to the south side as early as the 17th. He has his supplies all up for a vigorous push on Atlanta. . . .

On July 16, 1864, Rawlins wrote a long letter, speaking of his "Democratic notions of life and its proprieties." He added:

. . . That I have not gone home is a matter over which thus far I have had no control, but I have been shaping everything with a view to seeing you before a great many weeks go by. I have urged and encouraged every one of the staff who had the least desire to go home, to do so, and all except Colonel Babcock have been off. When they return I shall have the aid of all of them, and their interest too, in getting away for a few days myself. Don't you think I'm something of a diplomat? . . .

City Point,

July 17, 1864

. . . . The General has ordered to this place the 6th and 19th Corps, sent some days ago to Washington, with a view to an attack on the enemy before Early can get back. Whether the Government will let

206

them leave Washington is somewhat doubtful. There is evidently much anxiety still there for the safety of the city, and I fear an uneasiness as to the effect the recent raid may have upon the fall election. The blame will, I have no doubt, be laid at the General's door. For my own part I see nothing serious that can come of it. Certainly the General acted as promptly as he could in the premises and but for the despatches saying they thought they had troops enough to defend the city, sent by one authorized to speak for them, and who ought to be regarded as capable of judging, one whole army corps would have been there three days earlier than it was. Say nothing of this. We shall see what we shall see.

It turns out that General Wilson was not confirmed by the Senate, although we had, in answer to inquiries long ago, been made to understand that he was. He has, however, been appointed again to rank from his former date. This is treating very badly an enthusiastic, able young officer, but time will make all things even, it is said, and I trust it is true. . . .

City Point,

July 18, 1864

. . . . Another delightful day has closed with nothing worthy of mention, except that General Grant has in view the responsibility that may be laid upon him for the enemy's recent raid into Maryland, asked to have a Military Division constructed out of the territory now comprising the Departments of Washington, Middle and Western Virginia, with Major General Franklin to command it. If this is done the General can be answerable for the safety of the Maryland border; otherwise he should not be so held.

The two corps ordered to be returned here are en route for this place.

The regiments whose term of service expires between this and the twenty-fifth of August next, have been ordered to Washington. They will tend considerably to steady the nerves of the people of Maryland and not materially weaken us here; for the fact is those regiments whose time is nearly out, do not evince the alacrity of regiments who have a long time yet to serve. There is good reason—or at least it is not unnatural—that this should be so.

General Ord and staff arrived here this evening. Honorable Mr. Kellogg of Michigan is here. He talks to suit me, and his visit, I have no doubt, will be fraught with good to the service. I like to entertain such men . . .

Enclosed I send you photograph with autograph of <u>Major General</u> <u>Winfield S. Hancock</u>, one of the best and most gallant of soldiers. Put it along side of the lamented Sedgwick in your album of heroes. . . .

City Point, Va.,

July 19, 1864

. . . . We have had one steady and continuous rain all day. The dust is effectually laid and it will take several days to resurrect it into the clouds, which seemed so long to delight in enveloping us. Never were people more glad to have rain than we.

The 19th Corps is beginning to arrive. The news from Sherman is very favorable. He has crossed the Chattahoochee with his entire army and is moving directly on Atlanta and Decatur. He has already struck and broken the railroad east of Atlanta. Since crossing the river he has encountered only the enemy's cavalry. It may be possible they intend giving up Atlanta without a battle. The tone of the Atlanta papers favors this supposition. If they do, my own conviction is that the major part of Johnston's army will be brought here. Should they do this, there is no doubt of our ability to hold our present position, even against both Lee and Johnston. The danger will be of a movement against Washington. But why speculate upon the uncertainty of future military movements? All we have to do is what we can do in the living present, not forgetting, however, to prepare for future dangers, as time may develop them.

General Grant today relieved Major General William F. Smith from command and duty in this army, because of his spirit of criticism of all military movements and men, and his failure to get along with anyone he is placed under, and his disposition to scatter the seeds of discontent throughout the army. . . .

City Point,

July 20, 1864

. ... No news today from Sherman. General A. J. Smith, after a fight with Forrest at and in the neighborhood of Tupelo, Miss., on the Mobile & Ohio Railroad, defeated him, with a loss to the enemy of full twenty-five hundred. Our loss was small in men and no loss in anything else . . .

The President has finally called for five hundred thousand more men. This is better late than never. Had Congress given him the power to conscript, with the commuting clause left out, at the beginning of the last session, instead of at its close, and he had exercised it, the end of the war, so much hoped for, would have been reached in the campaign begun last May, but such was not the action of the Government and hence the unfinished work yet to be done. . . .

City Point,

July 21, 1864

. ... A most delightful day has closed with still the same momentous quiet along our lines here, that has prevailed for the last month.

News from the South is that [Confederate General Joseph] Johnston has been relieved and General [John Bell] Hood, who is said to be a fighting General, has been put in command of his army, from which we infer that the enemy will give Sherman battle at Atlanta, and that if we can only whip them, is the very best thing they can do for us. The enemy beaten in battle at Atlanta, would give us the whole country, whereas if they simply fall back from that place, keeping their army intact, it will be a constant menace to our position which at best is difficult to hold.

We shall so operate here as to prevent the enemy from sending troops to Hood to defeat Sherman as Beauregard did from Corinth in 1862 to defeat McClellan, and as Lee did last September to defeat Rosecrans of the operations of our Eastern and Western armies this spring and summer, this much at least can be said—they have so moved and fought as to prevent the enemy reinforcing in either front, to our destruction, as they have in every instance heretofore.

News from General Wright is encouraging. He and Crook had crossed the Shenandoah yesterday, near Berryville and were driving the enemy, with a prospect of capturing their trains. The day before they had driven Crook back from his attempt to cross the river before the arrival of Wright. . . .

City Point,

July 22, 1864

. ... I mail to you an article which I desire preserved, from the *New York Herald*, vindicating General Hunter against attacks, which have been made upon him in the *Western Press*, and which article is near the truth. The only question being whether General Hunter should not have gone by the way of Charlottesville to Lynchburg instead of by

Lexington. His orders were to go to Staunton, Charlottesville and Lynchburg, if possible, destroying thoroughly the railroads from those points to Richmond. In this way the Valley of Virginia would always have been open to him.

I send you also a copy of a letter from General Scott, touching what he understands someone has reported he should have said about General Grant. He is mistaken, however, in his supposition, for the General had never heard of his speaking unfavorably of him. I am pleased at his writing the letter.

. . . My cough is still annoying me, but I have a fresh gallon of very old Bourbon and a bottle of cod liver oil, but how I wish the necessity for its use no longer existed. . . .

City Point, Va.,

July 23, 1864

. . . . No occurrences of interest to the historian. No, I cannot say so much, for every day some of the brave defenders of our country are taken away to a better land, and in their death help to swell the roll of honor . . .

News from Sherman today brings sad intelligence that Major General J. B. McPherson was killed yesterday by a bullet through his lungs, fired from the enemy's works while he was making a reconnaissance of them. McPherson, my friend, with whom I have shared the same blanket, messed at the same board, endured the fatigue of the march, the exposures of the storm and faced dangers of battle. Brave, patriotic and gifted, his country will weep his loss as irreparable, and every friend of freedom will find for him a tear. My mind would be to say more of him but I have not the command of language to do justice to his worth and fame. . . .

City Point, Va.,

July 24, 1864

. ... I send you in this mail a *Galena Advertiser* in which you will read an article advocating your husband's being appointed Secretary of War, which will surprise and amuse you as much as it does him. . . .

City Point,

July 28, 1864

.... On my return yesterday from Washington I touched at Cherry Stone Point and there received your despatch, for which accept my thanks....

I find the General in my absence digressed from his true path. The God of Heaven only knows how long I am to serve my country as the guardian of the habits of him whom it has honored. It shall not be always thus. Owing to this faltering of his, I shall not be able to leave here till the rebel movement in Maryland is settled and also the fate of Atlanta....

City Point,

July 28, 1864 [later]

.... Matters are now such that it is impossible for me to leave here at present. Active operations have commenced, which with the fact of the General's forgetting himself, in that one danger of which I wrote you this morning, renders my being here of an importance that you can appreciate as fully as any person living, although it deprives you of an immediate visit from me, a visit which my health demands . . .

Since writing the foregoing I have had a long talk with the General and Colonel Bowers, and they conclude I had better go as early as the first of next month, and I have thought, all things considered, I can perhaps as well be spared by that time as at any time thereafter. So you may begin to look for me about next Wednesday if I have no delays....

From the foregoing correspondence it will be seen that from the time Grant assumed command of our armies as Lieutenant General till he crossed the James River and besieged Petersburg, Rawlins had been his inseparable counsellor and his ever-vigilant guardian. He had from the first thrown the weight of his influence in favor of the Overland Campaign, and what is still more important, in favor of manoeuvring the enemy out of his entrenched positions, instead of trying to drive him out by direct attack. He had constantly urged that the army should be reinforced by all the troops that could be spared from elsewhere and that Congress should authorize a conscription from which no man could escape by purchase. He points out that had this measure been enacted at the beginning of the current session of Congress instead of at its close, the army would have been strengthened in the right way and the war would have been ended much sooner. Withal, it is evident that in a strictly military sense his influence had begun to wane, and that in the daily operations of the army others of inferior judgment had acquired greater influence than himself. In the more important fields of personal conduct and military policy he still remained without a rival. When the President invited Grant to Washington, it was Rawlins whose fears and arguments prevented his going, till it was certain that the trip was absolutely necessary.

It is also evident that while Rawlins had at first a high regard for the abilities of W. F. Smith, and concurred in his condemnation of the assault at Cold Harbor, he ultimately came to censure his criticism of those in authority over him for their responsibility and part in it, and fully approved his relief from duty with the Army of the James as the shortest way to the restoration of harmony and discipline. In common with Grant, Rawlins appears to have been disappointed in regard to Butler's merits as a soldier as well as to his importance as a politician and statesman.

On the other hand, Smith was an open, imprudent, and even an acrimonious critic of both men and measures that he did not approve, and while he was careful to limit his censure to those whose function it was to regulate details, the latter were doubtless ingenious enough to make it appear that his shafts were aimed at the chief commander as well as at the plans upon which the army was then operating. The letters quoted above show that Rawlins not only came to this opinion but to the belief that Smith, whom he knew to be an honest and able man as well as a good friend of Grant, had been actuated rather by disappointment and selfish ambition than by a spirit of helpfulness in advocating the plan of operations by the way of Albemarle Sound, which Franklin was first to bring forward, but which his friend elaborated and supported, as Rawlins thought, with obstinate persistency. When it is recalled that both Grant and Rawlins at first concurred in considering Smith's success at Petersburg as having been all that could have been expected, and that Rawlins, at least, joined in the condemnation of the futile and costly attacks directed against the enemy's entrenched positions at Cold Harbor and Spotsylvania, it will be seen that powerful influences must have been brought to bear to weaken his control and to bring about Smith's overthrow.

It is not known what Butler's own attitude was in respect either to these operations or to what finally came to be designated by the critics as the "Policy of Attrition," but it is fully established that he used the criticism contained in Smith's letters, as well as what Smith said in person to Butler's officers at Fort Monroe, to secure his own reinstatement and Smith's dismissal from command in the field. This is one of the most interesting but obscure episodes of the time, and whatever may have been the open or secret influences underlying it, it may well be regarded as an instance of retributive justice that, notwithstanding Butler's immediate triumph and Smith's downfall, Grant shortly found himself compelled to relieve Butler for incompetency and to place his army under the command of the steady-going Ord, of the regular army. Moreover, it is certain that, whatever may have been the part taken by Rawlins in these transactions, he fully approved of Butler's relief by a professional soldier as a sound and judicious measure which called for no public defence.

To those who knew Grant and his Chief of Staff in the West and were aware of their peculiarities and personal relations, and to such as read with care the letters which I have quoted, it will be apparent that the friendship or hostility of Rawlins was an important factor in the fate of many of the leadings generals, and that he gave his approval, on the one hand, or his disapproval, on the other, from none but the highest and most unselfish motives. While it is to be regretted that he did not more fully describe the conduct and characteristics of those with whom he had to do, and did not more fully set forth the genesis and course of the various plans and movements which came under his observation, there is much in his correspondence which the student of history will thank him for. His revelation of self is complete. It shows him to have been a fearless friend, an unselfish patriot, and an official adviser, of ability and independence. Lacking technical military knowledge, to which he made no pretension, but possessing moral qualities and character of the highest order, he nevertheless rendered the greatest service to his chief, who had had military training and experience in abundance, but was lacking in other important qualities which Rawlins supplied. It was a rare and fortunate combination; and while it was far from including all the attributes of a perfect general, it may well be contended that without the contributions of both, Grant could scarcely have hoped to achieve the splendid success which finally crowned his military career.

It is to be noted, on the other hand, that notwithstanding the vein of hopefulness which pervades these unstudied letters of Rawlins to his wife, the work and exposure of the campaign were proving too much for his strength, and that in spite of his indomitable will and his pathetic desire for health, the disease from which he was suffering was making slow but steady progress to its inevitable end.

NEARING THE WAR'S END

IT will be observed that the confidence, which Rawlins expressed on July 29, in a successful assault of the enemy's lines at Petersburg, like that of the month previous in regard to the extension of the national lines to and across the Weldon Railroad, was misplaced. The latter should have succeeded because of Grant's superiority of numbers, if not by good management, but the former was based upon the belief that the explosion of an extensive mine in Burnside's front would make an opening in the enemy's entrenchments through which a vital thrust might be made. The mine was exploded, an enormous breach was made, but unfortunately it was bottomed by a crater of great depth, with sides too steep to be surmounted by a rush. The enemy was stunned and scattered by the explosion, and quite a quarter of an hour passed before his shaken battalions could be rallied and put into position to resist the assault which should have followed at once, had proper dispositions been made to that end.

Grant, in accordance with his general rule, had left the details to Meade, who unfortunately left them in turn to Burnside, the immediate commander. It was clearly their duty to make the necessary arrangements for following the explosion, with an assault which should pass around, not through, the breach, drive the enemy back, and take possession of the works on either side. But it appears that neither general had had much confidence in the mine; hence, neither made any adequate preparation to insure the success of the assault following the explosion. Instead of telling off two divisions of the best troops under the guidance of experienced officers, and preparing others to support and cooperate with them, Ledlie's division of white troops was assigned to the task of assaulting the breach made by the crater. Ledlie, although a civil engineer and contractor, was an officer of but little aptitude and no special training for such serious work, and while he was supported by two divisions of colored troops, one of them commanded by an ex-dancing master at West Point, the movement after the explosion was not only slow but badly managed throughout. The advancing men piled into, the crater without method or adequate leadership, became hopelessly confused, and were killed by hundreds, mainly through the use of hand grenades, which were thrown down the slopes of the crater in great numbers. The operations instead of being conducted successfully by trained officers and competent commanders, ended, as might have been expected, in a bloody and discouraging disaster, which should have emphasized the failure to capture Petersburg, not only then but when the Union Army first closed in upon its defenses. In both cases it is now evident that the troops available for the undertaking were ample and within reasonable supporting distance, and that the failure was primarily due to defective organization of the army as a whole, and to the absence of all proper staff arrangements. There were too many links in the chain, too many separate heads through which orders must be sent, too much independence, too little cooperation between commanders, and a total absence of that promptitude, coherence, and efficiency of operations which are impossible without a competent general staff.

Grant was primarily responsible for all this. He had complete authority over such matters, but having committed himself from the start to the maintenance of the separate organizations in that theatre of operations, as well as to the policy of leaving the different generals free to carry their orders into effect in such manner as might seem best to them, he had thereby relieved his chief of staff from most of the responsibility that should otherwise have rested on him.

Nobody knew better than Rawlins that well-laid plans were failing far too often. Nobody knew better than he that the team was not only "balky" but badly driven, and finally nobody had been more severe than he in the condemnation of direct assaults upon fortified positions; but he allowed himself, apparently with good reason, to hope that the explosion of the mine would afford an exceptional opportunity, which might lead to a great success. The failure which followed was a sore disappointment to him as well as to his chief. His impaired health made him peculiarly susceptible to the influence of the hot weather, which was now becoming intense. Realizing that this, when superadded to the great disappointment which had overtaken the army, would necessarily put an end to active operations for a few weeks, Rawlins concluded to take a sick leave, with the understanding that he would return on short notice should any emergency arise. He left the army on July 25, with despatches for the President and Secretary of War. After seeing them both, he went on to New York and Danbury the next day. It is not known what passed between him and the Washington authorities, but it may be safely assumed that he posted them fully, not only as to the history of recent operations but as to the requirements of the army, forgetting neither the necessity for the draft nor for such other reinforcements as could safely be drawn from other departments.

During the absence of Rawlins, his faithful assistant, Bowers, kept him informed by daily letters, written the last thing at night, in reference to all matters of importance which took place at headquarters after August 1. These letters contain many interesting comments upon current events, and especially upon the operations that were undertaken for the purpose of preventing Lee from detaching further reinforcements to Early in the Valley of Virginia.

On August 2 Bowers reported the losses of the various corps of the army in the operations following the mine explosion as 4,400 men, of whom 1,960 were prisoners; and that the failure of our troops to break through the gap made by the explosion had produced a feeling of gloom and despondency which threatened to paralyze future operations. The next day he reported that he was having unusual trouble on account of whiskey permits. Nearly all the sutlers were asking for such permits, and the embarrassment was increased by the demand of the Chief Quartermaster in behalf of his own sutler, who wanted permission to introduce a large number of cases of liquor and bitters. Permission was refused and Colonel Bowers adds:

> . . . The Quartermaster General thought my course unreasonable and my objections mawkish, youthful sentiment. He said if you were here no objection would be interposed. I told him that he was much mistaken unless you had radically changed your views, that I had derived my education on the subject from you, that he could appeal to

Grant and I would do his bidding, but that so help me God, I never would voluntarily stock this army with liquor. Grant was not accessible and so the matter ended for the time. . . .

Early in the month of August, Grant went to Washington for the purpose of looking after its defence against [Confederate General Jubal] Early's army operating in that direction. Referring to this trip, Bowers wrote Rawlins, August 10:

... I have tried to induce the General to remove Halleck. While he confesses to having been deceived in him and having now his eyes open as to Halleck's position and conduct, he will not bring himself at present to take the step we urge. He has, however, settled Halleck down into a mere staff officer for Stanton. Halleck has no control over troops except as Grant delegates it. He can give no orders and exercise no discretion. Grant now runs the whole machine independently of the Washington directory. I am glad to say he is fully himself, works vigorously and will soon devise another plan for discomfiting the enemies of the country. . . .

Referring to a movement similar to that contemplated when Hancock and Sheridan were sent to Deep Bottom, he wrote, August 12:

... the troops are already in motion and everything is being conducted with great vigor and secrecy ... If the movement succeeds it will give us Richmond. The prospects are fair. Indeed my expectations are up to the highest pitch. After debating the subject seriously I this morning telegraphed you to come up by the first train. I was not only agonizing to have you here but I feared you would think me unfaithful if I neglected to recall you on the eve of important action. I know the General would be rejoiced to have you present but his solicitude for your restoration to health would prevent his sending for you as long as he could. I think when I see you, you will approve my action in telegraphing you to return.

On August 20 he wrote:

. . . The impression is becoming almost universal that for political considerations the President will suspend the draft. If he does, good-bye United States.

The General is fully himself, although in impaired health. . . .

The next day he wrote:

... I never before saw Grant so intensely anxious to do something. He appears determined to try every possible expedient. His plans are good but the great difficulty is that our troops cannot be relied upon. The failure to take advantage of opportunities pains and chafes him beyond anything I have ever before known him to manifest.

Each and every member of the staff daily requests me to present you his kindest remembrances. . . .

On the 25th he wrote:

. . . Anxious as we all are to have you return we trust you will: remain until your health has permanently improved, unless the necessities of the service here make your presence indispensable. In the latter case we shall promptly telegraph you to come. I will show portions of your letter to the General in the morning and tomorrow will give you his views on the subject. I regret to say that Grant has been quite unwell for the past ten days. He feels languid and feeble and is hardly able to keep about, yet he tends to business promptly and his daily walk and conduct are unexceptionable. . . .

This is the last of Bowers' letters, as he was about this time called home on account of his widowed mother's severe illness. But the daily reports from headquarters were continued by Captain Leet, who thenceforth kept Rawlins officially informed of what was taking place not only there but throughout the entire theatre of war.

The situation from the time the Army of the Potomac crossed the James and sat down before Petersburg was a discouraging one. Grant had early in the campaign committed the serious mistake of dividing his cavalry, thus making it easy for the Confederate leader to use his entire mounted force supported by a moving column of infantry, from a central position on shorter or interior lines against our detachments, as well as for the reestablishment and maintenance of his communications with the Confederacy. Rawlins's letters, as well as the Records, show that Sheridan, instead of going on to Hunter, which he might have done, or rejoining the army immediately after the fight at Trevilian's Station, pursued a circuitous route to the White House and then lost eleven days in getting from the White House to the left of Grant's infantry front, when the distance of about fifty miles, including the passage of the James, might have been covered easily in two, or at most three, marches. My discomfiture at the close of the movement against the Danville and Southside Railroads was the direct result of this division of force and of Sheridan's unnecessarily long absence north of the James. Both should have been entirely successful had we been directed to operate together, first north and then south of Richmond.

Immediately after I began the operations confided to me, the army made another failure, which was a great disappointment not only to Rawlins but to every general in it. I refer now to the effort to complete the circumvallation of Petersburg on the south side of the Appomattox, which was an essential part of Grant's general plan. While it was not absolutely necessary to my safe return, both Grant and Meade confidently said that it would be accomplished on the twenty-second and twenty-third of June and that in any event the door would be kept open for me. It will be remembered that all of Grant's efforts to rest the left of his army on the Appomattox were frustrated till April 2, 1865, or for a total period of nine months. The energy and skill with which Lee during that period held and extended his line of defence from the Appomattox below Petersburg to Five Forks, nearly forty miles straight out into the country, and thus covered both the city and its railroad connections, while he kept up his connection with the Confederacy, are among the marvels of modern warfare. They are worthy of the most careful study and consideration by military men. Grant did his best from time to time to break through or turn this line of defence, but after making due allowance for the mistakes and mismanagement which are always liable in military operations, it must be admitted that the efficiency of the army had been so lowered that it seemed unequal to the task before it. Grant had a considerable preponderance of force over Lee throughout the campaign, but withal he did not have sufficient to hold his own works, cover his base, maintain his line of communication, and detach at the same time a force strong enough to turn Lee's right flank completely and drive it from the field, till after the other Confederate forces operating elsewhere in Virginia had been overthrown. Had Rawlins's policy in favor of the prompt and rigid enforcement of the draft and of fetching reinforcements from other departments been earlier and more vigorously carried into effect, it is now conceded that the end might have been reached just so much sooner.

During the excessively hot weather of August and September the army in front of Petersburg remained on the defensive, or its operations were desultory and inconclusive. Consequently many of the officers took leave of absence. Rawlins, who was among the first to go, was again encouraged and anxious to return to duty, but with that thoughtful kindness which never failed him, Grant insisted upon Rawlins remaining away till rest and care should completely restore him. His brother-officers, with most of whom he was a strong favorite, in spite of the favorable reports he sent back, had begun to feel anxious on account of his prolonged absence, though as yet it is far from certain that any of them realized that he was in the clutches of a fatal disease. On September 25, Babcock strongly advised Rawlins by letter to give up the idea of further service in the field and to establish headquarters at Washington. He reinforced this advice by saying that all his friends concurred in the opinion that this would be the best course for him. While Grant's name was not mentioned, it may be regarded as certain that the letter would not have been written without his permission.

But in spite of this solicitude for his health and welfare, Rawlins remained firm, and after nearly three months spent with his family, mostly in the bracing air of the Connecticut highlands, returned to his post of duty at City Point, somewhat improved in strength and looks, but still far from as fit as he ought to have been for military work. While absent he had consulted a specialist in New York, who pronounced his lungs sound, but said he was suffering from chronic bronchitis, which would yield to proper treatment. Dana, who held him in the highest esteem, saw him while passing through Washington, and wrote me that he was sorry to notice in him "the signs of increasing disease." He added ominously: "I fear there is no escape for him." Both Porter and Bowers held similar views and wrote in the same strain, but I am persuaded that none of them yet realized that the indomitable Chief of Staff was hopelessly ill. After his return he took encouragement from every flash of sunlight and every passing breeze, and thenceforth remained steadfastly at his post to the end. But whether from impaired strength and the wish of his Chief to spare him from the drudgery of his position, or from other causes, it is certain that he took less and less part thereafter in the detailed work of the staff.

When he arrived at headquarters the heat of summer had given way to cool and comfortable nights. But it was still a period of great anxiety. While his faithful assistants had kept him fully informed of what was going on during his absence, and the newspapers with what had taken place throughout the entire theatre of military operations, there was still much pertaining to present and future plans which he could learn only at Grant's headquarters. It was painfully apparent to him, as well as to the country at large, that the failure of all efforts to turn, or dislodge, the Confederates from their strongly fortified positions covering Petersburg and Richmond had not only greatly discouraged the Administration, the army, and its leaders, but had correspondingly encouraged the Confederates, and begotten a feeling on the part of Lee that the time had now come for a countermovement against Washington and the country to the northward.

The tacit truce and the feeling of uncertainty were rudely broken by the detachment of Early with a mixed but considerable force of infantry, cavalry and artillery to move first into the Valley of Virginia and thence across the Potomac against the National Capital. The Confederate advance was soon discovered, and the country was at once alive with apprehension. Gold, which was already high in terms of greenbacks and National bank currency, rose rapidly. The disastrous failure of the campaign against Lynchburg had shaken the confidence of the Administration in Hunter's capacity as a leader. Halleck, the Chief of Staff, was in Grant's absence its main dependence, but the public had no confidence in him, While there were plenty of troops within reach, there was no one at hand to command or lead them efficiently, consequently Early's advance met with but little serious opposition until it encountered and defeated the unfortunate Lew Wallace at the crossing of the Monocacy.

As the danger became more and more apparent, the Sixth Corps and one division of cavalry were detached from the Army of the Potomac and hurried by transport to Washington. Sheridan was shortly afterwards assigned to the command and at once called for another division of cavalry. All the troops within reach, or that could be spared from other departments, were ordered to the point of danger. Meanwhile Early, who was a cautious as well as a resolute commander, after reaching the outer fortifications of Washington, where he first got wind of the real storm gathering against him, began his retreat, without tarrying to strike home for victory. After a few days he was safe behind the Blue Ridge.

But Sheridan was now in the field, though it is to be observed that that vigorous officer took hold but cautiously at first. The stakes were great, but as this was his first independent command, he naturally felt the importance of making no mistake. Gathering his forces as rapidly as possible, but manoeuvring them cautiously, two months and more passed away without a serious engagement. The country began to doubt the propriety of giving so young a man as Sheridan so important a command. Gold, which was the country's military barometer, rose to a point never reached before. The mine explosion and the assault at Petersburg were everywhere regarded as a disastrous and expensive failure, all aggressive operations had come to an ominous standstill, and the feeling of gloom and despondency which had settled on the country were accentuated by Sheridan's caution, till Grant finally went in person to the Valley and told him to "go in!"

The battle of Winchester, resulting, as it did, in a complete victory over Early, which was followed by the battle of Cedar Creek and the ultimate destruction of Early's army, restored public confidence and, what was still better, enabled Grant later to gather up and concentrate in front of Petersburg an overwhelming force with which to move against Lee and his dwindling army.

Rawlins, being absent for much of the time, had but little to do with the preliminary dispositions that led to these important results. He returned to headquarters at City Point on October 3, and the next day wrote to his wife in Connecticut as follows:

... I arrived here last evening at 7 P M.

... The General goes to Washington today to see if he cannot hurry up the reinforcements for this army. The situation here is more than flattering. All we want is a few thousand more men to enable us to strike a blow that will tell and tell to the death of the Rebellion. I find here every convenience for my comfort, a room with a grate in it, neatly fixed up for my occupation. The fact is I could have no more convenience in the city of Washington than I have here.

My cold is a little improved but I fear a little the dampness of the weather. A few days will test my ability to remain here. . . .

City Point,

October 7, 1864

. . . . General Wilson has been recommended for a brevet major general and ordered to Sherman to command his cavalry. It was or is necessary that he have such rank to enable him to command, for most of the brigadiers out with Sherman are his superiors in rank. . . .

City Point, October 8, 1864. . . . Yesterday in company with Colonel [Ely] Parker and my friend, Mr. Felt of Galena, I went to General Butler's front, arriving there just at the conclusion of the fight, but before the excitement and confusion consequent after an attack, had subsided. ...

General Grant has not yet returned. We look for him today and unless the weather was too heavy last night for his boat to run on the bay, he will most certainly be here.

Troops are arriving very slowly. How long it will be before we are ready to make a determined move against Richmond I am unable to say. A heavy and organized force will perhaps reach here during the ensuing week. If it arrives we shall not remain long idle, and stirring news may be expected from this quarter. I am getting along quite comfortably. The weather is dry and fine but my cough has not left me although my appetite and digestion are good. . . .

City Point,

October 10, 1864

. . . . Hood has adopted a bold plan of campaign. He has abandoned every point south and struck out with his whole army northward. On the 9th he was crossing the Coosa River twelve miles south of Rome, which is far north of Atlanta. He was moving westward evidently with the view of getting onto the Mobile & Ohio Railroad, in the State of Mississippi, now in operation to Corinth, or to move towards the Ohio River via Nashville. I cannot myself see other than great disaster to him, if Sherman pursues him as is his character to pursue. Of course this movement was unexpected and makes even Grant scratch his head. But with the rebels it is desperation, and even despairing as they are, nothing but an underestimate of Sherman's forces could have induced them to undertake it. Sherman is strong enough to hold Atlanta and move a sufficient force to defeat Hood, for as he nears the Tennessee River he gathers up many men on the line of the railroad and also comes closer to his supplies.

Here all is quiet and will be until reinforcements arrive which we are daily expecting. In the last ten days a little upwards of seven thousand reinforcements have joined us. So you see less than a thousand a day come forward. But we will have here before Monday some of the old organized and reliable heroes of the war. . . .

City Point,

October 12, 1864

. . . . General Dodge of the Western Army is here. It does one's heart good to meet one from the army that has made such a bright record for its country's honor and its own fame. I can shake the hands of these veterans and heroes with something of the thrill of joy and pride that pervades my being when I take hold of the hand of my own dear wife after months of absence . . .

General Quimby, formerly of the old army, is also here. He is, however, not in the service at present, having long since resigned. Major General Doyle of the English service is here. He is the least English and most American of any Englishman I have ever met. He sympathizes with us in our struggle to maintain our governmental authority, and furthermore he believes we will succeed. . . .

City Point,

October 13, 1864

No news of any importance from any quarter . . . On the 10th General Grant upon my putting the unreliableness and insubordination of Rosecrans clearly before his mind, and showing him that should Hood get well up in Tennessee, he would have great difficulty in getting troops from Rosecrans to help resist Hood, he telegraphed to Washington and asked to have Rosecrans removed and someone sent out there who would take at once the offensive and defeat or at least drive Price clean out of the State, and on the 11th he sent up the name of General Crook as the one to relieve Rosecrans. Whether this order will be made I cannot say, but I deem it most important to the public service that it should be made.

What course Sherman will pursue now that Hood has thrown himself north of him, so as to threaten his communications, is not fully determined, but if he carries out the plan he proposed to General Grant, and which was approved by General Grant, conditioned that Thomas had force enough to hold the line of the Tennessee, why you may look for Sherman within a few weeks to come out at some one of the great Atlantic or Gulf cities. This of course you will keep to yourself . . .

I learn from a letter of Rowley to Colonel Parker, that Lemon has enlisted, so has Obediah Taylor. This is the spirit that animates the Western country and makes Western troops invincible —the spirit which sends young men of first standing and respectability to the field to fill up the thinned ranks of our veteran regiments. Jarradd writes me from California that he is coming on here in February and will enter the service as a private. So you see our children will not be ashamed to hear the mention of their family name in connection with this bloody strife. . . .

City Point,

October 15, 1864

. ... We are expecting Secretary Stanton here tomorrow to confer with the General upon the field of operations for all the armies. No news has been had for several days from Sherman. I suppose, however, that he is following up Hood, who at last accounts was at Dalton on the railroad north of Atlanta about one hundred miles, and south of Chattanooga thirty-eight. It may be that Sherman has cut loose and gone down through Georgia, but I think not. Too fine an opportunity presents itself for the entire destruction of Hood's army for Sherman not to avail himself of it. . . .

City Point,

October 16, 1864

. ... We have here today Secretary Stanton, the Quartermaster General, the Commissary General and the Surgeon General, also the Secretary of the Treasury and many of the public men of the country. I suppose they will leave tomorrow.

Mr. Antrobus, the artist whom you met at Chicago and who painted the General's portrait, is also with us. He is glad that he did not then get a sitting of me for the reason that I now look so much fleshier than then. I was weighed today and find that I am ten pounds heavier than my usual weight which is 155 pounds. I now weigh 165, and am daily getting heavier. My cough is also better. . . .

City Point,

October 18, 1864

. . . . Never since I used to work on the farm have I had such an appetite as now. My digestion is good and I have no doubt of my recovery. News from Sherman about the same as yesterday. Everything here very quiet and will remain so for some days.

Mr. Antrobus is painting a portrait of me for Russell Jones. I have already gone through one sitting. . . .

City Point,

October 19, 1864

. . . . Despatches from Harpers Ferry say that from five o'clock this morning and up to late this afternoon heavy and continuous cannonading was heard near Strasburg, which we suppose was a battle going on between Sheridan and Longstreet who succeeded Early. We feel great confidence if such is the case that Sheridan will defeat him. A few hours will fix the fact whatever it may be . . .

Hood has lost more men than Sherman in this recent move and his men must feel more despondent than ever, now that all the promises made them by Hood and Jefferson Davis have proven so fruitless to them. I wish we had this army of Lee's in as bad condition as the army of Hood necessarily must be.

Everything here is very quiet. Men arrive very slowly. We have received the sad intelligence today of the death of Major General [David Bell] Birney of this army. He was a noble, true man. The country will lament his loss, and the army feel it as almost irreparable. . . .

City Point,

October 20, 1864

. . . . Today has been very fine and brings us news of Sheridan's glorious victory of yesterday, snatched as it were from the jaws of disastrous defeat. Early attacked our forces early yesterday morning, near Strasburg, Va., and succeeded in turning our position and driving our whole line in confusion a distance of four miles, capturing from us twenty pieces of artillery, when Sheridan arrived on the field (he having been to Washington) took command of our retreating forces and by his masterly generalship brought order out of the confusion, repelled a fierce attack of Early and attacking him in turn routed and defeated him, capturing forty-three pieces of artillery, many prisoners and a large number of wagons and ambulances. The losses on both sides were heavy, but our victory was complete.

Everything here is quiet, no news from Sherman today, nor have we any from Missouri. I have been urging the removal of General Rosecrans ever since my return, and General Grant has asked to have it done, but the thing hangs fire for want of someone to take his place. Rosecrans seems to desire that Price should remain in Missouri. I judge so from his inactivity, for since Price entered the State there has been no hour but Rosecrans had sufficient men to defeat and drive him from it. . . .

City Point,

October 21, 1864

. . . . More detailed report from Sheridan of his victory on the 19th instant increases the number of pieces captured to over fifty, and also informs us of driving the enemy's rear guard from Fisher's Hill.

News from Sherman is to the effect that Hood is rapidly retreating to the South and he is following. Missouri news is very unsatisfactory, as to all save one thing, and that is the unfitness and incompetency of Rosecrans for his present command. Whether any order will soon be made to relieve him I cannot tell. General Grant has certainly done his duty in the premises and cannot be held responsible for any failures in that quarter, even if it should be the blockading of the Mississippi River again. This latter, however, cannot well happen for General G. H. Thomas is looking to its safety with the troops he has in Tennessee. . . .

City Point,

October 23, 1864

. . . . Another beautiful day has closed. No news of interest save in regard to General Sherman's intended campaign, the details of which I fear to write lest my letter might fail to reach its destination. All quiet here. Sheridan followed the enemy to Mt. Jackson in the Shenandoah Valley. . . .

City Point,

October 25, 1864

. . . . Today has been clear and cold. No news of note, except that the Mexican Minister Romero from President Juarez, is on a visit here. He is accompanied by a major general and a colonel of the Mexican service, and was received in the manner prescribed for the reception of foreign ministers. How it will be with the Minister Maximilian sends, I cannot say.

News from Sherman is satisfactory. All progressing well with him. . .
.

City Point,

October 26, 1864

. ... We have had no news from Missouri nor from Sheridan. A despatch from Sherman shows all well, with abundant supplies in the country for his army. Indications are that Hood has not yet abandoned his intention of invading Tennessee. Proposed movements of Sherman will, however, without doubt, compel Hood to look to affairs south. Otherwise the heaviest blow yet dealt will fall in that direction.

Here all is quiet save the preparations that have been going on for a movement tomorrow morning against the Southside Railroad, which I have but little doubt will bring on a great battle, one perhaps decisive of the fate of Petersburg. Should the railroad, however, be found too strongly fortified, we shall not risk an attack. The General and staff go to the front tomorrow morning. I shall of course go with the party. In God who has thus far protected us from danger, I place my trust. . . .

City Point,

October 28, 1864

. ... We got back last night but I was so tired, I put off writing till this morning. We were along the line of our march, to the very front of our advance and up to half-past three P M. of yesterday had found no place favorable to us, for an attack. Being so far separated from our base of supplies, and not having what we conceived to be a sufficient force to warrant cutting loose from it altogether, we determined to return to our entrenchments. The General and staff started for City Point. Up to the time named, there were no indications of a battle, except some artillery firing to which we were perhaps as much exposed as any others. Although the shot and shell came exceedingly near, no one was hurt. About an hour after we left, however, the enemy made an attack on Hancock and a very heavy battle followed in which neither party gained anything of permanent advantage. The losses on both sides were heavy. We, however, repulsed the enemy and held possession of the field at dark, but during the night commenced to retire.

News from Missouri is cheering. General Price has been severely defeated and General Marmaduke and another general captured. Price lost ten pieces of artillery and over a thousand prisoners. . . .

. . . Full reports of the battle fought yesterday afternoon show the result to be a splendid victory for us. Hancock retained his position, repulsed the enemy and held possession of the battle field until midnight when he commenced his withdrawal in pursuance of orders issued to him before the battle. The loss in killed and wounded on either side is not yet stated but we captured 910 prisoners and lost but 60. Among the rebels killed was Brigadier General Dearing. On the north side of the river, however, we did not fare so well. General Butler, although acting under positive orders not to attack the enemy in fortified position, did so attack and lost for us full one thousand men, killed, wounded and prisoners, without any corresponding damage, if damage at all to the enemy. I am free to say I fear the continuance of General Butler in command will someday work disaster of a serious character to our arms. But General Grant has had to deal with such men from the beginning and has succeeded. I therefore have hopes he may succeed with this one.

General Halleck is expected here tomorrow on official business the nature of which has not yet been communicated to the General.

I have been urging General Grant to bring here at once fifteen thousand of the veteran troops of the West, to help end this campaign against Richmond. I have said to the General that if half the pains and energy had been shown in getting troops here that have been taken in sending them unnecessarily to Missouri, to drive off Price, we could have broken the enemy's lines yesterday and held in our hands today the long coveted prize of Richmond. He listens favorably and I have hopes he will adopt my views. I am still quite well. . . .

City Point,

October 30, 1864

. . . . No news here of any kind. That from Sherman is that Hood is heading towards Middle Tennessee via Decatur, but trusts that Thomas, with the force he has sent him, will be able to prevent Hood's advance north of the Tennessee River.

All orders to General Rosecrans for troops of Sherman's command to be returned to Tennessee, where they are likely to be greatly needed, having failed to get them, I have received orders and instructions from General Grant to proceed at once to St. Louis, with full authority in the premises to enforce obedience to these orders. I leave here this morning. The trip I do not much like, and were it not for the confidence the General has in my ability to discharge the duties imposed, over any other member of his staff, I would get myself excused. But the importance to the public service, of the faithful execution of my orders, will tend to the interest of my going, and will lighten in a great degree the wearisomeness of it.

I shall perhaps be absent two weeks, and unless I find a letter from you at Washington as I go west, will not hear from you until my return. Major General Halleck is here and I go with him on a special boat to Washington. . . .

St. Louis, Mo.,

November 3, 1864

. . . . Until today, I have not had a moment for writing since I left Washington, which place I left on the 31st ultimo. Without missing a connection I arrived here this morning at one o'clock in as good health and spirits as when I started, save a slight cold which does not trouble me much. I have not yet seen General Rosecrans. He is absent from the city but a despatch from him states he will return this evening. Until he does, or at least, until I see him, I shall be unable to state when I shall leave for City Point.

I have met two or three of my old friends of the Army of the Tennessee, among them General Grierson of cavalry celebrity. They were delighted to see me. My mission will I trust greatly aid the success of General Grierson's trip here, he having come for the express purpose of trying to get General Rosecrans to return to Memphis the cavalry of West Tennessee, which are a part of the troops, I am also here with orders to send back. . . .

St. Louis, Nov. 4, 1864

. ... I met General Rosecrans this morning and transacted with him the business on which I was sent. I was delighted to find that in pursuance of orders previously telegraphed to him, he was moving the troops for which I came here, to the river for embarkment. It saved me a long and perhaps perilous journey to the interior of the State, which is infested with bands of guerillas. General Rosecrans received me with great cordiality and assures me that the orders I brought to him from General Grant shall be promptly complied with. I also saw this afternoon General A. J. Smith, who confirms all that General Rosecrans said to me of his (Rosecrans) disposition to obey the orders of General Grant. My orders were to remain here until the troops for which I came were embarked and off but as matters were promising so well when I came here, and as I am assured they will continue so, I deem it unnecessary to remain longer, and I have so telegraphed the General. Unless he thinks differently I shall leave here for City Point on Sunday evening. . . .

St. Louis,

Nov. 5, 1864

. ... I have been very busy this evening getting off orders to troops and despatches to General Grant, and was in hopes I would be able to leave here tomorrow, but I have learned some things that may detain me two or three days longer. I still hope to get away but I fear I shall not.

I was out to see Mrs. Grant at her father's. She is in excellent health and inquired most affectionately after you and your welfare. She is very anxious to have you visit her at Philadelphia and go with her to City Point on a visit to the General and myself. We will discuss this when we meet which I hope will be in New York Thursday or Friday. . . .

It should be noted that the detachment of my division from the Army in front of Petersburg to join Sheridan in the Valley, and my

232

subsequent detail to command the cavalry of Sherman's Military Division in the Southwest, separated me entirely from Rawlins, with or near whom I had been serving for over two years. As before related, I first met him in Northern Mississippi and during the Vicksburg and Chattanooga campaigns was his constant companion and intimate friend. As Engineer and Inspector on the same staff, till promoted and ordered to Washington, I knew both his daily life and his inmost thoughts. After taking the field in Virginia, with the cavalry, I saw him often and enjoyed his confidence without break or intermission; but from the time I left the Army of the Potomac on August 5, 1864, I did not meet him again till after the war had ended. Although he was never a ready correspondent, it was our custom to write to each other on subjects of common interest from that time till the date of his death. During my service in Tennessee, Alabama, and Georgia, and especially after Sherman had begun his "March to the Sea" and Hood had begun his invasion of Middle Tennessee, I kept him fully informed of all important matters in regard to which I felt that he and the Lieutenant General should have accurate and disinterested information. But my correspondence with the headquarters of the army was not confined to Rawlins. Porter, Babcock, and Bowers, at first, and Badeau afterwards, participated in it, and the information which I sent was, when deemed necessary, communicated also to Grant. In this way he had an independent source of information, especially in reference to the disposition and the preparation of the troops, the condition of the country and the roads, and the character and efficiency of the leadings officers, their relative deserts, as well as their claims for recognition and promotion.

As occasion offered I pointed out to Rawlins that Sherman had taken the flower and pick of the army on the "March to the Sea" and had left Thomas with the dismounted cavalry and the poorer infantry, which was widely scattered, to make head against Hood and his veterans, whom Sherman had left behind, still aggressive and unbeaten. I also pointed out the danger of defeat, and the urgent necessity for the concentration of all the forces available in Tennessee, Kentucky, and Missouri, and especially for the remount of the cavalry.

Whatever may have been the confidence of others in immediate success, Rawlins indulged in no illusions. He appeared to see from the first that Thomas might be overthrown before he could gather his widely scattered forces together and weld them into an efficient army, and it was doubtless for this reason that Grant sent his Chief of Staff to Missouri with full authority to hurry the idle troops from that department to Nashville for the purpose of reinforcing the army in front of that place. In spite of all Rawlins could do, however, in spite of all the promises made by Rosecrans, and in spite of the anxiety of A. J. Smith, the hardy and aggressive commander of the Sixteenth Army Corps, that corps was nearly a month, or four times longer than necessary, in moving from St. Louis to the scene of action. Rawlins never performed a more useful service than when he hastened the concentration of the forces with which Thomas finally won his splendid victory at Nashville. Rawlins, like the rest, was impatient at the delay in overwhelming Hood, but having far more faith, as we have seen, "in the infallibility of numbers than in the infallibility of generals," he took no rest till he had sent to Thomas every available man within reach.

The careful reader will not fail to note the many important suggestions contained in the extracts from Rawlins's correspondence; yet their bearing upon controverted historical points is not always clear. It has long been known that he was not in favor of Sherman's starting on his "March to the Sea," while Hood was marching northward, and this is now placed beyond controversy by what Rawlins wrote while the matter was under discussion. He thought that Sherman, having with him the bulk of the good troops of his Military Division, should follow Hood and bring him to battle, rather than permit him to march unmolested against the widely scattered forces left to defend the territory previously taken from the enemy. He rightly thought that Hood's march first to the west and then to the north offered a fine opportunity for Sherman to throw himself upon his rear, cut off his retreat, and destroy his army. That this would have been the policy of a Napoleon there can be but little question. It is also evident that when the intentions of Hood to move through Middle Tennessee against Nashville became apparent, Rawlins at once became the strenuous advocate of strengthening Thomas and making him invincible by sending to his assistance all the good troops that could be spared from other departments. This was clearly in accordance with the simplest maxims of war, and Grant could not have paid Rawlins a greater compliment than to send him on this mission. That it was necessary is abundantly shown by the fact that in spite of its urgency and the orders given to Rosecrans on November 3 and prior thereto, the Sixteenth Corps did not reach Nashville in time to participate in the battle of Franklin, which was fought November 30, while Grierson's cavalry, although the wounded Upton had been sent to Memphis to hurry it to its destination, did not join the corps in Northern Alabama till after Hood's army had been defeated and driven south of the Tennessee River.

When it is remembered that the national troops attached to the Military Division of the Mississippi amounted to something like 300,000 men "present and absent," and that counting those with Sherman and those gathered up by Thomas to make head against Hood, with his unbeaten army between them, there was scarcely 120,000 effective men with the colors in the entire Military Division, it will be seen that Rawlins, who knew the dangers of the situation perfectly, had abundant grounds for apprehension. It is now evident that the country was justly alarmed, and that Hood's well-directed campaign failed solely because he had neither men nor resources sufficient to make it a success. Strategically his plans were not only brilliant but in accordance with correct principles. They failed because his battalions, brigades, and divisions lacked weight, while a scarcity of supplies caused him to lose thirty days on the banks of the Tennessee before beginning his Northern march. It was during this period that Schofield succeeded with the heterogeneous forces under his command in delaying the earlier stages of the Confederate advance, and at last, through the reinforcements sent by Rawlins and the work done in concentrating and remounting the cavalry, that Thomas finally found himself at the head of an organized army strong enough to defeat Hood in the great battle at Nashville, on December 15-16, and to destroy his exhausted and decimated army as it retreated, broken and despondent, during midwinter towards Central Alabama.

When these facts are considered, it may well be admitted that Rawlins, who was the first to propose the transfer of fifteen thousand veteran troops from the West to assist in closing the campaign against Lee, was, as usual, giving sound advice. It should also be remembered that the Sixteenth Corps belonged to the Army of the Tennessee, and after participating in Banks's ill-starred campaign on the Red River, where there was no real call for its service, was sent to Missouri. It is this circumstance that gives point and force to Rawlins's declaration on October 28 that "if half the pains and energy had been shown in getting troops" to the Army of the Potomac "that have been taken in sending them unnecessarily to Missouri ... we could have broken the enemy's lines yesterday and held in our hands today the long-coveted prize of Richmond."

That Rawlins's counsel was conclusive in this case is shown by the fact that as soon as Thomas had driven the Confederate army out of Tennessee, Grant ordered the transfer of troops from the West to the East in great numbers. And it was this wise measure, made feasible and safe solely by the great victory at Nashville, that enabled him to bring the war to a close by concurrent movements the next spring. It is to be noted, however, that Grant was to the last impatient of Thomas's deliberation, and wanted him to continue active operations through the winter, while he permitted Sheridan to remain idle at the same time in the Valley of Virginia, with no enemy whatever confronting him.

This is not the place to argue the case in behalf of Thomas. It was his fate to be doubted and misunderstood from the first, and when his relations with Grant, as they are elsewhere pointed out, are considered, it will not be thought strange that he was left practically unemployed while younger and perhaps more deferential men were permitted to finish the great work of overthrowing the Confederacy and reestablishing the Union. That Rawlins in some degree shared the prejudice of his chief cannot be denied, nor can it be denied that he was partial to men of more aggressive temper and less formal habits than the stately and deliberate Thomas. There is no room to doubt that he admired the erratic Sherman and the impetuous

Sheridan more than he did the more formal Meade, the more brilliant Warren, or the more imperturbable Thomas.

VIEWS ON SHERMAN'S CAMPAIGN

AFTER finishing the business that took him to the West, Rawlins went East and rested a few days with his family at Danbury, with apparent benefit to his health, but with real disadvantage to his influence at headquarters. While he was far from being a loquacious man, he never sought to disguise from his brother officers his opinions on questions of either personal OR public policy. His views in regard to Sherman's proposed campaign, which in its earlier stages was far from being settled in favor of the Atlantic coast, but for a while confessedly looked towards the Gulf of Mexico, were well known to the rest of the staff. They may have been approved for a time by some of the officers, but his absence from headquarters and the necessity he was under of passing through Washington both going to and returning from the West, gave an opportunity, after it was known that Sherman as well as Thomas had succeeded, to circulate the report that Rawlins had been bitterly opposed to the "March to the Sea." It is personally known, however, that Rawlins was cognizant of the first suggestion leading to that march, and gave it his unqualified approval, but there was nothing in the condition of affairs when it was first made, that contemplated the necessity of meeting such a counter-campaign as Hood afterwards conducted. It will be apparent that the defeat of that general and the destruction of his army settled many military problems, and greatly simplified those that yet remained to be settled.

Before leaving this subject, it may be well to call attention to the following quotation from Grant's *Memoirs,* published years afterwards:

> ... I was in favor of Sherman's plan (for the March to the Sea) from the time it was first submitted to me. My Chief of Staff (Rawlins), however, was very bitterly opposed to it, and as I learned subsequently, finding that he could not move me, he appealed to the authorities at Washington to stop it.

I have purposely delayed the discussion of this statement till all Rawlins's letters concerning this period were within reach. They show conclusively both the ground of his opposition and the extent to which it was carried. They make it evident that his anxiety related solely to the timeliness of the proposed movement and the advisability of delaying it till the defeat of Hood could be counted upon with absolute certainty. When all the circumstances connected with the double campaign of Sherman and Hood in opposite directions, and the consequent anxieties which the Government and the country passed through during the months of October, November, and December of that year, are reviewed, it must be admitted that Rawlins's apprehensions were well founded, and that his views were supported by the soundest principles of the military art. It should also be remembered that the statements of the *Memoirs* were not formulated till twenty years after the end of the war, and that they are not supported by any corroborative evidence whatever. If Grant personally wrote the lines of the *Memoirs* bearing on this subject, it is altogether probable that he did so on the report of others, who must have had it themselves upon hearsay. The only other supposition consistent with the established facts of the case is that Grant's memory, like that of his informant, dulled, as might well have been the case, by the lapse of time, may have confounded the well-known opposition of the Chief of Staff to the time for commencing the "March to the Sea," till the necessary measures had been taken to resist Hood's advance, with the statement that "he was very bitterly opposed" to the march itself.

It is also due to Rawlins to say that I have found no evidence whatever, beyond the simple statement of the *Memoirs,* to support the declaration that he "appealed to the authorities at Washington to stop it." No letter to that effect has ever been published, and hence, if any appeal was ever made to the authorities, it must have been as he was passing through Washington, October 31, 1864, on his way to the West, or as he was returning therefrom to headquarters. There is no evidence that he saw any of the authorities on either of these occasions, but if he did see them, it was doubtless at their instance, in which case it would have been clearly his duty when questioned to give his views frankly and honestly both as to the facts and as to the military policy which should have been based upon them. There was nothing to be concealed in all this. The entire country knew the general situation and was greatly alarmed by Sherman's abandonment of the pursuit of Hood, by the aggressive attitude of the latter, and by the divided and scattered condition of the forces left at the disposal of Thomas for the defence of Middle Tennessee. It was one of the great crises of the war, and now that it is long since over, and we know how well-founded his apprehensions were, we may well pardon the Chief of Staff for whatever grain of truth there may have been in the statement of the *Memoirs*. That nothing more serious than this was ever brought against him shows conclusively that he was a man of good judgment and sterling worth.

Rawlins arrived at City Point November 15, and the next day wrote to his wife as follows:

... I arrived here last evening having left New York on Sunday evening.

. . . The General is satisfied with my execution of his orders in Missouri. How delightful was my little stay in Danbury. . . .

City Point,

Nov. 16, 1864

. . . . Brigadier General T. Kilby Smith is here—so is Dr. Kittoe. General Grant goes tomorrow to Burlington, N. J., to see Mrs. Grant. Colonel Badeau accompanies him. Colonels Porter and Duff are both absent on duty, one at Indianapolis and the other at Louisville. . . .

City Point,

November 17, 1864

. . . . General Grant accompanied by Colonels Comstock and Badeau and Captain Robinett, started today for Washington and Burlington. I hope he will keep all straight during his absence, which will last till about the 22nd instant. General Sherman was to leave Atlanta yesterday on his Southern campaign. I have every hope he may succeed to his fullest expectations, but have many fears that he may fail. That he will damage the enemy terribly I have no question, but whether he will cause such commotion in the Confederacy as to loosen their hold on Richmond, is not so certain. And regarding Richmond's fall as of the first importance to our arms, I can but feel solicitous at every movement of troops that looks not directly in that direction.

The country need feel no uneasiness as to the movements of Beauregard for Thomas has a much larger army than Beauregard, and should if the latter persists in pushing North, defeat him. . . .

City Point,

Nov. 18, 1864

. ... It began raining at dark and I fear it will continue some time. Last night the enemy captured some pickets of General Butler's command in front of Bermuda Hundred; the number has not yet been reported, but they will probably not exceed one hundred. No news whatever from other quarters, nor have I heard from the General since he left.

At this moment heavy musketry firing is heard in front of Bermuda Hundred. It is very dark and it is not at all unlikely that the enemy under cover of it have attempted to break through our lines. Such an attempt has been looked for and I suppose General Butler's troops are in readiness to repel it. . . .

City Point,

Nov. 19, 1864

. . . . Today has been excessively stormy. It has rained with little intermission since it set in last night. General Butler, Senator Wilson, ex-Governor Gardner and other gentlemen of distinction were here today. The firing in front of Bermuda Hundred last night was our pickets attempting to recover the line the enemy drove them from last night, but they did not succeed.

No news from the enemy's lines in this vicinity. We have had no newspapers from Richmond since one dated the 16th. It is with much anxiety we now look for them, for in them we hope to see something of Sherman's whereabouts. He was to have started from Atlanta on Wednesday morning last and this is the fourth day of his march. Moving as he does many miles must now intervene between him and his starting point. May providence prosper and preserve him is my earnest prayer, and may the road, though marked with ruin as it will be, along which he passes, prove in the end the pathway to Peace.

General Wilson is at Nashville organizing the cavalry of the Military Division of the Mississippi. I was in hopes he would accompany General Sherman, for in so doing he would have secured his confirmation as a brigadier general, and perhaps as brevet major general too. As it is he may have difficulty. I hope, however, he will receive his confirmation for he is a brave and deserving officer. . . .

City Point,

Nov. 20, 1864

. . . . The rain continues with no indications of ceasing soon. Richmond papers of yesterday show that Sherman has commenced his campaign from Atlanta southward and that he has reached Jonesboro. They also show that an attack from the armies here is daily expected. From other sources we have certain information of the return to Richmond of Kershaw's division, which was with Early in the Valley. This would indicate the intention on the part of the enemy to withdraw from further offensive operations in the Shenandoah Valley.

The General being absent leaves us here without news from the West, other than that which reaches us through the newspapers all of which you see before we do. All quiet along our lines, and will perhaps remain so for some time to come.

I see by the papers gold has gone down. I shall write to Colonel Hilyer to purchase $200 more [about $3,000 in 2015] and send it to you by express.

Headquarters, in the absence of the General, is quite a lonesome place. The only excitement we have is the news we get from Richmond papers and scouts, and digesting and sending it to the General and to Washington. . . .

City Point,

Nov. 21, 1864

. . . . The rain still continues. Richmond papers of this date state that Sherman was on the 19th, within thirty miles of Macon, that great consternation existed on the first news of his approach, but they were now becoming quiet and preparing to meet him. The papers editorially urge the people in the line of Sherman's advance to destroy everything in the way of supplies. Marching with the rapidity that Sherman marches they will in this, be able to do but little to delay him. Should he hesitate, or delay, they might greatly jeopard his advance by the destruction of everything in his front. This much, however, in that event he could and would do, namely, turn either to the right or left and get supplies or compel a general destruction of everything in the country.

There is no news here of any interest. All is quiet and the rain is pattering as it has pattered for several days and nights on the tent flies.

No news reaches us from the west. The fact is the weather is so unfavorable for army operations that I do not anticipate anything of importance from any quarter for some days, save what we gather from the Richmond papers in regard to Sherman's movements.

I have just received a despatch from General Grant dated today at New York City. This somewhat surprises me for when he left here it was his intention to be back tomorrow. Now I do not know when he will return. It makes, however, little difference, so far as there is anything to do here, because of the prevailing storm, but I would like to have him here for it is not with these armies as it was with the armies of the West. There any orders that went from his headquarters over my signature were the same as if the General were present.

Everything is going smoothly and quietly. . . .

City Point,

Nov. 22, 1864

. ... We must be patient, and content our minds to the performance of the duties demanded by the times in which we live. The privations consequent upon our being so much separated, and at times of sickness too, when we could be of so much comfort to each other were we together, we will bear and submit to without complaint, knowing that in doing so we are but fulfilling the requirements made upon hundreds of thousands of our countrymen and countrywomen, and feeling too in so doing we are but filling the measure of service we owe our country.

Richmond papers of this date have but little news. They state that Sherman was yesterday eighteen miles from Macon. No news from the West. All quiet here. A despatch just received from the General dated at Washington says he will be back to this place Thursday.

I am I suppose what might be called a man in perfect health. In all the stormy weather we have had I have not felt or had the slightest cold, and my appetite and digestion are perfect. . . .

City Point,

November 23, 1864

. . . . Today has been clear and cold—a most delightful change from the cloudy and rainy days that have preceded it the only additional news from Sherman through Richmond papers is that he was near Macon on the 21st instant and a battle at that place was imminent, and also that he had cut the railroad between Atlanta and Macon, twenty-five miles from the latter place. This looks very favorable to his success. The Richmond papers of today have not yet come in. Deserters report that a South Carolina brigade and two North Carolina regiments have been sent from Petersburg probably to Georgia to meet Sherman. With this exception there is no news here. From the West we have no report.

I see by the *New York Herald* that a member of General Grant's staff at the complimentary serenade to the Governor elect of New York, appeared and very neatly and delicately advertised the General's great modesty, by stating and requesting that no notice of the General's presence in the city be taken by the papers, till the next Tuesday thereafter. Now I have high respect and regard for modesty but this thing of making too much of it I deprecate exceedingly. I know the General is a modest man but if he allows it to be proclaimed too loudly in immediate advance of his presenting himself, the credit he has for it will fast depreciate. What object he could have in desiring the papers not to mention his presence in New York, I cannot conceive. It certainly was not that he would prevent people from calling upon him, for the fact that he was at the Astor House being known at all would spread sufficiently among those of that city, who since his congratulation of the President upon the double victory achieved in the peacefulness of the recent election, would consider it an honor to call on him, to occupy his entire attention in receiving them during his short stay. If it was that the rebel leaders might suppose him at City Point, it was entirely unnecessary, for they had already the news of his absence and drew the deduction therefrom that the expected attack on their lines would not soon be made. The General from his long labors was entitled to respite and rest, and if he desired to visit New York, he should have gone there and not permitted his military secretary, Colonel Badeau, to ostentatiously announce his desire that his presence should not be noticed. This whole thing is not General Grant, but solely Colonel Badeau.

Colonel Bowers started for Washington this morning. He will be absent for perhaps a week.

I look for General Grant tomorrow, which is Thanksgiving Day. We have received several Turkeys for our dinner, and the good people of New York and vicinity have sent here about eighty thousand pounds of turkey for distribution, and they are now being divided among our men. This remembrance of them by their friends at home is truly encouraging. Some of them may not get any but the greater majority will. . . .

City Point,

November 24, 1864

. Today has been most delightfully beautiful and everyone seemed to enjoy Thanksgiving most heartily. I am sorry to say, however, that one boat containing a portion of the turkeys for the soldiers' dinner got aground and was detained till late today, but those who were by this cause deprived of their turkey for dinner will have it tomorrow, and except the little annoyance, the disappointment and the causes, it will be just as well. Turkey in camp is a luxury all can appreciate . . .

The following is as nearly as I can repeat it a proclamation from General Beauregard and shows the trepidation he is in:

"Corinth, Miss., Nov. 18, 1864. ... To the people of Georgia: Arise to the defence of your native soil. Rally around your patriotic Governor and gallant soldiers; destroy all bridges and block up all roads in Sherman's front, flanks and rear, and he will starve in your midst. Be confident, and trust in an over-ruling providence, who will crown your efforts with success. I hasten to join you in the defence of your homes and firesides. P. G. T. Beauregard, General Commanding."

I have written the above as I remember it from reading it once. It may not be exactly correct but is substantially so. This looks as though he would move Hood's army after Sherman, but as information from Thomas places three corps of Hood's army North of the Tennessee, it would seem to be beyond hope of successful pursuit of Sherman.

Richmond papers of today have not yet come to hand. General Grant, and Colonels Porter, Comstock and Badeau and Captain Robinett of his staff, returned this morning all in excellent health except the General who sat up too late last night. Mrs. Grant went with the General to New York. They breakfasted with Colonel Hillyer. . . .

City Point,

Nov. 25, 1864

. . . . Today is clear and fine, all quiet here. News from Thomas is meagre. Hood appears to be advancing towards Nashville, with three army corps, but he moves slowly. Thomas is sufficiently strong for defensive purposes and will soon have his forces so concentrated as to take the offensive should Hood not attack him.

Nothing new from Sherman save confirmation of the report that the capital of Georgia is in his possession, and that he has cut the railroads between Augusta and Macon.

The General and all the members of the staff except Colonels Bowers and Duff are at headquarters. The General has written Mrs. Grant to come down here week after next and asked me your address for Mrs. Grant, as she intended or had spoken of inviting you to come with her.

Now I would like very much to have you come, were it not that I disapprove of having officers' wives in camp. It does not look like war to me, to see it heralded throughout the country by the press that the wife of the General and also the wife of his Chief of Staff are at City Point, and would be what I would avoid unless some good end could be subserved by it, besides the item of expense and the disposition of the children during your absence, is something to be considered. However, I leave the matter to your decision, after having stated my views, and whatever it is will meet with my concurrence and approval. . . .

City Point,

Nov. 26, 1864

. . . . Richmond papers of yesterday seem studiously to avoid any reference to Sherman, except a despatch which mentions the fact that his cavalry had been repulsed in its attempt to cross the Oconee River. Their failure to give details of Sherman's movements is construed here to be significant of his success.

News from Thomas is to the effect that Hood is advancing on Columbia, Tennessee, where our forces are being concentrated. General A. J. Smith with his command from St. Louis passed through Nashville on the way to Columbia. There seems to be little doubt now that Hood will give Thomas battle, and if Thomas can get his forces concentrated in time we are confident of victory.

All quiet here, General Hancock today took leave of his old comrades and soldiers of the Second Corps. He goes to Washington to organize a veteran corps to be composed of soldiers who have served out their time and have reenlisted. General Humphreys succeeds him in the command of the Second Corps. He is a brave and fit successor to the heroic Hancock.

Generals Grant, Meade, Warren, Crawford, Ingalls and others went up this morning to General Butler's front and are still there witnessing experiments being made with Greek fire. . . .

City Point,

November 27, 1864

. . . . Around our lines the greatest quiet prevails. Since I wrote last night we have had no news from Sherman or Thomas, and that from Sheridan is to the effect that all is as quiet with him as with us here. Colonel Bowers has returned, and now all of the staff except Colonel Duff are at headquarters.

The steamer *Grey Hound* with General Butler and Admiral Porter on board caught fire today and was burned below Fort Powhattan. No lives were lost. Butler and the Admiral continued their trip to Fort Monroe in a tug boat. . . .

Steamer *M. Martin* off Norfolk, Va.,

November 29, 1864

. . . . General Grant having business with Admiral Porter left City Point this morning accompanied by myself and other staff officers, for Fort Monroe, off which place the Admiral lay in his fine flag ship the *Malvern*. We reached there about three o'clock p m., met the Admiral and General Butler on his ship, transacted the official business, and then as we could just as well get back to City Point by breakfast, by starting for that place at twelve o'clock tonight, the General decided to come down here and attend the theatre, to which place he with all his staff save myself have gone. To have gone there would have afforded me no pleasure. Besides in times like these I do not approve of those to whom the country looks for leadership and guidance through the terrible storm still swelling with unspent fury, going to such places, and shall not myself by going give countenance to it although I might go without any injury to the cause of my country. Still the brave men in front can't have this privilege, if they desired it, and I will not take the benefit of it though the privilege is mine. The look of a thing is sometimes a great deal.

News this morning from Richmond is to the effect that the enemy has sent off either Kershaw's or Field's division to meet Sherman, and indications in front of General Sheridan are that the enemy has withdrawn Gordon's division from Early. Whether he has gone to Richmond or to resist Sherman has not yet been ascertained, probably however the latter is his destination. General Grant has ordered movement of troops to take advantage of this on the part of the enemy. Breckenridge's troops in West Virginia and East Tennessee, from all the information we can gather from Richmond, will be sent, and are now perhaps on the way to reinforce the force opposing Sherman.

Hood in Tennessee is slowly advancing on Thomas but both Sherman and Thomas are supposed to have men enough for the purpose each had in view. Great battles will no doubt soon be fought. May God grant us victory.

The Confederate war steamer *Florida* captured in a Brazilian port sank near Fort Monroe the other day in fifty feet of water. Nothing can be seen of her but her masts. What will be the result of this I do not know. I am decidedly in favor of doing exact justice to the sovereignty of Brazil. This, however, is left to our Secretary of State who has thus far prevented our becoming entangled with foreign powers, and I have full confidence, he will get us through this difficulty and I trust honestly, too.

Richmond papers state that thirteen thousand of our prisoners at Salisbury, N. C., attempted to make their escape on the 24th instant but that artillery was brought to bear upon them and some forty were killed and a large number wounded, when they submitted. I have hopes that many of them got away; poor fellows, my heart bleeds for them when I think of their sufferings. A just God will not always permit this state of things. . . .

City Point, Va.,

Nov. 30, 1864

. ... We reached this point from Norfolk this morning at sunrise. No news from the West today and information from Sherman very meagre. All quiet here.

General John Pope was here today and will perhaps have added to his Department of the Northwest the Departments of Kansas and Missouri. General Grant has recommended this. Generals Hardee and Beauregard are at Augusta, Georgia, and General Bragg with Western troops has left Wilmington for Augusta. So the Confederates have Generals enough if they can find troops enough to give Sherman trouble, but that they have troops enough, we do not believe, and without troops these generals are no match for Sherman. . . .

City Point,

December 1, 1864

. ... I fear my answer to your despatch of this date in regard to your reply to Mrs. Grant about coming to City Point, was not such as you had hoped for, but I could not decide that you should answer affirmatively for the reason that I could not approve of your coming, unless you should yourself decide to come after reading my letter on this subject, written to you last week. You know that when headquarters are established in a city whether in Washington or some Southern one, I will send for you, but not while they are in the field in front of an enemy, and when everything at headquarters should be indicative of readiness for immediate movements should they be required. Besides the orders are against officers wives being with them in camp and I am opposed to their being disregarded at headquarters, while enforcement of them is exacted of officers in the field. If you came you probably would not be able to stay more than one or two days and the fatigue of the journey to you in your weakened condition would not be recovered from in that time.

You will not think less of me for entertaining the view I express in this letter and the one written last week. They are based upon firm principles which I trust will find in you a hearty support. This is written with no view of influencing your decision, for that you have already made, but only to show you why the answer your sweet despatch invited, was not sent you instead of the one which was sent. Until I receive a letter from you I shall write my letters in fear that you will not get them for some time, as may be the case if you start for this place with Mrs. Grant.

News from the West is that Hood has attacked Thomas's army at Franklin, Tenn., a place about twenty-seven miles South of Nashville, at four o'clock yesterday and was repulsed with a loss of from five to six thousand men including one thousand prisoners, and among them one brigadier general. Our loss was from five to six hundred. This will prove a heavy blow to Hood and will, it seems to me, compel him to withdraw to the South bank of the Tennessee. Thomas's army by tomorrow, according to his despatches, will be ready to take the offensive. No news whatever has been received from Sheridan. All quiet along our lines here.

I stated in a letter to you some time ago, speaking of General Grant in New York, that Colonel Badeau probably requested that the press should not speak of the General's presence in the city. It was not Colonel Badeau who did this but Mr. Beckwith our cipher operator.

I see gold is going up again. I wrote some time ago to Colonel Hillyer asking him to purchase for me and send to you two hundred dollars in gold, but fear he did not do so.

In my trip to Fort Monroe I caught cold, which causes me to cough somewhat, but does not affect my general health. I went with Colonel Parker today to get weighed. My weight is now 173 pounds, or seven and a half pounds more than when I was last weighed.

The Richmond *Examiner* of today, just received, gives it up that Sherman will get through to the coast, and is now across the Oconee River. This looks most favorable for our military situation. . . .

City Point,

December 2, 1864

. . . . The news from General Thomas today is not so favorable as it looked yesterday, for notwithstanding our repulse of the enemy at Franklin on the afternoon of the 30th ultimo, at 3 A M. of the 1st instant, we fell back to within the fortifications at Nashville and Hood's advanced infantry was near there. General Grant has ordered General Thomas to attack Hood at once and before he has time to fortify. So you may expect news of a battle from that quarter at any time, yes, before you read this . . .

General Gregg commanding the cavalry of the Army of the Potomac attacked Stoney Ford Station on the Weldon Railroad and succeeded in capturing it with two pieces of artillery, one hundred and seventy prisoners, among them Major Fitzhugh of General Hampton's staff and a brother-in-law of Colonel Dent. He destroyed by burning the depot containing five hundred bales of hay, three thousand sacks of corn, large quantities of bacon and ammunition; also one train loaded with supplies. This was a very brilliant affair and reflects much credit upon the cavalry and its commander.

General Dodge will be assigned to command the Department of the Missouri. General McClernand has resigned his commission in the army.

General Grant expects Mrs. Grant here within the next four or five days and says she has invited you to come with her. I merely mention this to show how much she has put her heart upon having your company. You of course have decided this and as you have not telegraphed me I take it for granted that you have decided not to come. . . .

City Point,

December 4, 1864

. . . . News from the West is that Thomas will in two or three days from this be in condition to give Hood battle.

News from Sherman through Richmond papers is that he is still progressing towards the coast without serious opposition. Colonel Markland with Sherman's mail and Lieutenant Dunn with despatches for him, start for the blockading fleet off Savannah this morning, to remain there till General Sherman gets through. All quiet here. . . .

City Point,

December 4, 1864

. ... No news of army movements from any quarter away from here. The First Division of the Sixth Corps, which has been in the Valley with Sheridan, arrived here today. The Third Division will commence arriving tomorrow and the Second and last division will be here in a few days, unless movements of the enemy in the Valley should require it to stay in that section.

I see in *Harper's Weekly* of the 10th instant a wood cut of myself, with a short (but as to my being wounded in battle incorrect) notice of my career. If you have not already seen it, you can, by procuring that copy of the paper, have the pleasure of doing so. I have no doubt it will amuse if not interest you. . . .

City Point,

December 6, 1864

. ... I was kept in my room all day yesterday by a severe cold. Otherwise I was quite well and this morning I am out but not entirely well of my cold. The day is beautiful and I shall take a ride on horseback which I hope will much improve me.

News from Sherman through Richmond papers is still favorable to him. From Nashville matters do not look as it seems to me they should. The enemy day before yesterday captured two transport steamers going down the river, but Captain Fitch in command of our gun boats recaptured them and drove back the rebel battery from the river bank. Everything quiet here. . . .

City Point,

December 7, 1864

. ... I am delighted to know all is satisfactory to you. I felt it would be. Mrs. Grant telegraphed yesterday she will start for City Point on the 8th. Colonel Dent has gone with the steamer *Washington* to meet her. News from Nashville is unchanged save that General Thomas intends to attack the enemy today.

Nothing from Sherman. Warren with a force from the Army of the Potomac started this morning to break up the Weldon railroad so as to deprive the enemy of any benefit of it for some weeks. His command is large and sufficient for the purpose. I am getting better of my cold. It is raining here quite hard this morning.

Colonel Babcock goes to Sherman this morning with orders of the right ring I assure you. Richmond ere long will tremble at the Union soldiers' march, if the orders which Babcock has for General Sherman are carried out. Mail time is up. . . .

City Point,

December 9, 1864

. . . . This morning is clear and cold. No news from Warren, Sherman or Thomas.

The expedition for the capture of Wilmington, under General Butler and Admiral Porter got off last evening. They should reach there day after tomorrow. Colonel Comstock accompanied General Butler. . . .

City Point,

December 10, 1864

. ... It commenced to snow, sleet and rain here last night, and this morning everything was white as age. Today has been really disagreeable.

Colonel Clark of the old Army of the Tennessee is here; he will leave for Washington tomorrow. Hon. E. B. Washburne and General Logan arrived this afternoon. They are both in excellent health and spirits. News from Thomas is that all there is quiet and a freezing storm prevailing. Nothing of any kind whatever from Sherman. General Warren has not yet been heard from. He should be back tomorrow. The expedition against Wilmington is off. In a day or two we shall hear from it, and I trust the news will be such as to cheer the country throughout its borders. . . .

City Point,

December 11, 1864

. . . . Tonight is very, very cold but clear as a bell. One consolation I have is that I have blankets enough to keep me warm and shall suffer no inconvenience from the change of weather. Would to heaven I could say the same for all of our brave men.

General Warren has been heard from. He is on his way back and will be in tomorrow. His raid has been most successful having destroyed the Weldon railroad from Jarrotts Station to Hicksburg including several bridges of considerable importance. No news today from Thomas. Richmond papers place Sherman East of the Ogeechee River and moving towards Savannah. The expedition against Wilmington has been delayed at Fort Monroe by the recent storm. Mrs. Grant arrived yesterday morning. She had your letter, also your despatch, and is considerably disappointed that you did not come. She says she thinks you must be a very considerate and obedient wife to ask your husband if you should come to see him, that she intended having your visit here as a surprise to me and the next time she sees you she intends to give you some instructions as to how to manage me. . . .

City Point,

December 12, 1864

. . . . Today has been clear and cold. This evening, however, the wind has laid and we hope the expedition against Wilmington got off from Fort Monroe today. News from Sherman through Richmond papers of this date, is that yesterday afternoon he was within twenty miles of

Savannah and they think it more than probable that the battle for the possession of that city is progressing today. If they meet Sherman outside of the city in battle he will most certainly beat them. We are anxiously expecting direct news from Sherman daily. From Thomas we have not a word today. General Warren is coming in from his raid to Hicksburg. It is a great success. The last division of the Sixth Corps has arrived. All quiet in our front today. . . .

City Point,

December 13, 1864

. . . . We have no news from General Thomas today. The last was on Saturday. He then could not attack Hood because of the sleet that covered in one icy glare the whole country about Nashville. Still Hood had been able to move against Murfreesboro and at the same time to cross some three thousand men into Kentucky. General Grant has ordered and repeated over and over again his orders to General Thomas to attack Hood, but it seems, first from one cause and then another, he will not or at least has not attacked. General Logan who was here has been ordered to Nashville and when he gets there, if Thomas has not attacked Hood, will relieve Thomas and whip Hood if it can be done. We can depend on these old soldiers of the Tennessee.

News from Sherman is quite satisfactory. Richmond papers say he is within five miles of Savannah, and drawn up in line of battle, and that they have a large force confronting him. . . .

City Point,

December 14, 1864

. . . . Today has been warm and cloudy. The General with Mrs. Grant and lady friends, accompanied by Colonels Bowers, Dent and Morgan, and General Barnard, left here tonight for Washington, and unless he receives other information than he had when he started from here, the General with Colonel Bowers and General Barnard will go on to Nashville. Notwithstanding the positive orders sent General Thomas to fight Hood, he had up to the 13th made no move whatever in that direction.

We have just received a despatch from Sherman's army, dated the 9th. He was then within ten miles of Savannah. The despatch came through from General Howard, commanding the right wing of Sherman's army, to Admiral Dahlgren, and on the 12th instant was forwarded by the latter to Washington. Admiral Dahlgren was going at once to open up communications between Sherman and the fleet off Savannah.

Through rebel papers we learn that Sherman has already invested the place. General Foster holds a point near the railroad between Savannah and Charleston, with batteries in twelve hundred yards of the road and prevents cars from passing between these places. All quiet here and nothing yet from the Wilmington expedition. . . .

City Point,

December 15, 1864

. . . . No additional news from Sherman and none whatever from Thomas. All quiet here.

Through Richmond papers we learn that a part of Burbridge's forces reached Bristol on the 13th and captured the place and destroyed three trains of cars. Bristol is a point on the railroad near the boundary line between Tennessee and Virginia. This is a decided success to us, as it must relieve East Tennessee from further pressure from Breckenridge. Richmond papers also show that the forces that we sent out from New Berne a few days ago failed to reach the Weldon railroad. Whether it accomplished the purpose for which it was sent—mainly the capture of some guns and a force the enemy had at work fortifying a place called Rainbow—the papers do not state.

I have received no word as yet as to whether or not the General has reached Washington. . . .

City Point,

December 16, 1864

. . . . Today has been quite warm, too warm in fact for good health, still I am getting along finely.

Despatches this morning from Nashville inform us that at 9 o'clock A M. yesterday General Thomas attacked Hood and drove his left and centre out of their entrenchments and back from three to five miles, capturing fifteen hundred prisoners and seventeen pieces of artillery. This, if no reverse has since followed it, is glory indeed for our arms.

Through Richmond papers we learn that the force which captured Bristol is pushing towards Salem, Virginia, having already captured

Abingdon and reached a point only two miles distant from Marion. They fear the salt works at Saltville would fall into our hands. This force is in the rear of Breckenridge and will I have no doubt compel him to withdraw from East Tennessee. The same papers also state that Sherman has carried Fort McAllister on the Ogeechee River by assault, capturing the garrison and entire armament thus opening up full and complete communication with our fleet, which can run up to that point with the heaviest class of ships. All this is very cheering news I assure you. . . .

City Point, Va.,

December 17, 1864

. . . . Accompanying this is a badge or medal of honor of the 17th Army Corps, General McPherson's old corps. It was presented to me by the officers of that corps as evidence of their friendly regards. I desire it preserved for Jimmie. In the meantime I think it is beautiful enough for you to wear. It might answer as a brooch for your splendid new cloak. . . .

City Point,

December 17, 1864

. . . . Today has been like several preceding it, too warm for winter and good health.

Colonel Porter went home several days ago on account of sickness and Colonel Badeau starts in the morning for the same reason. He is very sick with fever. General Grant will be back Monday next.

The news from General Thomas is glorious, a victory complete as any yet obtained in open field, with little loss of life to us.

A despatch dated 14th from General Foster states that he met General Sherman that day, that he was then investing Savannah, the right of his army resting on the Ogeechee River and the left on the Savannah, three and a half miles from the city—that he was sending a division to the East bank of the Savannah River, to prevent Hardee's escaping with the garrison in that direction, and also to connect with Foster's forces: that Sherman intended summoning the city to surrender on the 16th instant and in the event of refusal would open on it with artillery at once. His army is in fine spirits.

Here all is quiet. In the morning a salute of one hundred guns will be fired in honor of our victory at Nashville. . . .

City Point,

December 18, 1864

. . . . The salute of one hundred guns in honor of Thomas's victory was fired this morning.

City Point,

December 20, 1864

. . . . Yesterday was a damp day with no news from any quarter. General Grant got back from Burlington where he had gone with Mrs. Grant from Washington.

Colonel Babcock arrived from Sherman this morning, bringing very satisfactory report. All there is well and Savannah must soon fall. It is in much the same situation Vicksburg was after we invested it.

News from General Thomas is still favorable. We have hopes he may get a force in Hood's rear to destroy his means of recrossing the Tennessee River. One has already been started for that purpose and if it succeeds Hood will be entirely ruined. . . .

City Point,

December 21, 1864

. . . . Today has been one of storm and wind without, and it admonishes one that within doors is the best place to find comfort tonight.

The news from General Thomas is cheering and his prospects of preventing Hood from recrossing the Tennessee River are hopeful.

Nothing new from Sherman. The fleet of the expedition against Wilmington had appeared off that place yesterday and a brigade of troops were sent from Richmond to reinforce Wilmington. It is to be hoped they will be too late. This information we have from Richmond papers and deserters. . . .

City Point,

December 22, 1864

. . . . Today is clear and cold. All quiet here, no news from Thomas or Sherman. Richmond papers state that Butler and Porter's expedition against Wilmington has done nothing as yet, that two divisions of Sheridan's cavalry were approaching, one on the Virginia Central and the other on the Virginia & Tennessee Railroad. This latter is no doubt true as Sheridan had ordered the movement some time ago. . . .

City Point,

December 24, 1864

. . . . We have no news from General Thomas nor from Sherman, save that a telegraph operator from Richmond yesterday says that Beauregard telegraphed on the night of the 20th to Davis that Savannah had surrendered to Sherman unconditionally on the morning of the 20th, and that papers of this date say that there is a report that Hardee had evacuated Savannah and Sherman had taken possession.

The Wilmington expedition has done nothing yet. All quiet here. . . .

City Point,

December 25, 1864

. . . . This has been a most beautiful Christmas and news from Sherman in Savannah made it merry indeed. He telegraphs through General Foster his occupation of the place on the 21st; evacuation of it on the afternoon of the 20th. His captures consist of 800 prisoners of war, 150 heavy guns, much ammunition, three steamers, 32,000 bales of cotton. The enemy burned their navy yard and blew up their three ironclads.

The news from General Thomas is quite cheering and he is still pursuing Hood with hopes of inflicting greater damage upon him. No news whatever from the Wilmington expedition. General Butler is with it. You remember what I wrote about him some time since. I fear I was right. Whenever he does anything to change my judgment I shall commit that change to paper. . . .

City Point,

December 26, 1864

. . . . Today has been quite misty and very foggy. Everything here is quiet. News from Thomas is still good. General Wilson's cavalry appears to be doing excellent service for which I am truly glad, not only on the country's account but on his own. The General has written out his orders for Sherman. They are not in accordance with my first views, but they are all right, and when the result of them is seen, the country will fully approve their wisdom . . .

The Wilmington expedition has failed—failed too, I am sorry to say from what I can learn, from the tardiness of the navy, which delayed two clear days of good weather, during which time the enemy had only one thousand men in all the defenses of the place, including Fort Fisher. At the expiration of these two days a storm set in which drove our fleet to sea and gave the enemy time to get into the place some eight or ten thousand men and thereby destroyed every vestige of a chance for our success.

The powder boat of which I wrote several days ago was exploded near Fort Fisher and so little damage did it do that the enemy thought it only one of our gunboats that had been run aground and blown up by us to keep it out of their hands. The terrible danger they escaped they little dreamed of. Our entire casualties in the land forces do not exceed sixteen. . . .

City Point,

December 30, 1864

. ... We have here today Frank P. Blair, Sr., and Montgomery Blair. Their mission is one with which I have not been made acquainted. It does not, however, relate to military affairs. . . .

City Point, Va.,

December 31, 1864

. . . . Today has been very stormy and tonight a heavy gale is blowing but within my cozy, comfortable quarters I could wish you with me, laugh at the storm, so far as it might affect me personally, and even though you are absent, I am delightfully enjoying myself, in the anticipation of your soon being with me. Those of our brave men without shelter, wherever they may be, I do most sincerely pity, and wish within my heart of hearts, this war were ended and they in the bosom of their beloved families.

We have no news from any quarter. Tomorrow the rebel army of General Lee has a New Year's dinner gotten up by their friends in the same manner as was our Thanksgiving dinner, and as they claim not to have fired on our lines to annoy us when we were enjoying our Thanksgiving dinner, General Grant has issued such orders to our troops as to prevent any firing tomorrow unless it be in answer to shots from the enemy. We are never to be outdone, either in fighting or magnanimity. . . .

City Point, Va.,

January 1, 1865

. ... Today has been very fine. No news from any quarter. The mine intended to open out the canal was exploded but the result was not as favorable as was anticipated. It will require several weeks more work to complete it. . . .

It will be observed that in his letter of December 7, Rawlins speaks of the orders sent to Sherman from City Point the day previous by the hands of Colonel Babcock, as having "the right ring." They were conveyed by an autograph letter from General Grant, containing this phrase:

My idea now is that you establish a base on the sea coast, fortify and leave in it all your artillery and cavalry and enough infantry to protect them, and at the same time so threaten the interior that the militia of the South will have to be kept at home. With the balance of your command come here by water with despatch. Select yourself the officer to leave in command, but I want you in person. Unless you see objections to this plan, which I cannot see, use every vessel going to you for purposes of transportation.

On its face, this was the natural and proper order to secure the concentration of the overwhelming force against Lee, which had been the object of Rawlins's, as well as of Grant's, constant solicitude. It was approved by Halleck, the Secretary of War, and the President, but when water transportation came to be considered, it was found that ships enough could not be got to transfer 60,000 infantry from Savannah to City Point in less than sixty days, or say, before the middle of February. Such a movement, preceded as it must have been by a separation of the cavalry, artillery and trains from the army, would necessarily result in a certain amount of disintegration and a consequent impairment of its efficiency. These considerations were not lost sight of for an instant, but besides this, and the lost time it would entail, there was another which soon found a lodgment in Grant's mind. I refer now to the suggestion that, if possible, it would be better for the Army of the Potomac to overthrow Lee, alone and unaided, rather than by the help of Sherman's army, which had never suffered a defeat, and by "marching through Georgia," although unopposed, had added so greatly to its fame. It was thought that if it were permitted to be in at the death it would claim, and the country would accord it, a share of praise beyond its due, and this might promote a feeling of sectionalism, rather than one favorable to national unity and harmony.

It must be recalled that Sherman's entire army was in the highest condition of mobility, could doubtless with all its impedimenta make the overland march in a considerably shorter time than it would take to land its infantry alone at City Point, that in making the march it would necessarily destroy the entire railway system upon which Lee depended for his connection with the Southern Atlantic States, and would besides, constantly interpose itself between the Confederate forces it was leaving behind and those under the immediate command of Lee in Virginia.

It has been frequently shown that, strategically considered, Sherman made a serious mistake in going to Fort McAllister near the mouth of the Ogeechee, and then to Savannah, instead of marching directly through Augusta and the Carolinas, by the shortest and most practicable route to Southern Virginia. It will be observed that it was through his loss of time and distance, by going to Savannah, that Johnston was enabled to gather up the scattered remnants of the Confederate forces, and interpose himself between Sherman and Grant. Had Sherman gone by water to City Point, as had been at first proposed, Johnston would doubtless have been enabled to form a junction with Lee early in February, or before the troops which came by rail from the West under Schofield could have intercepted him in North Carolina.

Fortunately Thomas's victory at Nashville, December 15 and 16, shook Grant's confidence in the soundness of his first view as to the proper movement of Sherman's army, and gave the foregoing considerations their proper weight in deciding that he should have both the duty and the privilege of marching northward overland and giving South Carolina a real taste of the war she had done so much to provoke.

It has been charged that Rawlins opposed this view of the case, and adhered to the orders sent Sherman on the sixth of December; but his correspondence shows beyond question that he at first opposed those orders, and fully approved the change as soon as it was made. The military arguments which justify the change, were as easily understood by him as by any professional soldier in the army, while such of them as were based upon political considerations, if not actually brought forward by him, were more in consonance with his known views than with those of any other man on the staff. Watchful as he was of his Chief's real fame, he would naturally have been the first to see the desirability of beating Lee without the actual presence of Sherman and his army. And when not only the possibility of this was shown, but the probability of still greater injury to the Confederacy from the overland march was pointed out, it might well be assumed as certain, in the absence of positive testimony to the contrary, that Rawlins was in full accord with the change of orders that left Sherman free to carry out his own preferences. Had it been otherwise, Rawlins was not the man to have stated as he did in his letter of December 26:

> . . . The General has written out his orders for Sherman. They are not in accordance with my first views, but they are all right, and when the result of them is seen the country will fully approve their wisdom.

Evidently he had as much right to change his views as had Grant, Halleck, and Stanton, and in doing so gave additional evidence of his real ability as well as of his independent judgment. This was indeed one of his strongest characteristics. It will be remembered that he had approved the action of Grant in retiring W. F. Smith and restoring Butler to the command of the Army of the James. But his correspondence shows that he soon came to doubt the wisdom of trusting Butler with such grave responsibilities. This is made manifest by a pointed remark in his Christmas letter, referring to the Wilmington expedition:

. . . General Butler is with it. You remember what I wrote about him some time since. I fear I was right. Whenever he does anything to change my judgment I shall commit that change to paper.

While Rawlins's correspondence shows that he was firmly attached to such men as Logan, Dodge, Gresham, Ransom, Crocker, and Legget, who had entered the service from civil life and had become great soldiers from long experience in actual campaign and battle, it also shows that he had no abiding faith in mere political generals, like Butler and Banks, who failed to prove themselves equal to the great opportunities which had come to them rather by their prominence in civil affairs than by their just deserts as military men.

Rawlins's attitude in respect to this important matter receives increased importance from the action of the appointing power in respect to certain promotions in the regular army after the Spanish War. In the days of the great rebellion, highly educated officers who had served creditably both as regulars and volunteers from the first, either in confidential staff positions or in actual command of troops, were not infrequently passed over in silence, or actually rejected by the Senate, because they had neglected to advertise themselves in the newspapers, had not otherwise sufficiently demonstrated their fitness for high rank, or had not thought it necessary to invoke the aid of political friends to secure their confirmation. Intrigue was as common then as now, but fortunately the Senate's approval was hard to secure, and grew harder towards the end of the war for men who had not honestly won their advancement to the higher grades by creditable deeds. It is due to Rawlins to say that, although from civil life, no officer was a greater stickler than he for the promotion of only such men as had shown themselves by actual service to be worthy of it. He kept himself well informed as to the character and services of the leading officers in all the armies, and when I notified him by letter that there was a feeling prevalent in the Western Army that Generals Thomas, Schofield, Wood, Cox, and Stanley had not been properly recognized, he at once earnestly advocated their advancement and exerted all his influence not only with his Chief but through Washburne in Congress to secure favorable recommendations to the War Department and favorable action from the Senate. He was the ardent friend of every good man in the service, and the implacable opponent of every man who sought promotion by meretricious methods, and this came to be generally recognized throughout the Eastern as well as the Western army. His merit has received no better attestation than that derived from the character of the men who gained his friendship during the troublous days of the war, and held it to the end.

For the first three months of 1865 there are but few letters from Rawlins in existence. The winter was a severe one, characterized by heavy rains, swollen streams, and almost impassable roads, and although Grant was justly anxious that the Union armies should not go into permanent encampments but keep constantly in motion, he could neither move the Army of the Potomac himself, nor prevail upon his subordinates in that region to carry on effective operations till spring. In fact, the weather as mentioned in Rawlins's letters, made this impracticable, and hence both the Union and Confederate armies in Virginia continued to confront each other sullenly and defiantly, but without serious intentions, while their commanders made themselves as comfortable as possible in winter quarters.

Rawlins, like his Chief, finally brought his wife to City Point, where she remained till after the final campaign began. During that period, he of course wrote her no letters, and being but a poor general correspondent and keeping no diary, I am forced in the remainder of my narrative to confine myself to the Official Records and to the memoirs of the times, for the particulars of his career. As a staff-officer, without initial or independent authority, his part was then and always a subordinate one. Sherman found no occasion to mention him in his account of the visit to City Point in March, but enough has been said by both Grant and Sherman in their *Memoirs* to indicate that Rawlins was neither a silent nor an insignificant factor in the determination of policies and plans. The fact is that he took an important part in both, and, as usual, displayed sound judgment and marked independence of character.

It is well known that after authorizing Sherman to make his overland march northward from Savannah, issuing his orders for the transfer of Schofield, with an army corps of 21,000 veterans, by rail from Middle Tennessee to the coast of North Carolina, and directing Thomas to resume active operations in various directions from his Department, Grant made his dispositions to gather all the forces within reach for a movement against Lee. To this end he directed Sheridan to send back to the Army of the Potomac the Sixth Corps and such other infantry as could be spared, but instead of recalling the cavalry, which had grown steadily for the past year in aggressive temper and efficiency and now believed itself to be invincible, while the infantry of the Army of the Potomac, with its nine months of killing but inconclusive work had gained but little in steadiness and nothing in confidence, he ordered the great cavalryman to move up the valley with his horsemen, clean up the remnant of Early's force about Staunton, break up the railroads and canal, cross the James River, destroy the Southside Railroad, and, after thus isolating the Confederate Capital and cutting off its supplies, to continue his march through Southern Virginia and North Carolina to a junction with Sherman's victorious army, wherever it might be found. This seems to have been a favorite though fallacious idea with Grant, for he had included it as an alternative in the instructions sent Wilson the year before.

Sheridan had no difficulty whatever in overrunning all that part of Virginia north of Richmond, but the Confederates, perceiving his purposes, beat him to the bridges above Richmond, and effectively destroyed them. His own bridge train was inadequate for the passage of so wide a river as the James, and as he believed in concentration rather than in a further dispersion of forces, he doubled on his track and after a wide and destructive march, through Central Virginia to the eastward reestablished connection with the Army of the Potomac at Harrison's Landing, March 25.

After a full description of the operations which brought him to this place, Sheridan says in his *Memoirs*:

. . . Very early next morning, in conformity with a request from General Grant, I left by boat for City Point, Merritt meanwhile conducting the column across the James River, to the point of rendezvous. The trip to City Point did not take long, and on my arrival at Headquarters the first person I met was General John A. Rawlins, General Grant's chief of staff. Rawlins was a man of strong likes and dislikes, and positive always both in speech and action, exhibiting marked feelings when greeting any one, and on this occasion met me with much warmth. His demonstrations of welcome over, we held a few minutes' conversation about the coming campaign, he taking strong ground against a part of the plan of operations adopted, namely, that which contemplated my joining General Sherman's army.

266

His language was unequivocal and vehement, and when he was through talking, he conducted me to General Grant's quarters but he himself did not enter.

As that was the most critical juncture of the war, everything which throws light on the plan of campaign and its evolution is most important. And inasmuch as there is considerable divergence in the various narratives as to the parts played then and afterwards by the great actors in the drama, what Sherman says, although it was written long after the events but while still in the full possession of all his powers, should be considered in connection with what Grant himself says. It seems to be certain that the Lieutenant General was somewhat reluctant to give up the idea of detaching Sheridan to join Sherman in the Carolinas, as he mentioned it in his final letters to Sherman and incorporated it in his final orders and instructions. His subsequent declaration that it was a "blind" has the appearance of an afterthought as it throws no light whatever upon who was to be deceived by the "blind." Both Sherman and Sheridan were certainly entitled to his fullest confidence. It is also certain that Sheridan thought the General's purpose was a serious one which he did not like any better after rejoining the Army and talking it over than he did when it was mentioned in his first orders and repeated in Grant's formal programme. Referring to this subject again, Sheridan makes the following explicit statement:

... When I had gone over the entire letter I showed plainly that I was dissatisfied with it, for, coupled with what the General had outlined orally, which I supposed was the "other instructions," I believed it foreshadowed my junction with General Sherman. Rawlins thought so too, as his vigorous language had left no room to doubt, so I immediately began to offer my objections to the programme. These were that it would be bad policy to send me down to the Carolinas with a part of the Army of the Potomac to come back to crush Lee after the destruction of General Johnston's army; such a course would give rise to the charge that his own forces around Petersburg were not equal to the task, and would seriously affect public opinion in the North; that, in fact, my cavalry belonged to the Army of the Potomac, which army was able unaided to destroy Lee, and I could not but oppose any dispersion of its strength.

All this was said in a somewhat emphatic manner, and when I had finished he quietly told me that the portion of my instructions from which I so strongly dissented was intended as a "blind" to cover any check the army in its general move to the left might meet with and prevent that element in the North, which held that the war could be ended only through negotiations, from charging defeat. The fact that my cavalry was not to ultimately join Sherman was a great relief to me, and after expressing the utmost confidence in the plans unfolded for closing the war by directing every effort to the annihilation of Lee's army, I left him to go to General Ingalls's quarters. On my way I again met Rawlins, who, when I told him that General Grant had intimated his intention to modify the written plan of operations so far as regarded the cavalry, manifested the greatest satisfaction, and I judged from this that the new view of the matter had not previously been communicated to the chief of staff, though he must have been acquainted of course with the programme made out on the 24th of March.

But the substantial accuracy of Sheridan's statement does not rest solely on his own recollection. It is confirmed by Major General James W. Forsyth, who was chief of staff to Sheridan from the time he joined the Army of the Potomac to the end of the war, in a letter dated at Columbus, Ohio, May 28, 1904, which runs as follows:

> ... I shall begin this communication with a conversation that I had with General Sheridan when he received his instructions in the early part of February, 1865, in regard to the movements of his command.

Upon receipt of General Grant's communication giving him his orders, he opened it, read it, and then handed it to me to read. He was directed to move up the valley with his cavalry, clean up the remnant of Early's force located near Staunton, then move over into Southern Virginia, destroy all railroads, and, if possible, the James River and Kanawha canal. Having accomplished this, to cross the James River, break up the Southside Railroad, then to move south and join Sherman in the Carolinas. After reading these instructions I said: "General, are you going to join Sherman?" He said: "No." I said: "How are you going to get out of it? This order is positive and explicit." He said: "I am not going to join Sherman." I said: "Why?" He said, in substance: "I'll tell you why; this campaign will end the war. I have been anxious for fear Lee would commence moving west before we could get to Grant's army. The Army of the Potomac will never move from its present position unless we join them and pull them out. The cavalry corps and the Army of the Potomac have got to whip Lee. If I obeyed these instructions and crossed the James and joined Sherman, the Army of the Potomac would rest where they are and Sherman, with our assistance, would close the war. If this should happen it would be disastrous to the country, for there would be no balance of power between the East and the West. This cavalry corps and the Army of the Potomac, of which it is a part, have got to wipe Lee out before Sherman and his army reach Virginia."

We moved out from Winchester, finished up Early, destroyed the railroads in Northern Virginia, swung over on to the James River and destroyed the James River and Kanawha canal. Prior to our departure from Charlottesville, where we rested two days, a force of cavalry was sent south to a bridge across the James River near a place called Dugansville. Fitzhugh Lee's cavalry division and Longstreet's corps had been detached by Lee and sent west on the Southside Railroad to watch us. When our cavalry made a dash for the bridge at Dugansville, the rebels burned it up before our forces reached there. The result of this was that there was no bridge across the James River from Richmond to Dugansville. When the officer in command of this reconnaissance reported to General Sheridan at Charlottesville, he turned to me and said: "How are we going to cross the James River? Have you found any bridges on your map over the James River between Richmond and Dugansville?" "No, there are none," I said. Then he said: "How many pontoon boats did you bring?" I said: "We have eleven canvas pontoon boats." He then said: "Do you think we can bridge the James with eleven pontoon boats?" I answered: "No." He said: "Well, as we can't cross the James, we will now join Grant." A few days after that we reached a place on the James River and Kanawha canal called Columbia. In the destruction of the canal we had captured sixty canal boats loaded with ordnance and medical supplies on their way west to Lynchburg. This disturbed the General very much, as it indicated that Lee was preparing to move west into the Blue Ridge Mountains of Virginia.

From Columbia we sent two scouts north of the river and around Richmond, and two scouts down the river in a canoe, each of whom carried a copy of the same despatch notifying General Grant of our success, of the impossibility of crossing the James and, therefore, that General Sheridan further proposed to move around north of Richmond to White House Landing on the Pamunkey River, and thence south to the Army of the Potomac. He requested General Grant to have the supplies for our command at White House Landing ready for us upon our arrival there.

We joined General Grant about the 25th of March, the cavalry corps was ordered out on the left of the line of the Army of the Potomac, and orders were issued to move out on the 27th and swing around the left and try to cut up the railroads in that part of the country. This project was not carried out.

We fought the Battle of Dinwiddie C. H. on the 31st and the battle of Five Forks on the 1st of April. All the while we were moving and getting into position we had nothing but soaking rains. Our wagon trains were all stalled on the road. Prior to the battle of Dinwiddie C. H. General Sheridan went over to General Grant's headquarters every day for the purpose of seeing General Rawlins and helping him to brace up and sustain General Grant. The relationship between Sheridan and Rawlins, Grant's chief of staff, was exceedingly close, and there was no man in that army so determined and positive that we should continue to push on and crush Lee's army as General Rawlins. Sheridan agreed with him. I believe if it had not been for these two men that Grant would have dropped back into his original works at Petersburg. In fact, an order was drafted and printed, according to my best recollections, looking to that end. The location of the army wagons, the supply trains and the cattle herds were changed. The pressure brought on General Grant by General Meade and other officers of the Army of the Potomac and the desperate and continuous rains were the reason assigned for withdrawing. The men who prevented that withdrawal were General Sheridan and General Rawlins. When Sheridan arrived at City Point he clasped the hand of Rawlins and earnestly discussed the condition of affairs. A compact was made and they stood by each other all the way through.

This statement is further certified by a letter from General M. V. Sheridan, dated June 20, 1904, from which I make the following quotation:

Michael Vincent Sheridan (1840–1918) was a brother and Aide-de-Camp to Lieutenant General Phil Sheridan. In 1877, Michael Sheridan was assigned to take a detail of soldiers to the Little Bighorn battlefield to exhume and retrieve the remains of the officers of the 7th Cavalry who had been killed there the year before.—Ed. 2015

... Not having been with General Sheridan on his trip to Dabney's Mill, I have only my recollections that came from talks I have had with General Sheridan then and afterwards. These convinced me that Rawlins objected to the retrograde movement of the Army of the Potomac. I have always understood that the retrograde movement was suggested by General Meade, and that it was assented to by General Grant there is no question. The letter of General Grant corroborates this.

I care as much for the memory of General Grant as any man that lives today, but I regret to say that in writing his *Memoirs* he dismissed from his mind, with a few words, an incident which had a most important bearing upon the close of the war.

The history of the whole matter as given in detail by General Sheridan can be the only truthful and accepted one. When Grant wrote he was a dying man. . . .

The renewal of the forward movement of the forces under Grant's immediate command began on March 29, 1865, and on the evening of that day Rawlins wrote from the first camp of Army Headquarters to his wife whom he had left in his cabin at City Point, as follows:

Crossing of Vaughn Road, Gravelly Run,

March 29, 1865

. . . . Today has been very favorable for our movements; everything thus far meets our expectations. About 4:30 p m. the enemy with two divisions attacked Griffin's division of Warren's corps, but were handsomely repulsed, leaving in our hands one hundred prisoners and losing many in killed and wounded. Our loss was between two and three hundred. Warren followed the enemy until he retired inside his main lines. Sheridan has reached Dinwiddie Court House, and everything is ready for an advance early in the morning. The General feels like making a heavy push for everything we have hoped for so long, and I am not slow in seconding all such feelings. It does seem to me we must succeed.

I trust, darling, you are giving yourself as little anxiety as possible about me. I have coughed but very little and I ate one of the best dinners since dark I have eaten in a great while. My tent looks very tidy, for, you see, it is new; besides I have Jenny's little chair, brought by mistake of course, which reminds me all the time of you and her. Tell her I shall bring it back. Say to Mrs. Grant the General is in fine spirits and I believe she will ere long be happy in seeing the captor of Richmond in him. . . .

The next day the camp was moved further to the front, and aggressive operations continued, but it rained heavily that night and the next morning. The streams became flooded, and the country roads were converted into quagmires and quicksand. It looked for much of the day as though the forward movement would have to be abandoned. Sheridan had met with fierce resistance in his effort to advance from Dinwiddie Court House. Warren had been greatly delayed by swollen creeks and muddy roads in his night march to the support of the cavalry, and consequently a feeling of discouragement and gloom began to spread throughout the army. It is certain that operations were temporarily suspended at the front, because of the rain, and that this was with Grant's concurrence is shown by his letter of March 30 to General Sheridan, in which he directs him, after leaving a force to protect the left, to "send the remainder back to Humphreys's station where they can get hay and grain."

At that juncture Rawlins wrote as follows:

Dabney's Mill,

March 31, 1865

. . . . Owing to the rain last night and this morning, making the roads movable quicksand, the proposed movement of General Sheridan had to be postponed indefinitely. So one of my bright visions of hope has for the present passed away. Today we have had considerable fighting,

272

and the losses in Warren's corps in prisoners are, I fear, pretty heavy, as usual, with him. He sent out one division to seize a road, and instead of sending his other divisions to support it, suffered it to be beaten and driven back on his second division, which in turn was driven back on his third, which checked the enemy's further advance. Had he sent up his second and third to the fight when it began, we should have had a splendid victory and would have saved Sheridan's cavalry from imminent peril. But thanks to God and Sheridan, the cavalry has been saved without his aid. Warren is now moving with his whole corps to get in the rear of Pickett's division, which has been fighting Sheridan. I do hope he will succeed in getting where he is ordered. If so, all will yet be well if not glorious. . . .

Neither of these letters shows any hesitation or doubt on Rawlins's part, but the last quoted seems to make it clear, without giving details, that the rain was the principal if not the only cause of the delay which had apparently been decided upon. This view of the matter is fully confirmed by Sheridan's Memoirs, and Forsyth's letter. There is no intimation from any source that Rawlins had lost heart in the slightest degree or that his course at any time during the campaign was other than what it had always been, in favor of a persistent aggressive campaign to the bitter end. And yet, many years afterwards, Grant in his *Memoirs* makes the following statement:

. . . Although my chief of staff had urged very strongly that we return to our position about City Point and in the lines around Petersburg, he asked Sheridan to come in to see me and say to me what he had been saying to them. Sheridan felt a little modest about giving his advice where it had not been asked; so one of my staff came in and told me that Sheridan had what they considered important news, and suggested that I send for him. I did so, and was glad to see the spirit of confidence with which he was imbued. Knowing as I did from experience of what great value that feeling of confidence by a commander was, I determined to make a movement at once, although on account of the rains which had fallen after I had started out the roads were still very heavy. Orders were given accordingly.

In view of what Rawlins wrote to his wife, as well as of what has been quoted from Sheridan's *Memoirs* and from Forsyth's letter, the conclusion is inevitable that the memory of Grant—fully twenty years afterwards, and suffering from an incurable malady—was at fault in the allegation that Rawlins urged the return of the army to its former position "about City Point and in the lines around Petersburg." The only reasonable explanation of this statement is that Grant's letter directing the withdrawal of the cavalry from Dinwiddie Court House, as well as the retrograde movement, which it was supposed to foreshadow, was suggested by General Meade, because of the heavy rains or the stout resistance of the enemy, or by some other important person, and not by the Chief of Staff, who had always, up to that time, stood as the exponent of an unrelenting and aggressive policy. Undoubtedly the bad weather and the almost impassable state of the roads and fields, were the immediate cause of the suspension of all aggressive operations on March 31, as well as of the authorized withdrawal of the cavalry. But as the actual conditions were evidently quite as unfavorable to the Confederate as to the Union forces, the recall of the order for the retirement of the cavalry was not only timely but greatly to the credit of those who advised it. That Sheridan is entitled to the first place in this is made clear by Grant's own statement, and that Rawlins is entitled to the second, is made equally clear by the statements of both Sheridan and Forsyth.

In connection with the change of plan by which Sheridan was relieved from the necessity of again cutting loose from the Army of the Potomac, and making his way to a junction with Sherman in North Carolina, but little is said in any of the histories or memoirs of that period. Still less is said in regard to the origin of the order directing Sheridan on March 31 to leave a portion of his cavalry to protect the left and withdraw the rest to Humphreys's station on the railroad. Sheridan's ride to Grant's headquarters at Dabney's Mill, on the receipt of that order is mentioned in Newhall's *With General Sheridan in Lee's Last Campaign*, but it casts no light upon the occasion. Indeed, no mention is made of the incident except in the *Memoirs* of Grant and in those of Sheridan. Grant's letter to Sheridan has been frequently alluded to as authorizing a retrograde movement, but Humphreys and other writers of accurate memory refer to what actually followed as at most a suspension of hostilities for the day, or a part of the day, due entirely to the heavy rains. It is to be noted, however, that the rains having ceased on the morning of March 31 the roads dried out rapidly and were sufficiently improved to permit the partial renewal of operations that afternoon. There seems to be no doubt that Sheridan and his confidential staff officers for several hours thought that Grant's letter directing the withdrawal of the cavalry, foreshadowed an abandonment of the campaign then fully under way. It appears to be equally certain that Sheridan and Rawlins, in mutual confidence and support, stood together in the determination to prevent such an inglorious result.

Whatever may have been the precise facts of the case, it is to be observed that it presents the second occasion, during the entire period of the war, on which Grant ever allowed himself to question the conduct or the judgment of Rawlins, or to cast the slightest reflection upon the aggressive policy of which he had come to be generally acknowledged as the advocate. At most the incident as recorded indicates a temporary difference of opinion between the Lieutenant General and his chief of staff, from which no evil consequences resulted. Fortunately the difference, whatever its extent, led to the issuance of no formal orders for a "retrograde movement," of any corps except the cavalry, and if such movement was ever seriously thought of for the infantry, by Meade, or by anyone else, whether on account of the rain, or of the fierceness of the Confederate resistance in the vicinity of Dinwiddie Court House, it is a creditable circumstance that the thought never crystallized into definite orders, either written or oral. There is no evidence that any such orders were ever given or that there was ever anything more than a temporary cessation of the pressure which Sheridan and Rawlins, from the first, never doubted would end the war.

It should not be forgotten that while the Lieutenant General might have had at any time the opinions and advice of his subordinates for the asking, the responsibility of advance or retreat rested in that as in every other case, solely upon him, and it was infinitely to his credit that he decided after but a few hours' hesitation in favor of an unrelenting advance. It is evident from all accounts that the condition of the weather and the roads was, for at least two days of the campaign, most discouraging; but clear skies and sunshine soon brought a revival of hope which culminated in a determination to continue the movement as begun until victory should crown it with complete success. Fortunately, heavy rains and muddy roads are about as fatal to movements in retreat as in advance. If they paralyze one belligerent they are likely to have the same effect upon the other. Hence it is always well in stormy weather to wait a while for developments.

Whatever may have been the doubts and discouragements of the initial movements of the campaign, it is certain that the brighter weather of April 1 found Grant's headquarters, as well as the left of the army, glowing with hope and confidence. By the battle of Five Forks Sheridan literally pulled the Army of the Potomac out of its hesitation and delay, and started it in earnest upon its last and most victorious campaign. Nothing could now stop it, and nothing but a failure to press forward with the utmost speed could mar the completeness of its success. When the troops were in motion and the enemy on the retreat, Rawlins was not the man to interpose with suggestions. His letters to his wife, written in the evening after the results of the day's operations were known, were necessarily brief and to the point. So far as I know, they are the only ones hot from the very center of information, and while they are full of confidence, they bear unmistakable testimony to the fact that Sheridan held the post of honor and of interest in the drama that was then so rapidly unrolling itself before the world. As his turning movement acquired momentum, it brought the left wing and center of the army into closer relation, and made it unnecessary for Grant to break camp till April 2, for the purpose of following the marching columns. Consequently he held on for the day at Dabney's Mill, from which place Rawlins wrote, April 1, 1865, as follows:

. . . The hero of the Shenandoah stands afront of all on the Appomattox. His personal gallantry and great genius have secured to us a splendid success today, 4,000 prisoners, 8 pieces of artillery and many wagons, with the morale of victory to us. General Grant is making every exertion to prevent anything occurring to dim its brightness. Miles's fine division with all the reserves of the Second Corps move at twelve tonight to join Sheridan, to enable him to resist any attempt the enemy may make to retrieve their losses and to follow up his successes, as circumstances may determine in the morning. All the other corps will attack between this and morning. Sheridan relieved Warren of his command and succeeded him with Griffin. This should have been done yesterday. . . .

Southside Railroad,

April 2, 1865

. . . . Today has been one of battle and glorious victory. Thank God, the Lieutenant General has commanded in it himself and not permitted the spirit or, I might say, the genius of his orders, to be dampened by his subordinate commander.

We have captured as strongly entrenched positions as I have seen— many thousand prisoners and pieces of artillery. We hope to get Sheridan with the Fifth Corps and two divisions of the Second Corps to the north side of the Appomattox between this and morning, which will enable us to shut up the enemy's forces in Petersburg or compel them to evacuate that place. . . .

Sutherland Station,

April 4, 1865

. ... I did not write to you last night, for the reason that I had no opportunity of sending back. I now do so hoping for such an opportunity today.

The evacuation of Richmond and the apparently great demoralization of Lee's army have decided the General to follow it up to its final destruction, if possible to do so; hence it is not probable that I shall reach City Point for some time. So, please, after visiting Petersburg and Richmond, make your preparations to return to Danbury. You need not start, however, till you hear from me again. Colonel Bowers will let Harry go with you, I am sure. Speak to him about it. If we are brought to a halt by the enemy, or for the want of supplies, I may get to see you before you start home, which I desire so much to do. My health is much better than when lying still at City Point. The excitement of victory and of army life agrees with me. The letter of yesterday, which I expected from you, I did not receive. Don't fail to write me often.

The decision of the General not to let Lee rest is a wise one and augurs the early termination of the war. I had feared he might not so decide, but all is well now and promising early brightness of the national sky. . . .

With the campaign at last in full swing, the enemy's right wing doubled up and driven back, and his entrenchments covering Petersburg in possession of the victors, there was nothing left for Lee except to retreat. Richmond was no longer tenable. Davis and his cabinet had fled, and ruin was staring the Confederacy in the face. Sheridan and Humphreys's rapid advance resulted in a sure lodgment of the Southside Railway, fully nine months after it was first broken by Wilson's cavalry. All the roads south of the Appomattox were at last firmly in the grasp of the national army, and there was no way left open for the retreat of the enemy except by a circuitous route leading in the direction of Amelia Court House. It was now a race for life between Lee and his pursuers, with the short line in favor of the pursuers.

Rawlins was the constant companion of his Chief, sharing his labor and joining in his counsel, but, so far as is known, writing only orders and despatches. The hurry and rush of the campaign, which culminated in the disintegration of Lee's army and its final surrender at Appomattox Court House, overwhelmed the staff with work. There was but little time for rest and sleep, and none for personal correspondence. Even the diaries and itineraries were left to be filled up after the campaign was ended. Only the reporters were making contemporaneous records. The great actors now occupied the stage in front of all others. Grant and Lee held the center, with Meade, Sheridan, and Humphreys on one side, and Longstreet and Gordon on the other. The staff officers had their part, but it was the part of subordinates. Rawlins, worn and pale with disease and impaired strength, met all demands upon him. At the supreme moment he was by the side of his Chief, and when Lee's letter came asking for an interview he was the first to see it after Grant had opened and read it.

It will be remembered that Grant first wrote to Lee, April 7, 1865, saying in substance that the results of the last week's operations should not only convince him that further resistance must be hopeless but were such as to justify a demand for the surrender of that portion of the Confederate forces known as the Army of Northern Virginia. Lee replied the same day, asking what terms would be offered. This letter did not reach General Grant till the eighth, but was followed immediately by a reply that as "peace" was "his great desire," there was but one condition which he would insist upon, namely that the men and officers surrendered should be disqualified from taking up arms again till properly exchanged. This communication reached Lee late in the afternoon, and the use of the word "peace" was at once seized upon by that astute and wary commander with the hope of broadening the meeting into one for a treaty of peace between the contending belligerents. In his reply he put forward the declaration that he had not intended to propose the surrender of his army and did not think the emergency called for such a result. He added:

> . . . But as the restoration of peace should be the sole object of all, I desire to know whether your proposal would lead to that end. I cannot therefore meet you with a view to surrendering the Army of Northern Virginia, but as far as your proposals may effect the Confederate States' forces under my command and tend to the restoration of peace, I shall be glad to meet you at ten o'clock A M. tomorrow on the old stage road to Richmond, between the pickets of the two armies.

The phraseology of this note was adroitly framed. It was evidently designed to entrap a frank and generous commander who was anxious to bring his labors to a successful close, and yet not quite sure that he had the enemy in such position as would render his capture certain. It reached Grant at midnight, and, according to [Sylvanus] Cadwallader, the *Herald* correspondent who occupied the parlor of the farmhouse where headquarters had been located for the night, it was sent upstairs to the bedroom occupied by Grant and Rawlins. As customary, it was delivered to Rawlins, who tore it open and proceeded to read it in a voice so loud that both the correspondent and the junior staff officers below-stairs heard it as fully as Grant did. Rawlins caught its drift instantaneously, and pointed out Lee's disingenuousness and inconsistency in the declaration that he did not intend to propose the surrender of his army, but was ready to meet for the purpose of considering the restoration of peace. At this Rawlins flamed up, and, according to Cadwallader, addressing Grant directly, said:

Lee now tries to take advantage of a single word used by you as a reason for granting such easy terms. He wants to entrap us into making a treaty of peace. You said nothing about that. You asked him to surrender. He replied by asking what terms you would give if he surrendered. You answered by stating the terms. Now he wants to arrange for peace—something to embrace the whole Confederacy if possible. No, sir,—no, sir! This is a positive insult—an attempt in an underhand way to change the whole terms of the correspondence.

Thereupon Grant replied:

It amounts to the same thing—Lee is only trying to be let down easily. I can meet him, as requested, in the morning, and settle the whole business in an hour.

But Rawlins was inexorable and declared with all his strength:

It would be presumptuous to try to teach General Lee the force of words, or the use of the English language; that he had purposely proposed to arrange terms of peace to gain time and secure better terms; that the note was cunningly worded to that end, and deserved no reply whatever. He doesn't think the emergency has arisen! That's cool,—but another falsehood. That emergency has been staring him in the face for forty-eight hours. If he hasn't seen it yet, we will soon bring it to his comprehension. He has to surrender! It shall be surrender—and nothing else!

To this outburst Grant replied modestly and quietly:

Some allowance must be made for the trying position in which General Lee is placed. He is compelled to defer somewhat to the wishes of his Government and his military associates. But it all means precisely the same thing. If I meet Lee, he will surrender before I leave.

Then Rawlins took another stand.

You have no right to meet Lee, or anybody else, to arrange terms of peace. That is the prerogative of the President and the Senate. Your business is to capture or destroy Lee's army.

It will be observed that this was a strictly legal view of the situation, due doubtless to Rawlins's training as a lawyer. In bringing it forward he gave it additional force by reminding Grant that when he telegraphed for instructions in reference to meeting the Confederate Peace Commissioners at City Point a few weeks before, Stanton in his reply went to the verge of giving him a reprimand. This was the most notable despatch of the day, and if it had been sent to meet the emergency which confronted Grant in his correspondence with Lee, could not have been more explicit or more applicable. Rawlins dwelt with emphasis upon its terms which are as follows:

> The President directs me to say to you that he wishes you to have no conference with General Lee unless it be for the capitulation of Lee's army or on solely minor and purely military matters. He instructs me to say that you are not to decide, discuss or confer upon any political question. Such questions the President holds in his own hands, and will submit them to no military conferences or conventions.

Rawlins concluded the argument by pointing out that this despatch was sent when Grant had no thought of treating for peace, but had merely asked for instructions as to the treatment he should give to the Commissioners. It is well known that Grant, at the time, regarded the wording and scope of Stanton's reply as an open rebuke; but in view of its provisions, which were still more pertinent to the case under consideration, and finding that Rawlins was irreconcilably opposed to the meeting as modified by the provisions of Lee's last note, Grant yielded, and Rawlins carried his point, as he always did when his mind was resolutely set. But as Grant felt that it was his duty to give a respectful answer to all official communications, and that Lee was, under the circumstances which surrounded him, especially entitled to courteous treatment, he replied fully to his note. The discussion with Rawlins had cleared the case of all uncertainty, and laid the foundation for a reply entirely within Grant's discretion, but which was so clear and explicit that it could not be misunderstood. As this reply is a historical document, which owed its form and provisions to a most unusual discussion between a victorious general and his chief of staff, and was besides an essential link in events of far-reaching importance to the country, its provisions should not be forgotten. It was written at Clifton House, Virginia, in the latter part of the night of April 9, 1865, and, omitting the address, runs as follows:

Your note of yesterday is received. As I have no authority to treat on the subject of peace, the meeting proposed by you for 10 A. M. today could lead to no good. I will state, however, General, that I am equally anxious for peace, with yourself, and the whole North entertain the same feeling. The terms upon which peace can be had are well understood. By the South laying down their arms they will hasten that most desirable event, save thousands of human lives, and hundreds of millions of property not yet destroyed. Sincerely hoping that all our difficulties may be settled without the loss of another life, I am,

Very respectfully, Your Obedient Servant,

U. S. GRANT,

Lieutenant General, U. S. A.

It is worthy of note that as soon as this communication was despatched, Grant sent copies of the entire correspondence to the Secretary of War; and, as if to show that he had not lost sight of the instructions he had received on a previous occasion, he concluded with the significant remark that "there has been no relaxation in the pursuit during its pendency."

It was a busy and exciting time at headquarters. The fate of an army was at stake, while the victorious general was, on one hand, marring his fame, or, on the other, gathering new and imperishable laurels. Neither Rawlins nor any other staff officer got much rest or sleep that night. The Lieutenant General and his staff took breakfast with Meade, and as soon as it was light enough to find their way, they were on the road to join Sheridan, who had already planted himself squarely across Lee's only road to escape. The ride was a long and circuitous one, much of the way through fields and farms, over hills and ravines, and across muddy streams and bogs of quicksand. At eleven o'clock, or about that time, they halted for a rest; and while waiting they were overtaken by Major Pease, of Meade's staff, bringing Lee's reply to Grant's letter declining to meet for the purpose of arranging terms of peace.

The staff officer gave the sealed envelope to Rawlins, who tore one end open slowly, withdrew the enclosure, read it deliberately, and then, without a word of comment, handed it to Grant. The latter read it through with the same deliberation, and as he passed it back to Rawlins, directing him in a conversational tone to read it aloud. The staff officers and military suite were looking on with mingled anxiety and hope. They were expecting the surrender, but the impassive conduct of Grant and Rawlins left them momentarily in doubt. Grant betrayed no emotion whatever, but Rawlins compressed his lips, clenched his teeth and grew deathly pale. When Grant directed him to read aloud, he proceeded in a deep and solemn but somewhat tremulous voice as follows:

9th April, 1865.

GENERAL: I received your note of this morning on the picket line whither I had come to meet you and ascertain definitely what terms were embraced in your proposal of yesterday with reference to the surrender of this army. I now ask an interview in accordance with your letter of yesterday, for that purpose.

R. E. LEE,

General.

It will be observed that Grant's last letter had not only settled the purpose of the meeting beyond further question but had placed it as completely on the basis of a simple surrender, as it would have been had Lee not written his letter of the eighth at all, in which he sought so adroitly to induce Grant to enter upon the larger subject of peace. Grant's triumph was complete, while Rawlins had the satisfaction of seeing the course he had recommended fully vindicated.

Silence fell upon those who had just heard the momentous news, but this was broken in a few moments by a staff officer who sprang upon a log, waved his hat, and proposed three cheers. A feeble response was all that followed. While it was apparent that the end had come, that the war was over, and that all would soon be

283

reunited with friends, family, and home, not one of the party felt that it was an occasion for loud or jubilant exultation.

Grant broke the spell by penning the reply in which he acknowledged the receipt of Lee's note, explained that he had passed from the Richmond and Lynchburg to the Richmond and Farmville road, and that he would push forward to meet Lee at the place he wished the interview to take place. This brief but all-sufficient note was written by Grant while seated upon a log. When it was finished he passed it over to the Chief of Staff, asking with a smile:

"How will that do, Rawlins?"

The latter replied:

"I think *that* will do," laying strong emphasis on the word "that."

As soon as the necessary record had been made, and the note had been sent to its destination by one of his own staff, Grant with his headquarters and escort "pushed forward to the front for the purpose of meeting" Lee and bringing the business between them to an end.

The surrender took place at Appomattox Court House, on the same day, April 9, 1865, but the details have been given so often and so minutely that they need not be repeated here. Rawlins was of course present at the negotiations, made the record, and revised the official reports of the events now on file in the War Department. It is a circumstance of great interest that of the many officers present he was the only one who had served through the war with Grant. The first staff had long since been scattered. Some were dead, some disabled, and some had been left behind, or assigned to service in other fields. Rawlins alone had remained with his Chief from the first gun at Belmont to the last at Appomattox. Strangely enough, it was four years almost to a day since the young Democratic lawyer had made the modest ex-Captain his friend for life by his ringing words at the Galena meeting: "We will stand by the flag of our country and appeal to the God of battles!"

On the night after the surrender the General and his staff encamped at Prospect Station and were joined by their faithful friend and supporter, E. B. Washburne, who, it will be remembered, was the principal speaker at the meeting which brought the Buchanan Democrat, the Douglas Democrat, and the "Black Republican" together in the cause of the Union. They had stood by one another loyally and steadily from the first, and they shared one another's confidence and congratulations to the end. While the "infallibility of numbers rather than the infallibility of generals" had prevailed, yet each had acted well his part in his own sphere. No selfish ambition had marred the career of any one of them. The pure love of country, inspired all, and it may well be doubted if, in the great conflict between the States, history affords a more striking example of patriotic and successful effort on the part of three citizens of a single country town than that of Grant, Rawlins, and Washburne.

This account of the correspondence with Lee and the closing days of the campaign is condensed from the manuscript of S. Cadwallader entitled Four Years with Grant. *It will be remembered that Cadwallader was constantly with Grant's headquarters till after Lee's surrender, and based his narrative on his own note books, and his correspondence with the* New York Herald.*—note in original*

THE AFTERMATH

IMMEDIATELY after the close of the war in Virginia, Grant returned to Washington; but fortunately on the very day the President was assassinated went on to Burlington where his children were at school. During his absence Rawlins gathered up the headquarters of the army and made arrangements to reestablish them at the Capital, where they would be in daily touch with the War Department.

Before the end came, in recognition of his services, Congress, largely under the influence of Washburne, who was at that time one of the Republican leaders in the House of Representatives, had created the permanent office of Chief of Staff with the rank of brigadier general; and without question, or the consideration of any possible rival, Rawlins was appointed thereto on March 3, 1865. In the final distribution of honors he received the commission of major general by brevet, to date from April 9 of the same year, "for gallant and meritorious service during the campaign terminating with the surrender of the insurgent army under Lee." Through some oversight his name was left off of the first list of nominations, whereupon Grant wrote a special letter in his behalf, dated May 8, 1866, from which the closing paragraph is taken. It runs as follows:

> . . . General Rawlins has served with me through the entire war from the Battle of Belmont to the surrender of Lee. No staff officer ever before had it in his power to render as much service, and no one ever performed his duties more faithfully or efficiently. He is eminently entitled to the brevet rank of major general, and I earnestly but respectfully request that his name be yet sent in for consideration.

Nothing can be added to this statement. It bears conclusive testimony to the high regard in which Grant held his chief of staff and the great value he attached to his services from the beginning to the end of the war.

It will be remembered that the terms granted by Sherman for the capitulation of Johnston's army and "the reestablishment of peace" were rejected by the Government, and that Grant, who had returned at once to Washington after the assassination of the President, was sent to North Carolina for the purpose of supervising the final arrangements for the surrender of the Confederate forces east of the Mississippi.

Meanwhile, Grant having arrived at Washington, Rawlins was making his dispositions for the continuance and completion of the report at that place. Aided by Bowers, Parker, and Leet, he gave his first attention to the collection of the reports and the preparation of materials for Grant's final report of operations. As was customary Grant prepared the outlines of the report himself but the details of every statement were wrought out, tested, and arranged in their proper places by Rawlins and his assistants; so that the report as finally sent to the War Department and published was the best one ever submitted to the Government and one of the most accurate and complete known in the annals of war. It has successfully withstood the test of time, and while the wisdom of some of its statements in reference to the principles upon which the army was administered has been questioned, the whole document may well be studied by military men as a model of arrangement, style, and completeness of statement.

As soon as peace was assured the work of mustering out the army began; but before this was finished, measures were taken to rid Mexico of the French and Spanish interposition, which had resulted in the establishment of an ephemeral empire under Maximilian. Sheridan was sent to Texas with a force of cavalry, infantry and artillery, to make good our demands in behalf of the sister republic. I, with my cavalry corps, was also under orders for a week to proceed from Georgia to the Mexican frontier.

Rawlins, who was, after all, more of a civilian and statesman than a soldier, was a strenuous advocate of the Monroe Doctrine, sympathized deeply with the Mexicans, and gave his Chief the most ardent support at that important juncture.

It should also be remembered that as soon as it became certain that the French would evacuate Mexico and leave Maximilian to his fate, public attention was strongly directed to a settlement with Great Britain for the unfriendly part taken by her in behalf of the Southern Confederacy. The depredations upon American commerce by the *Alabama* and other Confederate cruisers fitted out in British ports, had aroused the deepest feeling of resentment throughout the army, as well as in commercial circles. The rank and file, as well as the higher officers, manifested the liveliest disposition in favor of an enforced indemnification for our losses. Many of them wanted no money settlement, but openly advocated a campaign for the occupation of Canada and the expulsion of the British flag from North America. It is now known that Grant was for a while strongly in favor of this policy, and in view of the fact that we then had the most powerful navy in the world, and could have turned an army of 500,000 veteran soldiers in the direction of our northern frontier, there can be but little doubt as to what would have been the result. Even so late as Grant's own administration it seems likely that this would have been the policy, but for the political quarrel between President Grant and Senator Sumner, Chairman of the Senate Committee on Foreign Relations, who had become its most powerful advocate.

In this great question Rawlins shared the feelings of the army and, through Grant, did all in his power to give them effect. What would have been the result, had the more important questions connected with the reconstruction of the seceding States not been complicated by the assassination of Lincoln and the memorable quarrel between Andrew Johnson and the Republican party, must always remain a matter of conjecture.

It will be remembered that at first both Grant and Rawlins were disposed to approve the methods and uphold the hands of President Johnson in reference to Reconstruction, mainly because they supposed he was carrying out the benignant policy of his great predecessor. Both accompanied him on the memorable tour which he made through the Northern States, ostensibly for the purpose of delivering an address at the dedication of the monument to the memory of Senator Douglas, at Chicago, in September, 1865, but really for the purpose of winning the people of the Northern States to the views which he held in regard to the political rehabilitation of the Southern States, and the readjustment of their relations to the Union. In respect to this important matter a radical difference of opinion began to show itself between Congress and the President, shortly after his inauguration, and ended finally in his impeachment, trial, and acquittal. Although generally regarded as an astute politician, Johnson was slow to recognize the fact that the Northern people were against his policy. He was surrounded by office seekers and political parasites, who concealed the truth from him and told him only such things as they thought would gratify his vanity.

Secretary Seward, Secretary Welles, Admiral Farragut, and many other officials and ladies accompanied the President in the trip to the West. Speeches were made at the principal cities; but after the first few days it became manifest that the President was delivering substantially the same speech everywhere. It was a vague, incoherent appeal to the country in behalf of the readmission into the Union of the States which had taken part in the Rebellion, without terms or conditions, and had this policy been advocated with the gravity, decorum, and kindliness that Lincoln would have given to its discussion, it might have prevailed. But the trip soon degenerated into an undignified, if not a disgraceful, junket, which the newspapers designated derisively as "Swinging Around the Circle." Grant and Farragut doubtless consented to accompany the party because they considered the wishes of the President, as Commander-in-Chief, quite as obligatory upon them as his orders would have been. Rawlins went because Grant did, but having been a Douglas Democrat, and a great admirer of that distinguished statesman, he doubtless felt besides that it would afford Grant an excellent opportunity to show himself to the people, while attending the dedication of the Douglas monument. The war having come to a favorable ending, the time was now at hand when Grant could do this without incurring the criticism of even his bitterest enemy. As it turned out, however, Grant also soon became disgusted with the undignified exhibition the President was making of himself, and took leave of the party at Buffalo, going with Rawlins by lake steamer to Detroit. They rejoined Johnson at Chicago and accompanied the party to St. Louis, where they finally left it, ostensibly for the purpose of visiting Grant's father near Cincinnati, but really because, as Grant expressed it, he did not "care to accompany a man who was deliberately digging his own grave."

Rawlins, who was a politician before he became a soldier, soon saw enough to convince him that Johnson could not be renominated, and that Grant's chances for the succession would be injured by a further identification with Johnson or his policy. But notwithstanding its melancholy features, it must be admitted that the trip was a novel and interesting experience to the General and his Chief of Staff. To the latter it was a relaxation from the routine of army administration, for which in times of peace he had but little taste. Suffering, as he was, from impaired health and failing strength, he had grown exceedingly tired of the life in Washington. He realized, in fact, that his military services were at an end. They had been imposed upon him by the "Appeal to the God of Battles" which he had accepted and advocated in the Galena speech, as the only proper response that could be made to the overt acts of the secessionists. The work which it brought to him as a soldier was now done, while that which devolved upon him as a civilian and statesman was about to be extended to a wider field.

But before considering the concluding period of this patriotic and useful life, it may prove interesting to allude briefly to an association of officers in which Rawlins took the greatest interest, and which was doubtless suggested by the "Order of the Cincinnati," organized immediately after the close of the Revolutionary War.

In this connection it should be observed that the end of the Civil War and the disbandment of the volunteer army were followed almost immediately by the formation of a number of military societies, intended to keep alive the memories and foster the fraternal feelings which had grown up between the officers and men of the national army. The first and most important of these was started in the Senate Chamber at the Capital of North Carolina on April 14, 1865, during a pause in Sherman's march Northward through the heart of the Confederacy. The meeting was necessarily a preliminary one, but it was followed by another at the same place on April 25, at which time the organization was completed, and a constitution was adopted which entitled to membership every officer who had served with honor in the Army of the Tennessee.

The name selected for the association was the Society of the Army of the Tennessee. Instead, however, of electing one of its living commanders as its first president, it passed over the names of Grant, Sherman, Howard, and Logan alike and unanimously conferred that honor upon Brigadier General John A. Rawlins, U. S. A., Chief of Staff to the Lieutenant General, in consideration of his eminent services to our country in connection with the Army of the Tennessee and also for his ability for the position.

Inasmuch as he was not within four hundred miles of that army at the time, but had been absent from it over a year, this was not only an unexpected but a marked compliment which shows better than any other event that ever took place the esteem in which Rawlins was held by the leading generals. It also shows that the Society recognized and intended to certify him to the country as an officer of the highest character and most unusual services. No ordinary man either of the regular army or of the volunteers could have counted upon such a distinction. The proceedings show that the choice was not made by accident nor without full and careful consideration. Rawlins had not been consulted, and therefore had no reason to be prepared for or to expect that this honor would be conferred upon him.

The first regular meeting of the Society was called by letter, July 10, addressed to the officers of the Army of the Tennessee and was held at Cincinnati on November 14, 1865. Rawlins was of course present at that meeting, and delivered a careful and elaborate address which was listened to with marked attention by his comrades. It contains without doubt the best synopsis that has ever been made of the history of the Army of the Tennessee interspersed with anecdotes and frequent allusions to its most distinguished officers. It may be well to observe again, however, that Rawlins, with Grant and Sherman, persisted in the error that Bragg, at the battle of Missionary Ridge, moved his troops from the left and center of his line to the right, for the purpose of resisting Sherman's attack on the last day. Rawlins always took great pride in this society, and remained its president until his death. Its first Vice-Presidents were Logan, Blair, Oglesby, Giles A. Smith, Belknap, and Fairchild.

EXCEPT for his short visit to Chicago in the autumn of 1865, Rawlins had been constantly with his family since the cessation of hostilities, but his tour of the country with President Johnson and party again separated him from, and gave occasion for several letters to his wife, two of which are here quoted as follows:

Hudson River,

August 30, 1866

. ... We have been so constantly engaged that I have not had time to write sooner. I am well and improving all the time, but don't much relish the loss of my morning naps. However, I hope soon to get used to it.

The ovations to the President have been very fine all the way from Washington here. The one in New York perhaps has never been excelled in this country. General Grant and Admiral Farragut came in for a large share of the cheering, I assure you. And I am now more than ever glad that the General concluded to accompany the President, for it will do Grant good, whatever may be his aspirations in the future, and fix him in the confidence of Mr. Johnson, enabling him to fix up the army as it should be, and exert such influence as will be of benefit to the country. The Philadelphians gave the President a splendid reception, notwithstanding the action of their officers. Mr. Cadwallader has been very busy, and is likely to continue so. The General and all the party are well and happy.

I see by the papers that Admiral Radford is mentioned as having been with General Meade in the procession, when in fact Grant, Farragut, Meade and myself rode in the same carriage. . . .

Niagara Falls,

September 1, 1866

. ... I have been so constantly on the move since leaving Washington that I have been unable to write as I intended, but shall try hereafter to get off a line to you every day till we start back. We reached here at 4 P M. today and met a hearty reception from the people. The fact is the enthusiasm everywhere along the route has been unbounded, but there is more cheering for Grant and Farragut than for the President. The President's friends along cheer him, but all parties cheer Grant and

292

Farragut. I feel from what I see that the chances are favorable to the conservatives and Democrats in this State this fall. They claim that they will carry the State by forty or fifty thousand majority. Seward is delighted and is certainly a man unequaled in tact and shrewdness to manage an assemblage of men opposed to him in politics. I am not surprised that he was the leader of his own party when he was in membership with it. I can tell mother many things when I get back that will greatly please her and some, too, that will not.

They are having a grand ball here tonight. I shall take no part in it, but go early to bed and try to get some sleep. I have had very little since I left home. Still I feel refreshed with the trip already, and after tonight shall be in a condition to stand it better than I have. My cough is nothing like what it was in severity, which, under the circumstances, loss of sleep, etc., is a little surprising.

After dinner today Surgeon General Barnes got a carriage and, being well acquainted with the falls and vicinity, took me to see them. I can give you no description of them that would give you any idea of what they are, other than that you already have. You will have to come and see them yourself to properly appreciate their beauty, magnitude and grandeur. Simply to look at them and think, thus they have poured in their ceaseless roar from the beginning of time, and will continue to the end, sinks all thought of self in the sublime.

Mr. Cadwallader is well—the General is well—I am growing better all the time, and everybody with us is well.

The President makes innumerable speeches every day, and the people cheer him lustily. Grant was at first quite fidgety over the matter, but has finally grown quite tranquil and seems to enjoy himself very much. Admiral Farragut takes everything admirably and is having a happy time. Mrs. Farragut is delighted, and the only fears she seems to have are that the people will shake the Admiral's hands off. She is a most lovely lady and decidedly in love with you. She inquired very tenderly after you and Jenny, and said she should never forget your sincere affection for the sweet little girl. I told her we had a new baby, and she seemed perfectly enthusiastic over it and said that it would be another link in your love for the others. Of all that I have heard since I left home, this talk of hers pleased me most. This you believe, don't you, my darling wife? . . .

From the tone of this correspondence, although devoted mainly to public matters, it is apparent that Rawlins was a man of the warmest affections, who held his family and its interests above all considerations except those of public duty. As was his custom, he continued his letters to his wife during the whole of his trip, but as they relate mostly to personal and family matters, no further quotation from them seems to be required. It is evident that although he was encouraged by his physicians, and at times by his own feelings, to believe that he was mending, his health was really on the decline. It is also evident that the occupations of peace called less frequently for the exercise of his personal influence with Grant than did those of war. The load of his official responsibility had become lighter, and he felt correspondingly more at liberty to look after his own health and interests, and especially to study the drift of public opinion. As before stated, his earlier feelings inclined him to the support of Andrew Johnson and his policy, but the better he came to know the man and the politicians who supported him, the more certain did he become that they could not sufficiently command the support of the dominant party in the North to carry their views into effect. He was too good a lawyer to pronounce them illegal. The questions under consideration were of the highest importance. They were questions of policy upon which the Constitution was silent, and hence their solution called for the exercise of the highest patience, moderation, and wisdom on the part of the President as well as on the part of the Congress and as it soon became evident that instead of exhibiting these virtues towards each other the Chief Magistrate and the law-making body were drifting hopelessly apart, thousands of sensible men naturally began to fear that the most valuable results of the Union's victory might be put in jeopardy, if not lost entirely, and therefore began openly to favor Grant's election to the Presidency as the best possible means of restoring peace and quietude to the country. Rawlins favored the movement, but did not for a moment try to deceive himself into the belief that Grant was specially fitted for the solution of such questions as were then claiming public attention; but relying upon his sound judgment and his unselfish patriotism, and considering the fact that the victorious commander, in view of Lincoln's death and of the violent temper and consequent unpopularity of Stanton, was fairly entitled to the succession, without the slightest hesitation he declared for his nomination and election to succeed Johnson. While some thought him unfit for the office, and many of his best friends, such as Sherman, did not hesitate to declare that he would be foolish to give up the headship of the army for life in order to embark upon the uncertain career of a politician even if he should be elected President, Rawlins did not share their views. He felt that Grant, like every other citizen, must answer such supreme calls as his country might make upon him; that he would be entitled to the best help his countrymen could give him; and that if he failed for any reason fully to satisfy the highest demands made upon him, he would still be entitled to the grateful recollection of his fellow-citizens, not only for his military services but for standing as the exponent and guardian of the Union cause at a period during which its greatest interests were at stake, and its wisest statesmen were in doubt. Besides, Rawlins felt that under his Chief's leadership the war having ended in a complete suppression of armed hostility to the National Government, he was at perfect liberty to express the convictions which were growing in strength month by month, with the political unrest which gave rise to them. Rawlins early declared his feelings to his more intimate friends and as they regarded him not only as Grant's mouthpiece in civil as well as in military affairs, but withal as better able than was Grant himself to set his views fully before the public, they asked him to prepare and deliver an address upon the questions of the day, at such time and place as might best suit his convenience. His health was still failing, and Grant had already decided that he should make the overland tour of the continent along the line of the Union Pacific railroad, then under construction, in company with General Dodge, who had resigned from the Army and become Chief Engineer of the contracting company.

Yielding to the request of his friends, Rawlins prepared his speech with unusual care, and through them made all necessary arrangements for its delivery at Galena, on June 21, 1867. The manuscript was of course submitted to Grant, and received his approval. This fact became known at the time and gave to the address an importance and a circulation which it could not otherwise have obtained. It was justly considered as setting forth Grant's opinions and policy on the questions then uppermost in the minds of all. For this reason it was published shortly afterwards by the Union Republican Congressional Committee at Washington as a campaign document of the first importance.

As soon as Rawlins had completed the address and made arrangements for a protracted absence, he bade farewell to his family, and started for Chicago, where he stopped over for the purpose of conferring with his friend, Judge Drummond, who had already become greatly distinguished as the learned and fearless judge of the United States Circuit Court for Illinois, and also with J. Russell Jones, afterwards Grant's Minister at Brussels. They were both from Galena, and were besides the leading citizens of Northwestern Illinois. They were ardent Republicans, but cool, observant, and able men, who could hardly be mistaken as to the drift of public opinion. Nobody knew Grant's character or lack of qualifications for civil office better than did they. They were also his closest and most faithful friends; but nothing in their relations with the victorious soldier could be construed as indicating a willingness on their part to prefer his further promotion to the public welfare. After careful consideration, they fully approved Rawlins's proposed speech, and this gave him additional confidence in its timeliness and propriety as well as in the soundness of his views.

But in the midst of the satisfaction he had derived from seeing and conferring with his friends, Rawlins suffered a cruel and overwhelming blow to his affections. On June 13, 1867, he received a telegram announcing the sudden and unexpected death of his young son Willie. Naturally his first impulse was to give up his trip across the plains, and return to his sorrowing wife; but realizing that his duty to her as well as to others, required him to conserve his strength, he went on to Galena, where he received every mark of consideration and sympathy from his family and friends, and especially from his former brother staff-officer, General Rowley, with whom he spent his first night. From there he wrote that as soon as he had delivered his speech, which would not be delayed, he should continue his journey across the plains in hopes that their dry air would restore his health.

It is pitiful to contemplate how this able man, stricken in the prime of his usefulness by an incurable disease, was alternately buoyed up by the hope of recovery, and depressed by the certainty of increasing weakness. Distracted by a sense of duty to his wife and family, and by the necessity of doing all in his power for himself, he set forth bravely to make a supreme effort in search of health and strength, amid new scenes and new occupations, far from those he loved best on earth.

Under these distressing conditions, with a sinking heart and an enfeebled constitution, but sustained by an unfaltering sense of duty to his Chief and to his countrymen, he delivered his speech to one of the largest meetings of his fellow-citizens that had ever listened to him. The task was one which greatly taxed his strength; but he went successfully through with it, holding his audience in rapt attention to the end. It was a worthy tribute to their intelligence, and the honor that the citizen soldier, of whom they were so proud, conferred upon them, was returned to him tenfold by the unstinted approval which they gave to his eloquent periods.

After a few days' rest at Galena, during which he was soothed and encouraged by the ministrations of his relations and friends, Rawlins finally set out for the far West. From Dixon, Illinois, where he was forced to wait a few hours for a train, he wrote to his wife again; and after expressing his deep and abiding gratitude for the friendly and sympathetic letters which he had received from his brother officers of the staff, and for the present of a thousand dollars, which the people of Galena had given him, he continued as follows:

. . . The people of Galena have been very kind to me. On my leaving there this morning they handed me a letter, which on opening I found to contain one thousand dollars in a draft on New York. This amount I have at present a mind to invest in a few acres of land near Chicago, in yours and the children's name, with a view to its growing in value in a few years. I shall decide between here and Omaha. If I decide to make the investment I shall send it to Russell Jones from Omaha with the request that he make the investment for me; if not will send the draft to you.

... I made my speech in Galena. It met with the great approbation of my friends, and has been printed in the Chicago papers with favorable and, I might say, most flattering editorial notices. I shall send you some of the papers as soon as I get hold of them. Of course there are some typographical errors that are a little annoying; still it is generally correct. I sent you this morning a Galena paper containing it in full. The *Tribune* says: "It is the platform of the army; it is the platform of the Republican party; it is emphatically the platform of the country, and it is unquestionably the platform of General Grant."

On July 4, he sent his wife an interesting account of his march across the plains from Julesburg, at that time the end of the railroad, to the site of a new town, which he and his associates named Cheyenne. He was accompanied on this march by Major Dunn, his aid-de-camp and by Colonel Carling, of the Quartermaster's Department. Owing to the presence of wild Indians, the party was escorted through the country by a detachment of cavalry, under the command of Lieutenant Colonel J. K. Mizner, and it was an entirely new experience for most of them. Rawlins was especially interested in the glimpse of frontier life which the march, the hunting, and the encampments furnished him. It filled him with renewed hope that his health was greatly improved, that his cough had diminished, and that his appetite had increased. He thoroughly enjoyed camp fare, and on the fourth day out ate what he described as "the best meal he had had in four years." It consisted simply of antelope steak, rather poor biscuits, canned peas, peaches, cheese, and coffee. He was pleased with the scenery, the exhilarating atmosphere, and the free and easy life. He praised Carling, who had served on my staff as Chief Quartermaster of the Western cavalry, as "a most splendid gentleman and officer." He added buoyantly: "I feel greatly in hopes that I shall recover my health permanently," and one cannot suppress the thought that if the invalid or the medical profession had known at that time as much as is now known in reference to the proper treatment of such cases, it is more than probable that his hopes might have been fully realized.

On July 8, after alluding to the celebration held on the Fourth, 'to the arrival of General Augur at the site of the new town on Crow Creek, and to the expected arrival of General Stevenson with a detachment for the relief of his escort and the garrison of the new frontier post, Fort D. A. Russell, he wrote as follows:

> . . . Here will be the junction of the Denver branch of the road; here will be established one of the permanent military posts, the depot for years to come of all the posts this side of the Rocky Mountains. Crow Creek, a rapid stream of fine water, flows by here, and the great snowy mountains lift themselves up in full view, and every evening since our encampment here have breathed their icy breath upon us.

> General Dodge is here hard at work and looks badly. He is suffering from old wounds received in the service. I fear if he does not let up a little in his work he will be compelled to do so from physical inability to work longer.

While in this region Rawlins took a deep interest in the frontier life about him. He accompanied Dodge and the army officers in their explorations of the surrounding country and the location of the new army posts, taking part in all the preliminary work for extending the railroad towards Salt Lake. While the party was in no danger, the constant presence of Indians, with occasional rumors of outrages on their part, added to the interest and excitement of the life it was leading. This doubtless stimulated Rawlins's appetite and inspired him to ask for the New York papers and what they said of his Galena speech, which had been widely noticed and favorably commented on.

Rawlins was still at Cheyenne, July 20, 1867, where he was deeply interested in the case of a Swedish boy named Andrew Bomkersen, who belonged to a Government train from Salt Lake, was killed there on the 11th, and was the first person buried at that place. Having given his advice and assistance to Augur in locating the permanent post, he began to be eager to move on, and anxious about the importance given by the press to his Galena speech. He naturally wanted to know what the New York papers thought of it, though he felt sure his relations with the General would give importance to what he said.

From Fort Saunders, Dakota, he wrote an account of the journey to that place, which he greatly enjoyed, notwithstanding the fact that his party had been followed by Indians. He added with pardonable pride:

> ... I feel greatly flattered by the reception of my speech by the public. I know nothing of what the St. Louis papers say nor of what the New York papers say, except the *Tribune*. Rowley enclosed me some extracts from other papers, which I enclose herewith to you along with some I cut from the Chicago papers and the *Galena Advertiser*. The latter has the whole speech in it, with an editorial written by H. H. Houghton. However flatteringly the latter has written of me he believes every word of it. . . .

The party then advanced to the North Platte, where it located Fort Steele, but the march was quite trying to Rawlins. Much trouble and some delay were caused by the depth and rapidity of the stream; the cavalry horses and pack animals had to swim it, and this brought the party into a trackless region, farther and farther from the overland trail, as well as from water. Sixteen miles beyond the crossing they discovered a flowing spring, at which the party, and especially Rawlins, drank with great enjoyment. It was a veritable oasis in the desert, and later became the site of a flourishing town, which in due time Dodge named after his friend Rawlins.

From that point the party made its way to the Medicine Bow River, and thence across the Continental Divide to Fort Bridger, Utah. The march was varied by scouting and exploring, by fording rivers, climbing mountains, and shooting game. Elk, black-tailed deer, and bear were abundant; the mess was kept amply supplied, and Rawlins continued to feel stronger and better. Although he did not get rid of his cough, he still indulged in the hope that the trip would give him permanent relief. On August 19 he wrote:

> ... I see by the papers that General Grant has accepted the position of acting Secretary of War in the place of Mr. Stanton. I suppose of course he has good reason for doing so and that he thinks he can perhaps better serve the interests of reconstruction there than if someone inimical to reconstruction were placed there. For my own part I must confess that I am sorry any condition of things should have so turned out as to necessitate General Grant's accepting the position. It will

require a steady hand and clear head to keep out of the gulf that yawns between the President and the people. There is no friendship for the General with the President or any of his Cabinet in my judgment, and the party Butler represents and the bitterness he feels are neither dead nor sleeping. My faith in an overruling Providence is still strong, and Grant's star I believe to be still in the ascendant, but so the stars of my country pale not I shall be content. I have no letter from Washington since I left Galena, and of course know nothing of what is going on.

I received a letter dated July 26 from Russell Jones, in which he says: "I also received yours containing the $1,000 draft, and after talking with Bass, Bradley and Corwith I conclude to buy ten shares of our street railway stock instead of buying land. If I am not greatly mistaken there is no better place to put it. I hold it in the name of your wife and children, though standing in my name on the Company's books. Unless otherwise directed, I shall invest the dividends in new stock as fast as there is enough to buy another share." I am not so well satisfied with this as I would have been if he had bought land, but I have great confidence in the gentleman named and in his judgment. . . .

From Camp Douglas, Salt Lake City, he wrote:

. . . On Wednesday evening,

August 28

... we met Brigham Young, his last wife and two daughters at the house of Mr. Head, the Indian agent here. He looks to be a man of about forty-five years of age, but is sixty-six. Of the peculiar institution of these people one has a more favorable idea from letter writers than from observation. My own views of them are far less favorable than others of General Grant's staff who have been here before. I am in favor of the Conner rather than the Young party. On the 29th I called on Governor Durkee, Chief Justice Titus and Judge Drake of this territory. They are to call on us tomorrow. I like them very much. General and Mrs. Chetlain and Mr. Head are very kind to us. We shall leave here on the 2nd or 3rd of September for the East via South Pass. Shall reach Omaha about the 10th of October. . . .

On his way he sent the following letter:

Bear River Station,

September 6, 1867

. ... I am glad the General sent you the funds, but don't be uneasy about my hurrying home on account of the General's new duties, for be assured I owe too much to my family and my own health to hurry to Washington at this time. I could do nothing now. Had I been there I might have prevailed upon the General not to accept the position he has now. I certainly should have tried unless being there had put me in possession of knowledge I do not now have. May God guide him aright is my prayer. ... I am in very good health, except my cough, and I think I am getting better of that all the time. . . .

During this entire trip across the plains and Continental Divide to the Great Salt Lake, Rawlins had been the guest and inseparable companion of Dodge. As his letters show, they had been warm and devoted friends from the time they first met in West Tennessee, and had never lost an opportunity to say kind things of each other, but neither had come to appreciate the other thoroughly till they spent the summer and fall together, the one seeking health and the other trying to find the best possible location for a railroad to the Pacific Ocean. Hitherto Rawlins had been the industrious, austere, uncompromising staff officer, looking neither to the right nor left, but sternly working for victory over the public enemy. His high character had become known to all, but it needed this trip to reveal the genial and companionable nature of the man to his friend. During the relaxations by the camp-fire at night, he had let the light in upon his own nature, and the ruling principles of his life. As he told the story of his experiences from Belmont to Appomattox, he unconsciously revealed his unselfish character, his devotion to Grant, his persistence in the performance of duty, his exalted patriotism, and, above all, the high sense of honor by which he was guided through all the emergencies of his career. Dodge bears the most unmistakable testimony to all this, as well as to the fact that although a sick man himself, Rawlins was more worried about the health of his companion than about his own. While all looked out with anxious solicitude for his comfort, he was never for a moment neglectful of theirs. While all hoped that he would receive permanent benefit from the outdoor life of the plains, and it is probable that his disease was arrested and his life was thereby sensibly prolonged, it in the end became evident that the improvement was only temporary and that the unrelaxing hand of death had him firmly in its grasp.

While at Salt Lake City, Brigham Young and the Mormons made every effort to entertain and interest him in their affairs, but he respectfully declined their offers of hospitality and pitched his tent at Fort Douglas, overlooking the city. He treated all with politeness but acted throughout apparently on the theory that his official independence might be compromised by the slightest unnecessary intimacy.

On the return trip from Salt Lake City north to the Snake River Valley the party followed Brigham Young and his bishops, who were on their annual procession through the settlements. While Dodge and Rawlins were received at the settlements with respect, much to their surprise, but little personal interest was shown in their movements. In view of the friendly attentions which had been extended to them at Salt Lake this was difficult to account for and produced an unfavorable impression, which lasted Rawlins until his death.

As the party crossed the Green River Mountains, they discovered many signs of grizzly bears, which excited the sporting propensities of the younger men. A hunt was organized in which, against Dodge's advice, Rawlins and his aid-de-camp took part. They had not gone far before a wounded grizzly turned upon them and, but for the skill of a professional hunter, might have overtaken them. Both were glad to escape, and Rawlins did not hesitate to blame himself for this disobedience of orders.

The march to the eastward was varied by the excitement of bear and buffalo hunting and the fear of the Indians. A few gold camps were encountered, and claims were staked out, one of which, assigned to Rawlins, was sold for a small sum by his family several years afterwards.

After a wide circuit of several weeks through the mountains, north of the line on which it had gone to Salt Lake, the party reached Cheyenne in safety. Rawlins parted from it at the end of the railroad and on October 12, 1867, arrived at Galena, where he received a hearty welcome from his family and friends. He had been gone four months, during which he had been buoyed up by hope, but had derived little substantial benefit from the change.

Before passing from this period of Rawlins's life, it may be well to call attention to the fact that Stanton's dismissal from the position of Secretary of War, and Grant's appointment to that office *ad interim,* was followed by sharp collisions between Congress and the President in regard to the reconstruction of the Southern States, and this greatly complicated the duties which Grant was called upon to perform. Without the help, for the greater part of the time, of his trusted chief of staff, he continued to hold the office till relieved of it in accordance with the Tenure of Office Act. The Senate having refused on January 14, 1868, to concur in the suspension and removal of Stanton, Grant at once abandoned the position he had been filling, although the President alleged that he had promised to hold it against Stanton's reinstatement. A question of veracity arose between them. Grant denied that he had ever made any such promise, whereupon the President cited his Cabinet as-witnesses to prove that he had.

While the discussion was at its height Rawlins returned to Washington, and at once became interested in mastering the facts of the case and giving advice and counsel to his Chief. Through his legal acumen and his keen perception, he soon reached a clear understanding of the complications in which General Grant had become involved. All doubts were speedily dissipated, the damaging charges against the General were disproved to the satisfaction of the country, and he was nominated for the Presidency by a National Convention of soldiers and sailors gathered from all parts of the country at Chicago, May 19, 1868. Rawlins was known to be in favor of the movement, if not absolutely directing it. To his gratification, it culminated two days later in Grant's nomination by the National Republican Convention, substantially on the platform which Rawlins had outlined in his speech at Galena the year before.

During the month of October and a part of November, 1867, Rawlins remained at Galena, and wrote no letters. His health had received but little benefit from his life on the plains. Up one day and down the next, he had serious misgivings, and was driven almost to desperation at times. This is shown by the pathetic fact that while in camp on the plains one bright summer day he opened his shirt and bared his breast to the sun till it was almost blistered, in the hope that it would prove a counterirritant which would benefit his lungs.

It will be remembered that the Presidential election took place in November, 1868, and that Grant was elected by a great majority. While Rawlins was deeply interested in the outcome of the campaign, his health was not strong enough to permit him to take an active part in the canvass, even if the proprieties of his military position had allowed it. He was, however, constantly consulted by the politicians and gave them his best advice, especially in regard to the West. When the election was over he returned to Washington and took up his residence at Willard's Hotel, but while getting his house ready for his family he slept at his office, to the detriment both of his comfort and his health.

Early in December he wrote that, much as he would like to do so, he could not return home because his official duties forbade it. In common with many others, he soon began to feel some anxiety about the make-up of the Cabinet and the distribution of the great offices of the Administration. On December 10 he wrote:

> . . . The subject of offices is scarcely broached. In fact, among those whom I have met the chief speculation is as to what I am to have. All seem to take it for granted that the General is going to do something very handsome, more than he has ever done for me, but what he intends of course none of them know. The position I have is perhaps as good as any the General will have in his power to give, and to have it secured to me is all I want, and even this I should not want if I had the health I lost in the service. My arm pains me considerably and I do not as yet see that it relieves my cough, though it is hardly time.

> I met General Butler night before last and had a long talk with him. He tells me he intends to earnestly support Grant's administration, and I believe him, that is, if he is properly treated.

About this time both General and Mrs. Grant gave him an earnest invitation to make his home with them till he was ready to bring his family to Washington, but he persisted in living alone till after the holidays, which he spent with his wife in Connecticut. On his return to Washington he compromised what was evidently an embarrassing question by "sleeping at the office, taking his breakfast at a restaurant, and dining with General Grant." Curiously enough he was assured most positively about that time by the doctors that his lungs were not affected, and again took hope from the assurance; but nevertheless he was henceforth compelled to decline all social invitations on account of his enfeebled condition. He daily took a horseback ride on General Grant's black pony, "Jeff Davis" and scrupulously followed the regimen prescribed for him, but withal his disease was steadily making progress towards its fatal and inevitable end.

As the inauguration was approaching, he became more and more uneasy as to his own future. General Grant the President Elect, it will be remembered, was peculiarly reticent about his Cabinet and other important appointments, and kept the entire country in a state of suspense almost to the very day he took the oath of office. This doubtless added to Rawlins's anxiety. He had done his full part in making Grant's military career a success and in helping to place him properly before the country as a candidate for the highest office within its gift. He was too proud to ask what was to be done for him, or to even intimate that he would like to have a cabinet position, but his letters to his wife show clearly that he considered himself an important part of what Grant stood for, and did not want to be left out of consideration in the organization of the new Administration.

CLOSING EVENTS

It so happened that J. Russell Jones and I were visiting Grant for a few days shortly before the inauguration, and after the ladies retired, it was his custom to invite us into the library for the purpose of discussing both measures and men. On Friday night, February 19, 1869, he read us the draft of his inaugural address, and asked for our suggestions as to its form, as well as to several of the topics to be considered; but in doing so he warned us that, as he had not yet discussed the Cabinet "with anyone, not even with Mrs. Grant," he could not do so with us. He invited us, however, to talk freely about men for other places, and we did so. Before the conversation ended, I naturally asked him what he was going to do for Rawlins. He replied that he intended to assign him to the command of the Department of Arizona, in the confident belief that a prolonged residence in the high and dry atmosphere of that region would result in his complete restoration to health.

The next day, in reply to a direct question as to what Grant was going to do for him, I told Rawlins with Grant's permission what the General had said on that subject the night before, and was not at all surprised at the declaration that it would not be at all satisfactory to him. He said without reserve that he not only wanted but thought himself fairly entitled to the appointment of Secretary of War. He then gave a full summary of his views, and in conclusion asked me to make them known in my own way, but without unnecessary delay, to the President-elect. That night I complied with his request. The General showed neither surprise nor impatience, but without the slightest question or hesitation, he said: "You can tell Rawlins he shall be Secretary of War," but added, "He will have to wait a few days, possibly two weeks or a month, for I have asked Schofield to hold over a while."

I saw Rawlins early the next morning and gave him Grant's message, which he received with marked gratification, followed by the assurance that the arrangement would be entirely satisfactory to him.

Of course I made this known to Grant, and that terminated my connection with the matter. I naturally supposed that Grant would notify Rawlins officially of his intentions, but as the inauguration approached without his saying anything in confirmation of what he had specially authorized me to tell Rawlins, the latter became again discouraged, and went to Danbury with the declaration that he did not intend to return to Washington. From there he wrote to General Dodge, that he had come to the conclusion that he was not to be Secretary of War, but was to have a command in the West. Thereupon Dodge took the letter to Grant, who seemed surprised, but at once gave Dodge the same assurance he had given me. He explained again that it had been his intention to give Rawlins command in Arizona and New Mexico, in the belief that the high, dry climate of that region would be beneficial to him; but understanding that this arrangement would not suit Rawlins, he should call him to the Cabinet as Secretary of War. Grant made no explanation of why he had not already told Rawlins of his plans. It is of course possible that he may have entertained other views for a while, but be this as it may, he shortly confirmed what he had said to both Dodge and myself by letter or telegraph; for a few days later Rawlins returned to Washington and made arrangements for his family to join him there.

It will be remembered that Grant's first Cabinet, containing, as it did, several obscure and inexperienced men, was a great disappointment to the public, and still more so to the Republican party. E. B. Washburne, who was appointed Secretary of State for the purpose of increasing his prestige as Minister to France, soon gave way to Hamilton Fish, and in due time Schofield made way for Rawlins. As to Fish, although a distinguished man, who had long been out of active public life, his appointment was a genuine surprise to the country, while that of Rawlins was hailed by those who knew him best as one entirely proper to be made. It gave great satisfaction, especially to the volunteer army, by which he had long since come to be regarded as a man of unusual vigor, honesty, and independence. His principal friends among the higher officers were Dodge, Logan, and Gresham. They were also experienced politicians, who fairly represented the War Democrats as well as the

Republicans, and made haste to express their satisfaction to the politicians and the country at large.

Three days before Rawlins's appointment was announced, which was on March 11, Dodge, acting for himself and a few other friends who knew that Rawlins was a poor man, took up and returned to him the mortgage note and other papers connected with the dwelling house which he had purchased sometime before on Georgetown Heights. In performing this generous act, Dodge took occasion to say:

> ... I am enabled to do this through the kindness of a few friends, most of whom only know you by reputation, but who have watched your course through your entire public life. Their respect and high regard for you as a gentleman and a soldier, your strict integrity and ability, your disinterested services to your country and your Chief alone has prompted this gift. I trust you will receive it in the same kindly spirit it is given, and at some future time more appropriate than this I will furnish you the names of the gentlemen.
>
> Allow me to say, I never performed a duty that gave me more pleasure or satisfaction, and wishing you for them and myself that health and prosperity in the future that your valuable and distinguished services in the past entitle you to, I am truly your friend.

On March 11 Rawlins wrote to his wife as follows:

> . . . The excitement incident upon the organization of the Cabinet and the number of persons constantly around me have prevented me writing you earlier. The Cabinet is now organized, and, from what I learn from people here, is quite acceptable. I am congratulated by many for my position in it, and by some I am sure sincerely. Of Brigadier General U. S. Grant's staff as originally organized, I was the youngest member. So of President Grant's Cabinet I am the youngest and as a Cabinet officer shall try to serve my country and him with the same fidelity I tried to serve both as a staff officer.
>
> Enclosed I send you a letter from General Dodge which explains itself. . . .

Of course Rawlins, Secretary of War, was a much more powerful and important person than Rawlins, Chief of Staff; and while he had but few appointments in his own Department to give out, he was greatly run upon by his many military friends now in civil life for recommendations to the President and the other Secretaries.

On March 28 he wrote to his wife, who had not yet joined him, as follows:

... I am almost ashamed to write after having received three letters from you without having sent a single one in return for ten days, but I know you will pardon me when I tell you my friends have so pressed me, and the condition of my own department as left by the last of Secretary Schofield's orders so annoyed me, that I could not find a moment to sit down and write you as I would like to have done. Yesterday, however, I got permission and issued an order revoking the one of Schofield's, which virtually put the War Department under Sherman. The Department stands now as it did under Stanton, Grant and Schofield. The General of the army is subordinate to the Secretary of War.

I was out of ink in my room today, went downstairs to get some and started up, when in came Hillyer with a friend—of course he always has one. He remarked: "What are you going to do with your ink?" I replied: "I am going, if I can get an opportunity, to write to my wife, a thing I have not done for ten days." The only effect it had was to cause him and his friend to sit down and talk that ever-wearying twaddle about Grant, and the people being with him, etc., until it was too late to get this off in today's mail. I simply mention this to show you how considerate some are who call you friend.

The papers give you full particulars of what Congress and Grant are doing. To those particulars I can only add that God having for the last eight years watched over and guided the destiny of this people in spite of themselves, I have an abiding faith that in His watchfulness and guidance our destiny will be insured, and that it will be as grand as he designs it to be. But for this faith in God I should long since have despaired of my country's welfare and would not feel so hopeful as now. ...

To this he added, two days later:

. . . The great pressure still continues, but I stand it full as well as I had hoped to. . . . My health, I think, is improving. I certainly am not growing worse.

General Sherman felt badly over the revocation of Schofield's order, fearing it would put him in the light of losing Grant's confidence. He did not seem to think I had any special feelings in the matter, and as to that he was about right. A sense of duty to my country made me insist upon its revocation. I could not consent to have the authorities of a great civil office entrusted to me subordinated to the military authority.

Enclosed is a slip from a newspaper and also a letter from a friend, samples of what come to me on the subject. . . .

In further explanation of the reference to Sherman and Schofield in the letter just quoted, it should be remembered that Schofield's last act as hold-over Secretary of War was to issue an order by direction of the President, the practical effect of which was to place the administration of the army, as well as most of the business which had been assigned by law to the Secretary of War, under the immediate control of Sherman, the senior general of the army. All the heads of military bureau were announced as attached to his "General Staff." They were placed under his direct orders, and were required to transact all official business through him or by his authority. Whatever may be said of this as a measure of reform, it was not only adopted without proper consideration but was manifestly in contravention of many laws which had been duly enacted by Congress, and which could not be set aside by an executive order.

Rawlins, as might have been expected, was not slow to perceive the effect of his predecessor's order, nor was he slow to set about securing its immediate nullification. Sherman, general in chief, was to be the principal beneficiary of the order and naturally did all he could through his friend the President to keep it in force, but the case was too plain to admit of serious discussion. The briefest statement of it convinced the President that he could not uphold the revolutionary order, without a palpable usurpation of authority, which would not only discredit his new Secretary but arouse the antagonism of Congress. Rawlins, with his accustomed vigor, but with all due respect, made this entirely clear to Grant and thereby secured the necessary authority to countermand the unlawful order.

The case was a novel one, the outcome of which was watched with intense interest not only by the army but by the statesmen and politicians. It was regarded as a test both of the character and the influence of the new Secretary. His victory was complete, and it at once became recognized that he was a man to be reckoned with in civil as well as in military affairs.

From that time forth, although a confirmed invalid, he took an important part in all public measures which engaged the attention of the President and his Cabinet. His associates were comparative strangers to him as well as to the President. Not one of them had had the slightest acquaintance with the latter till after he had become the victorious commander of our armies. They knew nothing of his character and idiosyncrasies, and still less of his methods of business or of his mental operations. They knew, of course, that he had been educated at West Point, had served in the Mexican War and in the Indian country, and had resigned from the army. They, in common with the rest of their countrymen, knew also that he had been unsuccessful in civil life. They had heard rumors about his habits, and had shared the doubts of the country at large as to his real greatness; but they were well aware of the fact that he had won an unbroken series of victories which had overthrown the Confederate government and reestablished the Union. Without considering how much of this great result was due to Lincoln, Stanton, the Congress, the army at large, and to the patriotism and sacrifices of the people, they concluded, naturally enough perhaps, that he must be a very great man, richly endowed with wisdom and capacity for civil as well as for military affairs. They heard doubtless with surprise his reflections upon public affairs, which he was accustomed to express with unusual common-sense and directness, and attributed to them an importance to which they were not necessarily entitled.

Lacking familiarity with the Constitution and with the law of the land, unacquainted with the leading men of civil life, inexperienced in politics or statecraft, and being compelled, by the great office to which he had been elevated as well as by the condition of public affairs, to deal with questions of the greatest novelty and importance, Grant, more than any of his predecessors, needed the advice and guidance of the wisest and most independent statesmen of the day. With the generous impulse of a soldier, unchanged by contact with the world, he was naturally inclined to prefer his comrades and friends of the camp, whom he had learned to esteem and trust, to the politicians and statesmen, however experienced. It perhaps had not occurred to him that, in making up his mind upon questions and policies of his administration, he should seek the counsel of those who had gained their experience in civil life. He unconsciously treated his Cabinet rather as staff-officers than as his constitutional advisers; rather as clerks than as counsellors, and, unfortunately for him and for the country, this view of their relations was too frequently accepted without question by his new associates.

The simple fact is that the members of the Cabinet stood in awe of the victorious and taciturn soldier, and were prone to attribute to his views, a ripeness and wisdom which they did not always possess. Rawlins was the only one of their number who had seen him develop from the simple clerk in the Galena leather store to the victorious chieftain, commanding a million men. He was the only member of the Cabinet who knew that the President after all was only a plain, sensible man, of unselfish patriotism and excellent judgment, surrounded by grave responsibilities, and needing now, more than ever, an accurate knowledge of men and facts, together with sound and disinterested advice upon the complicated questions which were claiming attention.

Rawlins was besides the only member of the Cabinet who actually knew the capacities and limitations of the President, and while he held him in the highest respect, stood not in the slightest awe of him or of his opinions. Accustomed to think for himself on the questions of the day, and to accept no man's conclusions without the assurance of his own reason that they were sound, he was, for the brief period of his service in civil office, the same fearless, independent, and outspoken counsellor that he had been in military life. To those who knew what took place in government circles it was certain that the new Secretary of War wielded the same potent and controlling influence over the President, when he chose to exert it, that the Chief of Staff had wielded over the Commanding General. It is a circumstance creditable to both that this influence was never exerted except in matters of serious importance, and never failed to receive the attention to which it was entitled.

It is well known that Rawlins early became impressed with the importance of our relations with Cuba, which entered upon its first serious rebellion against Spanish authority in 1868. He was not only intensely American, but believed abstractly in the Monroe Doctrine, and in Senator Douglas's corollary of "Manifest Destiny." He was besides deeply sympathetic with all misgoverned people, and believed that it was our duty, as chief of the American republics, to extend an encouraging if not a protecting hand to such as were unduly oppressed. He did not disguise his sympathy for Cuba, any more than he did for Mexico. He was the open advocate of the Cuban Republic, and although it was not strictly within his province, he advised that the Administration should recognize the Cubans as belligerents, and hold the Spanish government to a rigid responsibility in all matters pertaining to the interests of American citizens. In this policy it is certain that he had at first the concurrence of his Chief and the support of his party as against the more conservative views of Fish, the Secretary of State.

In connection with this important subject, it should be stated that Rawlins had not concealed his views, but had given them fully to the world in his Galena address two years before. In that notable address, which was published and circulated broadcast by the Republican National Committee during Grant's first canvass for the Presidency, he gave his views on every important question then up for consideration. He openly rejoiced in the overthrow of Maximilian's Empire and in the humiliation of Louis Napoleon. He sympathized with the desire and efforts of Ireland to throw off the British yoke, and looked hopefully to the peaceful acquisition of the newly confederated British colonies in North America. He called special attention to the disposition manifested by the British Government after the withdrawal of the European invaders from

Mexico at "our behest" to pay the *Alabama* claims, but added, with a frankness not to be misunderstood:

> . . . Should she fail to properly adjust them, it may become the duty of the people's representatives to issue their writ in the form of a declaration of war for the seizure of her possessions in America in satisfaction of these claims, and thereby facilitate the departure of the last foreign power from this Continent.

Nor should it be forgotten that these were the views of the President-elect, as well as of Rawlins and the Republican party, at the time they were uttered.

Holding such opinions as these, it was to be expected that as a member of the Cabinet, he should avail himself of the Cuban rebellion, and especially of the *Virginias* affair, to favor Cuban independence as well as to hold Spain to a rigid respect for the rights of American citizens. At all events, that was the position Rawlins took, and there can be no doubt that he was both firm and vehement in maintaining it. Nor can there be any doubt that the more conservative and conciliatory Secretary of State, and possibly other members of the Cabinet, took the opposite view, and were disposed to regard the Secretary of War as going out of his proper sphere to influence and control the policy of the Administration.

It should be observed that the Spanish Government was at that time, as well as before, represented by able counsel, and had, besides, many influential friends to look out for its interests with the Administration and in the public press. Rawlins was an open and aggressive fighter, and, besides, held such close relations with the President as to make his success almost certain in any case that enlisted his sympathy and support. Although a man of modest and blameless life, he was not without enemies. His success had been too great and his elevation too high not to have brought upon him the envy of some he had left behind. While his arguments were rightfully enough combated by counsel, his motives were wrongfully enough assailed by others, who desired not only to defeat his measures but to injure his character and destroy his influence. They challenged his disinterestedness while living, and circulated reports to his discredit after he was dead, and, therefore, powerless to defend himself. The period of detraction and slander at Washington had already begun and no effort was spared to cripple those who were true to their own sense of duty and propriety.

With those who knew the austere and impassioned Rawlins in active life, his character needs no defence, and no defence will be offered. But for the information of those who come after, it is my duty to say that, having heard the innuendos and reflections made against him just after his death, and having become convinced that they were one and all without the slightest foundation, I have carefully gone through his correspondence, I have conferred with his family and friends, and I have pushed my investigations in every possible direction, without finding the slightest fact upon which to base even a doubt as to his private or official character.

In addition to being a sick and perhaps an irritable man, he was a bold and outspoken one, who never failed to denounce the foibles or the frauds of those in power, when occasion called for it. He thereby made himself a shining mark for envy and misrepresentation, and that envy and misapprehension should have followed him is but a tribute to his virile and aggressive qualities that should help to fix him and his services in the minds of his countrymen. As Dana well said:

> . . . Public servants of his quality will always be few, and there are plenty of men whose names will flourish largely in history, without having rendered a tithe of his unostentatious and invaluable contribution to the great work of the nation.

At the time Rawlins became Secretary of War he was under the constant care of a physician, who had prescribed a special diet suited to his case. He was already greatly enfeebled by the disease which had fixed itself upon him, but for the first two months the novelty of his new duties and the excitement which attended the organization of a new Administration, acted as a tonic to his system, under which he showed renewed strength and hopefulness. On May 9 he wrote:

> . . . Another week of official care and anxiety for the personal interest of my friends has passed. I had hoped on my return to find only the legitimate and proper duties of the Department to attend to, but found

things much the same as when I left. I hope only a short time will be required for matters to arrange themselves properly. Colonel Pride took charge of me in New York as usual until he saw me on the cars to Washington. Should Pride ever leave New York, I sometimes ask myself the question, could I get through New York at all?

On May 14th he wrote:

. . . Matters here are settling down, and soon I trust everything will move smoothly. Congress has mostly dissolved into the people, and applicants are left to press their own claims. I shall have the disagreeable duty to perform of reducing the clerical force of the Department, but am putting it off until the last moment. . . .

Shortly after this he again left Washington, and spent six weeks with his family in the hope that the more bracing climate of the New England hills would prove beneficial. The summer was somewhat dull, yet his position as a member of the Cabinet subjected him to constant pressure and annoyance. The newspapers seized every opportunity to quote him in speeches he had not made. The President and other Cabinet officers were more or less absent. The detention of the Spanish gunboats in American waters had been brought about by the interventions of Peru, and this gave him both pleasure and quiet.

But the end was now drawing near. Irreparable inroads upon Rawlins's constitution had become painfully apparent, and hope at last failed him entirely. It was at that juncture, July 17, that he ordered me to Washington and at his house in the presence of his wife, asked me to become his literary executor and to see justice done to his memory. He had become greatly emaciated, but had not entirely given up attendance at his office, although he showed much distress while performing his duties. Early in September he became so weak that he gave up going to the Department, but, notwithstanding his distress and failure of strength, he caused all important matters requiring his action to be brought to his residence for personal consideration, and kept this up till within two days of his death, which occurred September 6th, 1869.

One of the last and most complicated questions that demanded his personal attention, and gave him much anxiety and trouble, was the

Brooklyn Bridge, the plans for which the law required the Secretary of War's approval as a condition precedent to its construction. The bridge company naturally wanted to minimize the height of the span above the water which would have been injurious to the commerce of the port, while the shipping interests demanded an elevation, which the bridge company declared would involve an impracticable grade from the approaches to the highest point of the span. The case was argued with thoroughness amounting to prolixity. Maps, plans, and memorials covering every point at issue were submitted, and the severest pressure was brought to bear upon the afflicted Secretary by the parties in interest. All the important influences that could be enlisted were exerted to warp or control his judgment, but without effect.

The questions involved were too important to be decided without the most careful consideration, and to this end Rawlins gave several days and nights of minute and laborious study to the case. He found that the bridge company was willing to admit that a height of 130 feet above flood tide would give the maximum grade that could be worked, while the ship masters stoutly contended that 140 feet, or only ten feet more, would cause the minimum amount of annoyance with which the commerce of the harbor could be successfully carried on. Having got the opposing interests to within a few feet of each other, he thereupon decided to fix the height at 135 feet, with the remark that he would take the responsibility thereby of spoiling the bridge project, on the one hand, or of ruining the commerce of the port, on the other. Although greatly enfeebled at the time, he had the foresight to add to the order of approval a proviso that no part or appurtenance of the bridge should ever be below the limit of 135 feet above high-water mark. The wisdom of this provision was signally vindicated several years afterwards, when the bridge company was prohibited from giving a different construction to the order of approval.

In the short period of six months during which Rawlins held the office of Secretary of War, he was brought into intimate relations with many distinguished men both in civil and military life. His peculiar relations with the President had come to be pretty well understood by the public men of the day, and it is but fair to his associates of the Cabinet to state that they fully recognized his exceptional influence from the start, but apart from the former military relations which placed him closer to the President than anyone else, they soon became impressed by the singular force and independence of judgment which he displayed upon all occasions. He had, of course, met during the war many of the military men whom he found on duty at the War Department, but he had been intimate with none of them except Humphreys, the Chief of Engineers, and Meigs, the Quartermaster General. He had known Townsend, the Adjutant General, in the field; but with Marcy, the Inspector General, Barnes, the Surgeon General, Holt, the Judge Advocate General, and Meyer, the Chief Signal Officer, his acquaintance was but formal. These were all officers of experience and merit with whom he was destined to serve in the closest daily contact till the end of his career. He was, indeed, compelled to lean upon them, in the technical matters of their respective bureau, and reciprocally to expose to them his character and methods without reserve. It is but fair to those distinguished officers to add that while they were predisposed in his favor by the action he had taken in regard to the order placing them under General Sherman, they speedily came to respect him as a very able, self-reliant Secretary, irrespective of his civil training and military experience. His courtesy, tact, and equability of temper were in notable contrast to the violent and overbearing qualities displayed by Stanton, while his industry and promptitude of decision left nothing to be desired in an administrative officer. It is safe to add that no man ever died in the office of Secretary of War more thoroughly respected or more sincerely regretted by his subordinates of every grade.

In Sherman's order announcing the Secretary's death, a single paragraph is all that referred to the public services of this distinguished man. His letters show that he had been Sherman's faithful friend throughout the Civil War, yet he had not hesitated to disapprove the "March to the Sea" while Hood, with an unbeaten army, was just starting on his great movement against the widely-scattered detachments of the Military Division in the rear. He had approved Sherman's promotion as General of the Army over

Thomas and Meade, each of whom were regarded by many as his superior, in place of Grant, and yet he had not hesitated to insist on the reversal of the President's order, turning over to the general of the army the duties assigned by law and custom to the Secretary of War. It is hardly conceivable that Sherman should have regarded this action as in any way personal or intended to reflect upon him, but it is certain that Rawlins stood out tenaciously for the order, till the President became convinced that his duty required him to withdraw it.

This was a notable episode in the history of military administration, which aroused the attention not only of the army but of Congress. It was opposed by many Representatives and Senators at the time. But the most notable utterances against it were made by Senator Sumner in May, 1872, after he had broken with the President and his supporters. He characterized it "as an act of revolution exalting the military power above the civil." He even went so far as to say "that for the time there was a military dictatorship, with the President at its head not merely in spirit but in actual form."

While it is now evident that, however illegal the order may have been, it had no such sinister purpose, and was followed by no such hurtful results. Rawlins felt deeply about it. He was a civilian and a lawyer who had always been a close student and an ardent supporter of the Constitution, and although bound to the President by ties of personal and official friendship, he regarded it as his duty to secure the repeal of the offensive order even at the expense of his place in the Cabinet. Fortunately, the President yielded as usual to the legal advice of Rawlins, and accordingly, with his authority, the Secretary of War on March 26, 1869, issued a general order, directing that "all official business, which by law or regulation requires the action of the President or of the Secretary of War, will be submitted by the chiefs of staff corps, departments, and bureaus, to the Secretary of War." The result of this was to restore the business pertaining to the River and Harbor works, the fortifications, and to all branches of the military administration, to the channels prescribed by law and custom.

That Sherman, who liked power and had every confidence in his ability to administer it honestly and fairly, would have preferred to administer all the business connected with the military branch of the Government, there can be but little doubt. As his predecessors, from Scott down, had contended that all military business should be transacted through the General-in-Chief, it was not strange that Sherman should hold to the same view, or that he should resent the exercise of authority over him by one who had been subject to his command, as he afterwards did in the case of Belknap, who succeeded Rawlins in the War Department.

While he doubtless had but little feeling of resentment against Rawlins, it is certain that the order which he penned announcing the death of that distinguished man was of the most formal character and quite disappointing to the friends of the Secretary of War. It, of course, directed the closing of the Department, prescribed a military funeral, and fixed the usual period of mourning for officers of the army; but it contained no adequate account of the dead soldier's virtues, or of his services. Its only reference to them is contained in the following five lines:

> . . . The career of General Rawlins has been so brilliant and so closely connected with that of the President of the United States that it is familiar to all; it is an honor to the profession to connect his name with that army for whose welfare he labored so hard and with so much enthusiasm.

While many of the leading officers may have thought at the time that this general commendation was sufficient, they also knew that from first to last there was neither halt nor qualification in Rawlins's support of Sherman, no matter how great were Sherman's misfortunes. Neither his failure to fortify at Shiloh, nor the dissipation of his division on that field; neither his bloody repulse at Chickasaw Bayou, nor his opposition to the great turning movement against Vicksburg; neither his failure at the end of Missionary Ridge, nor the collapse of his campaign into Central Alabama brought a word of censure or in the slightest degree shook the confidence of Grant or of his Chief of Staff in the deserts of that brilliant, but not always successful, general.

321

But that Sherman had a deep interest in the subject is shown by a letter to the writer, dated January 13, 1885, in which after expressing his approval of the proposed *Life of General Rawlins*, he says:

> ... I would gladly aid you, but the truth is I know of him little more than the general public. He is a fine example of what an enthusiastic, ardent lawyer may become when war calls out the young and patriotic.

> To have begun as a volunteer at Galena, Illinois, to have been intimately associated with General Grant in his most extraordinary career to the end, and then to have been his Secretary of War, will give you an ample scope for your pen. I am sure you have ample materials and only need the encouragement of his friends to do justice to a worthy subject.

After alluding to Grant's financial misfortunes, the preparation and publication of the *Memoirs,* on which he was then engaged, and the completion of the picture by the story of Rawlins's connection with him, the letter concludes with the following graphic summary:

> . . . Rawlins was violent, passionate, enthusiastic, and personal, but always in the right direction. I know of no one who can do him and his memory justice better than yourself, and I am glad the task has fallen to your hands.

CONCLUSION

If the story, as I have told it, is true, and I am sure it is in all essential particulars, it must be admitted that this plain man of the plain people played a most important part in Grant's life as well as in the great events which took place about him. With perfect fearlessness and devotion, he was Grant's friend as well as his adjutant. With unfailing sagacity, he acted the part of mentor and counsellor in all the great emergencies of his Chief's remarkable career, from the first war meeting at Galena to the Presidency of the nation; never hesitating, never faltering, never failing to counsel him aright, yet always effacing himself, with a self-denial and an absence of egotism which are as rare as they are praiseworthy.

Love of country was indubitably his dominant passion—the controlling impulse of his life, but that the love of country could transmute a farmer lad, a charcoal burner, a country lawyer, into a soldier and statesman such as Rawlins had come to be, in the eight short and crowded years from the outbreak of the war to the end of his brief career in 1869, is of infinite credit to him and to our institutions, as well as of infinite encouragement to those whose duty it will be to uphold those institutions in years to come. Doubtless the work of the farm and of the charcoal pits did much to develop the muscles and the character of this typical American youth Doubtless the pious mother shaped his sense of duty and his conscience aright; doubtless the shiftless, but strong-willed, resolute father, had his helpful influence,—the one teaching by loving precept what should be done, the other by thoughtless example what should be avoided. Between the two, aided by the neighborhood school, the more pretentious Academy, and the Rock River Seminary, a strong, vigorous, self-reliant soul was shaped, which knew neither guile nor fear. The struggle with nature in the rough and exacting work of a Western community in its formative stage sharpened the faculties, strengthened the judgment, and aroused the ambition of the sturdy youth. The lives of our earlier heroes and statesmen were the staple food of every aspiring soul in those days. The debating society and the political club were the arena in which they fought their battles and gained the plaudits of their fellows. The practice of the courts and the encounters of political debate were the exercises which developed the intellect and prepared the minds of statesmen for the great task that confronted them at that important period. These were the schools of Lincoln, Douglas, and Washburne, no less than of Oglesby, Logan, and Rawlins. These were the school of patriots and heroes, and taught them how to live and how to die for their country in the hour of its dire distress.

No one who was not a witness of and a participant in the events which preceded and gave character to the great conflict between the States, can now properly understand the love which filled the heart of the Northern boy and man for the Union and for the Constitution which our forefathers framed and ordained for our protection. There were some who condemned slavery as "the sum of all villainies." There were some who would have even been willing to sacrifice the Union and give up the Constitution and its guarantees as "a league with hell and a covenant with the devil," to secure the abolition of slavery, but the great mass of the Northern people were inspired, above all, by the love of the Union and the Constitution, and were willing to fight for them and die for them, if need be, regardless of slavery and its iniquities. Glowing with patriotic pride in their institutions and in the happiness and prosperity they had enjoyed under them, they cared not in the last resort whether the negro should be slave or free, as the price of the Union and the triumph of our arms over the slave holder's Confederacy and their sympathizers. It was this supreme and all absorbing sentiment which filled the ranks of the Union Army and held it to its deadly work till its triumph was overwhelming and complete.

It is but a truism to say that this sentiment never had a braver nor a more self-sacrificing exemplar than John A. Rawlins. He believed in the Union from the bottom of his soul, and worked for it with every fibre of his body. He was the friend of Grant, and had an abiding confidence in his capacity to lead our forces to victory, but he was still more the friend of his country, and loved it above any man, and above every earthly consideration, and would not have deserted it to save his soul, much less to save his life. His letters to Washburne tell the truthful story of his devotion to Grant; but they also show that in his anxiety for Grant's success, he would go so far and no farther, and that he would be the first to withdraw his support, should Grant prove himself to be unworthy of it. His letter of June 6, from the camp back of Vicksburg to Grant himself, makes it plain that he held his official position not at the value of a cent as against his duty to Grant, to the army under his command, and to the country for which they stood.

In all the annals of war there is no nobler example of duty done, without fear or trembling, than in the remonstrance which that letter contained. The bravery of the officer or of the man in battle is the growth of discipline, strengthened by the spirit of mutual dependence and support. It requires that one should go with another and all together, shoulder to shoulder, but the bravery of that remonstrance and appeal to his Chief was of a higher order than that which was needed to lead a forlorn hope against a fortified position. It displayed the highest moral courage, which is much rarer and greater than physical courage.

No one can either read the utterances or consider the conduct of Rawlins without perceiving that he loved Grant, tenderly and patiently, and had an abiding confidence in his common sense, his ability, and his courage. That he was willing to defend him against unjust criticism, on the one hand, and to "stay him from falling/' on the other, is shown beyond question by his conduct from the time he joined the staff at Cairo till he yielded up his charge in death, at Washington.

But his fame does not rest solely on the silent records which I have quoted. His courage, his firmness, his judgment, and his fidelity to duty were known far and wide by his companions of the staff, by the subordinate commanders of the armies with which he served, and by the leading men of his own State at home. McPherson, Logan, Dodge, Crocker, Ransom, Gresham, and hundreds of other officers of high rank and untarnished character were familiar with his devotion to duty and to his Chief. They knew how solicitous he was for their welfare; and how anxious he was that none should be left behind on the day of battle. They knew also how strongly he favored the maintenance of the recruiting station and the enactment and rigid enforcement of the draft, in order that the ranks should be kept full, and that the trains and transports to the front should be kept crowded with recruits and reinforcements. He was one of the few officers, high or low, who felt deeply and spoke courageously on this vital subject. His declaration that he had more confidence in the "infallibility of numbers than in the infallibility of generals," deserves to pass into an axiom of war. It became known far and wide at the time of its utterance, and was the vital principle upon which Grant, Sherman, Thomas, and Meade alike won their final victories.

To Rawlins's fidelity and fearlessness in friendship Grant owed more than to any or all other extraneous influences, for without them and the support which Rawlins gave him with leading Congressmen and the representatives of the press, the work of the detractors must have been successful. Had that support been withdrawn after the Battle of Belmont, the capture of Fort Donelson, the trip to Nashville, the surprise of Shiloh, or during the delays of the campaign and siege of Vicksburg, though Grant had had the genius of a Napoleon or the fortitude of a Washington, his career must have come to an end. Nothing could have saved him from the public clamor, had Rawlins lost faith in him, or in his real merit, at any of these important epochs of his great career.

Among the most trusted correspondents of the war was S. Cadwallader, who joined Grant's headquarters at Jackson, Tennessee, in October, 1862, as the representative of the *Chicago Times,* then one of the most influential journals in the West. It was Democratic in politics and hostile to the Administration as well as to the war. On his way to the front Cadwallader made the acquaintance of Colonel Thomas Lyle Dickey, at that time Grant's Chief of Cavalry, and afterwards for many years a justice of the Supreme Court of Illinois. He also met en route Captain Bowers, then and afterwards Rawlins's principal assistant. Through these officers he made the acquaintance of Grant and Rawlins, and soon established most intimate relations with them. He messed with the staff, and while he held no official position, he was furnished with shelter and transportation and was treated in all respects as a commissioned officer. Having satisfactorily transacted the business which took him there, he resolved to remain, and during the Vicksburg campaign became the chief correspondent of the *New York Herald*. With the exception of Rawlins, Bowers, and Parker, he was the only other man of importance who accompanied Grant from that time to the end of the war. Throughout the whole of this period, nothing was concealed from him. He was fully trusted by both the General and his staff, and had early knowledge of everything that was taking place or under consideration. It is but just to add that he never forfeited the trust reposed in him, and was never in the slightest degree guilty of the imprudent revelations which too frequently made the war correspondent of those times an intolerable nuisance. After the war was over he was placed in charge of the *Herald* Bureau at Washington, and kept house for several months with Rawlins. Thus, from the beginning to the end of his association with Grant's headquarters, he shared the confidences and was entrusted with the secrets of those about him.

It will be recalled that Grant's death and the publication of his *Memoirs* gave rise to much discussion in the journals and magazines of the day as to his relations with Rawlins, Halleck, Smith, Butler, and others. Rawlins's Vicksburg letter to Grant and the correspondence between Rawlins and W. F. Smith were then published for the first time. The latter correspondence shows that an unbroken feeling of confidence and cooperation existed between Grant, Smith, and Rawlins down to the time that Smith asked for leave of absence from the Army of the James on account of his health. It shows also that Grant was loath to part with Smith "from the field even for a few days," and makes it clear that the rupture of the friendship between them did not take place till Smith had gone, and that it was due in all probability to the representations of Butler and his staff.

But, above all, the newspaper discussions which followed the publication of Grant's *Memoirs* brought the relations of Grant and Rawlins clearly before the public. Both were dead, and there appeared to be no necessity for further concealment as to the part each had played in respect to the other. Rawlins's friend Cadwallader was still living and felt called upon to give his testimony through the press as to the precise relations between the General and his Chief of Staff. Holding that the part contributed by the latter to the common success had been insufficiently stated in the *Memoirs,* he set it forth fully and circumstantially as he had recorded it from day to day in his own memory, or in his note books and correspondence. It not only upholds the estimate I have given of Rawlins's character and services, but is an independent and valuable contribution to the history of the times.

But it should be stated in addition that Parker the Indian, who lived at Galena before the war, and who joined Grant's staff at Vicksburg and remained with him to the end, had ample knowledge of all that took place at headquarters.

Ely Samuel Parker (1828–1895), was a Seneca attorney, engineer, and tribal diplomat. He was commissioned a lieutenant colonel during the Civil War. Grant appointed him Commissioner of Indian Affairs, the first Native American to hold that office.—Ed. 2015

Silent, reserved, and taciturn, he was a close observer and a good judge of character. His relations were specially close and intimate with Rawlins, whose assistant he was, and for whom he had the highest respect. In a funeral oration to the memory of his friend, he bears independent testimony to his great worth as a staff officer, lawyer, and statesman, and to the influential part he played by Grant's side as Adjutant General, Chief of Staff, and Secretary of War. While this oration contributes but little that is new, it throws a strong light from a disinterested source upon the personality, moral qualities, and character of the remarkable man it describes and commemorates. It emphasizes the fact that Rawlins played an unusual part and had a great influence upon the course of events with which it was his good fortune to be connected. Coming from a witness who knew both Grant and Rawlins while they were still plain citizens who had yet to achieve greatness, this tribute may be accepted as embodying the estimate and opinions of the Army of the Tennessee, to which they had all three belonged.

But the concurrent testimony of those who had the opportunity of knowing, and should have been able to judge dispassionately, seems to leave no doubt whatever as to the nature and extent of the influence exercised by Rawlins over the personal conduct and military career of Grant. Extending, as it did, over the entire period of their active campaigning, and coming, as it did, to the observation of many besides themselves, there can be but little room for mistake or misunderstanding in reference to it. In this period of their lives "they were, so to speak, as but one soul." They started in the war together from the level of a common citizenship and a common patriotism. If there was any difference in them, Rawlins was at the beginning the more important man of the two. While Grant was always singularly free from the assumptions and superiority of military rank, it must be remembered that he had tasted adversity, and was unusually modest as to himself as well as considerate to others. It was but natural, therefore, that throughout their campaigning days these two should have stood together, and been frank and free from restraint towards each other.

After peace came, however, and Grant had been chosen President by an overwhelming majority, he would have been less than human had he not begun to feel that there must be some personal greatness or some superior quality about him of which even he had been hitherto ignorant. It was but natural that he should consider himself fully able to stand alone, and therefore entitled to assume towards his Cabinet the headship and independence which were his right by both custom and law. He may have been changed by prosperity, but Rawlins was not. Rawlins continued to be bold, independent, and conscientious, although this required more self-possession and prudence on his part after Grant went into politics. Adviser, as he had always been, he doubtless grew more sensitive as well as more reserved and met with greater difficulty in seeing and conferring with Grant in his new estate than he had met in the field. It was but natural, however, that Grant should remain more unreserved and more outspoken with him than with the other members of the Cabinet. Doubtless it is true that in all matters of real importance their new relations were less intimate than those of the field, but it is evident that Rawlins still retained greater influence with Grant than did any of his associates. He was a bolder and more virile man, and naturally felt less restraint in the presence of greatness than the best of them.

It will not be forgotten that every other member of the first Cabinet was a comparative stranger both to the President and to Rawlins. The only one that either had previously known was Jacob D. Cox, who, on account of the high rank and fine reputation with which he had come out of the war, was appointed Secretary of the Interior. He was a good example of the cultivated and successful citizen soldier, but had never served directly under Grant's observation. What Grant knew about him, therefore, came largely from others. He was an able and learned lawyer, and afterwards achieved distinction as a judge and as Governor of Ohio. On account of his independence and conservatism he disapproved of Grant's policy and associates as President, and after a few months' service, resigned from the Cabinet to resume the practice of his profession. He had necessarily seen much of his official associates while in Washington, and hence his testimony in reference to them and to their relative influence with their common chief, based, as it was, upon actual observation, must be regarded as both trustworthy and important.

In an account of "How Judge Hoar Ceased to be Attorney General," which Cox contributed to the *Atlantic Monthly,* the following important and interesting statement will be found:

> . . . General Rawlins had died at the beginning of September, 1869, and his death was an irreparable loss to Grant and to the Administration. Other men might fill the office of Secretary of War, but no other man could be found who could be the successful intermediary between General Grant and his associates in public duty. His friendship for his chief was of so sacredly intimate a character that he alone could break through the taciturnity into which Grant settled when he found himself in any way out of accord with the thoughts and opinions of those around him. Rawlins could argue, could expostulate, could condemn, could even upbraid, without interrupting for an hour the fraternal confidence and good will of Grant. He had won the right to this relation by an absolute devotion which dated from Grant's appointment to be a brigadier-general in 1861, and which had made him the good genius of his friend in every crisis of Grant's wonderful career. This was not because of Rawlins's great intellect, for he was of only moderate mental powers. It was rather that he became a living and speaking conscience for his general, as courageous to speak in

time of need as Nathan the prophet, and as absolutely trusted as Jonathan by David.

In military problems Grant had a strong and almost intuitive sagacity in determining upon the path to victory, not always the easiest or the most economical in blood and treasure, but a sure one when his own indomitable courage and will had clear scope. He silently listened to the discussion of such men as Sherman and McPherson, he patiently turned the matter over in his own thoughts and after a while announced a decision which showed the aid he got from intelligent debate, whilst it was clearly marked with his own directness of purpose and boldness of action. Rawlins knew how to bring on such helpful discussion in Grant's presence. He knew how to reinforce the influence of those who deserved to be trusted and to expose insidious and false friendship. He had blunt, wrathful words of objurgation for those who put in Grant's way temptations which he knew to be dangerous. A moral monitor and guide, not hesitating at big oaths and camp expletives, seems a strange type of man, but no one could deny that Rawlins's heart was as true and his perception of the thing demanded by the honor and the welfare of his Chief was as clear as his manners and words often were rough.

It will not need argument to show how useful such a friend and counsellor might be as a Cabinet officer. He could give warnings that no one else could utter; he could insist upon debate and information before settled purposes should be adopted; he would know of influences at work that others would learn of only when some important step was already taken; his own openness of character would make him frank in action with his colleagues and an honorable representative of their general judgment and policy. Rawlins might have differed from Mr. Fish as to the foreign policy of his government, especially in regard to Cuba, but he would have seen to it that no kitchen cabinet committed the President to schemes of which his responsible advisers were ignorant. Indeed, there was no danger that a kitchen cabinet could exist till Rawlins was dead.

The extract just quoted caused me to write to Cox for further information, and my letter drew from him a reply, dated September 19, 1895, from which I quote as follows:

. . . General Rawlins was, as you know, in failing health when he entered Grant's Cabinet. The spring of 1869 was so completely filled with the business of organization and the making of appointments that very little opportunity was offered for general discussion of affairs which would have enabled me to form a satisfactory judgment of Rawlins's intellectual quality in civil affairs. What I saw of him I greatly liked, but he was not pushing in his method of dealing with others, a little shy and observant, rather than assertive at the beginning, and evidently weakened by disease.

Then he left Washington in the summer, as I recollect, and was taken more seriously ill and died at the beginning of September. I had not the privilege of more than a passing acquaintance with him in the army, for I never served in the columns with which he was immediately connected.

You will see, therefore, that my judgment of him was necessarily based upon what seemed the current opinion of those who knew about him, modified by what I learned from various sources, of his peculiar relations to General Grant and his extraordinary influence over him.

I am far from holding with any tenacity the opinion which you criticize, that is, that Rawlins had no great mental power. On the other hand, I so fully recognize the logical force of the evidence of his capacity, found in his influence over such a man as Grant, that I shall be among the first to welcome the evidence of his powers in every direction.

The noble traits which I have mentioned in several papers (including the one in the *Atlantic Monthly*) seemed to me to deserve a more emphatic recognition than they have commonly got, and this made me welcome an opportunity to bear testimony to them.

I am sincerely glad to learn that you have in hand Rawlins's *Memoirs* and shall hope that you may not be much longer delayed in procuring the officially completed records which will round out the materials for your work. . . .

Extracts and quotations from reports, addresses, and articles from the newspapers and magazines, and even from memoirs and histories of the times, bearing positive testimony to the high esteem in which Rawlins was held, might be indefinitely extended; but enough have been given to show even to the most skeptical that he was a man of extraordinary vigor and force of character, who exerted both a powerful and a beneficial influence not only over the personal fortunes of his Chief but over the policies and plans for which in the last resort his Chief was responsible. That he exerted that influence at all times and in all places to the personal and official advantage of his friend and commander as well as for' the advancement of his country's best interests cannot be doubted. Indeed, so much has been admitted with singular unanimity by all who knew him at the time, or who have contributed to the history of the period. But more might well have been said. All agree that so long as Rawlins was the final, if not the principal, adviser in all the great emergencies of Grant's life, and that in all military affairs from first to last Grant's efforts were crowned with marked success, and neither hurtful criticisms nor failures overtook him in the field or in the White House, till after death had deprived him of the counsel and advice of his faithful and fearless friend, it must now be evident that Rawlins was a vital and essential factor of the dual character which has passed into history under the name of Grant.

Moreover, it is the firm belief of many that had Rawlins lived in the enjoyment of health and strength, and continued to hold his place and influence with Grant, Grant's political career must have been much more successful than it was. Who can imagine Rawlins tolerating, or permitting Grant to tolerate, the false friends who afterwards brought so much discredit upon the Administration? He would have been the inflexible enemy of the foul brood of Post traders, fraudulent distillers, and rascally speculators in gold, who defrauded the Government and besmirched so many of the President's official associates. That Rawlins had protected him with a fair degree of success through his military life is ample to warrant the belief, and strongly supports the probability of a like success in political life.

Rawlins has been called by those who knew him but superficially a "fierce" and even a "violent" man. He has been characterized as rough and overbearing by those who felt the heat of his anger or of his indignation, but he was just, patient, modest, considerate, and fearless in the performance of what he conceived to be his duty. With remarkable self-control, with a strong and vehement vocabulary of plain Saxon English, and a full, penetrating voice, he was accustomed to express himself in language which no man could affect to misunderstand. Under the influence of deep feelings or in the advocacy of an important cause, he spoke with extraordinary clearness and deliberation. His dark and flashing eyes would light up with all the fire of an impassioned orator, his lips would curl and recede, leaving his strong and shapely teeth exposed while his dark and swarthy face grew pale and tremulous from the intensity of his emotions. Under these conditions, it was a bold man indeed who stood unbleached before him, or undertook to resist the force and logic of his argument.

It is literally true, as stated by Cadwallader, that, when strongly aroused and in earnest, Rawlins never failed to carry his General with him. It is equally true that when thoroughly interested, no sense of fear, no thought of danger or of personal consequence, ever seemed to enter his mind or to turn him aside from his purpose so much as by the breadth of a hair. Simple, honest, austere, and abstemious in all his ways, he expected the same virtue in all who were entrusted with power. He had but little patience with the petty foibles of full-grown men. He hated lying and prevarication in others so intensely that they were impossible to himself. He condemned drunkenness and gambling so unsparingly that he could not tolerate even moderate drinking or playing in those that were charged with the responsibilities of high command. Untiring in his industry, sleepless in his vigilance, and unfailing in his devotion to duty, he had no patience with those who wasted their time, or lost their opportunities, in idleness and inattention.

Possessing these high qualities and characteristics, he lacked only the technical education and practical experience of an officer commanding troops to have become, with the opportunities which were within reach, one of the leading generals of the army. While he was never a religious man, he had been brought up in the faith of the Methodist Episcopal Church, conformed to its discipline, and accepted its sacred offices and its consolation as he felt himself nearing the close of his earthly career. His funeral was conducted with the solemnity due to his high rank. The officers of the army wore the usual badge of mourning for three months. The President, who arrived in Washington after his friend's death, with the Cabinet, diplomatic corps, and many officers of the army, attended the ceremonies, while the newspapers of the country were filled with appropriate articles praising the high character, the valuable services, and the extraordinary worth of the departed Secretary.

He was buried in the Congressional Cemetery under a modest monument erected and paid for by his family and kinsmen. Later, a bronze statue, of questionable artistic merit, was erected to his memory by the Society of the Army of the Tennessee, at the south side of Pennsylvania Avenue, between 8th and 9th Streets, in Washington city. Still later his remains were reinterred in the National Military Cemetery at Arlington. "Pass them not by for the simplicity of their resting place. Few tombs hold nobler dust."

In the strong and unassuming modesty of Grant's character, in the unshakable quality of his courage, in his fine sense of duty, in his approved capacity to trample temptation under foot and to bear the responsibility which should not be shifted to another man's shoulders, and, above all, in the magnitude of his victories, as well as in the sufficiency of his rewards, he is undoubtedly great enough to have the simple truth told about himself as well as about the officer to whom he was so deeply indebted. Nor should it be doubted that in the days of his health and strength, and acting under his own generous impulses, he would have been the first to do full justice to the abilities, worth, and services of his only Chief of Staff, his first Secretary of War, and, best of all, his wise, fearless, and indispensable friend in all the emergencies of life.

THE END.

DISCOVER MORE LOST HISTORY AT BIG BYTE BOOKS

Made in the USA
Middletown, DE
27 December 2019